Idaho Anthem

by

Les Montgomery

ISBN 0-9662621-2-3
Library of Congress Number 00-132984

For additional copies:
Idaho Anthem
1906 Howard Ave.
Caldwell, Idaho 83605

Idaho Anthem

To George Willis Montgomery, M.D.
my father

Contents

Foreword

This book scores so well in so many different ways that a foreword is appropriate so that the reader may be forewarned that it is not your average buy. It is funny, irreverent, profound, light, reflective, outdoorsy, and engaging from first to last. It may or may not prove successful commercially. The trouble with producing a good book is that someone must bear the cost of production—good (or bad, for that matter) books don't just fall from the sky, edited, printed, and bound) nor are they found under cabbage leaves.

This book, which I would like to subtitle *The Life and Opinions of J. Lesley Montgomery, Gentleman, Physician, and Surgeon*, has much in common with the mid-18th century work of Laurence Sterne, *The Life and Opinions of Tristram Shandy, Gentleman*. Shandy, too, was conceived with little or no real expectations of commercial value, though the impecunious Sterne did have hope. Publishers are wont to have their expenses relieved, for they are not, ordinarily, philanthropists; hence they will not look at manuscripts that are funny, irreverent, profound, etc., etc., unless they also have reassurance that the conventional aspects of plot, progression, invention, and theme or thesis, are present in the text with public acceptance strongly implied. When manuscripts ignore these elements, their creators are usually told something to the effect that "While we appreciate your thinking of us as a possible publisher, we find that the work does not conform to our publication expectations. It is just not the right book for us." Fortunately, Dr. Montgomery's literary accomplishment did not die of rejection.

The book is apparently an anecdotal and carefully selective account of three generations—a Victorian grandfather; his grandson, who through native intelligence, hard work, and assiduity became a doctor; and his great-grandson, who survived the *angst* of medical school to become likewise a physician and surgeon, discovering that "once seduced by the high desert plateau (of western Idaho-eastern Oregon) the affair lasts forever." And read at this level, the account is extraordinarily engaging. But below the surface there are values that are equally engaging, illuminating the quality of mind that produced this valuable work. This tall, lanky physician-narrator can become philosophical without being pretentious and profound without the anticipated sententiousness. How refreshing that is. When, for instance he talks about philosophy, especially that branch of it usually called epistemology, without ever using the word "philosophy" he reminds us that truth often appears in irregular fragments that must be trimmed and honed until they fit into some kind of pattern. How like Herman Melville he is, who wrote of the ragged edges of truth attainable only in fiction.

And there is fiction here, the fiction of the tall tale, for instance. One cannot escape the conviction that Mark Twain would have loved this writing and its writer. There is also the folk tale quality of the account of how a lady's fox fur gets enmeshed with a gentleman's vulnerable trouser zipper.

Nowhere is this engaging book more engaging than when we learn about the preparation of a doctor. What Shakespeare said of a Jew may also be affirmed of medical students: if they are cut, do they not bleed? if they meet enchantresses like Portland's so-called Dolly Sisters (after a June Haver and Betty Grable movie) do they not feel passion? if they spend hours in the laboratory or with their textbooks when they should be sleeping, do they not languish and drink too much strong coffee? and if they memorize nerves and bones and mesenteries through traditional (and sometimes vulgar) mnemonic devices, do they not come to know these parts of the anatomy with absolute mastery? Indeed, one aspect of this book is the progress of medicine from the age of treatment by the administration of calomel (a mercury compound, for heaven's sake!) to the age of MRI. That is, we observe the study and practice of medicine from the time of a limited knowledge of chemistry when mercuric compounds such as calomel were often prescribed . . . to today's impressive knowledge of the great facts of nature. But Dr. Montgomery wonders between the lines of the text whether a modern medicine man knows more of human nature than did a man like Dr. Jones of Jordan Valley, whose funeral in Caldwell in 1963 is described in superb and affecting American English prose.

The reader may well rejoice in this material. In order that his (and I quickly add "her" lest the reader not accept "his" as genderless) rejoicing may be unconfined, the reader is urged to turn to the text and read it. A foreword is no substitute for what it introduces. So instead of lifting materials from their contexts and offering them as inducements—as enjoyable as that would be for the writer of this foreword—let those delicious swatches remain in their place to be discovered by the careful reader and savored in their rightful place.

However, the range of humor, wit, whimsy, irreverence, and profundity may be indicated without violating the integrity of the text. There is, for instance, a tweaking of the nose of the muse of history as Montgomery dares to suggest that those intrepid travelers Lewis and Clark may have had their unheroic moments and that the Indian maiden Sacajawea (this is how we came to know her, regardless of what authorities in Shoshone linguistics say about her name) may have been a real human being with authentic adolescent cravings and uncertainties. History is not sacred; it is, thankfully, secular. There is also a physician's revulsion at the breeding (or in-breeding) of marginal human beings who give no thought of the health of mother or offspring. There are priceless descriptions of river canyons, of dawns and sunsets in the Sawtooth Mountains, evocations of space and time and the ineffable loveliness of the wilderness that each generation of Westerners comes to know but in different terms from the earlier generations.

It is a life-affirming book, one that should be read whenever one is weary of considerations and the way ahead seems unclear. From it one can recover the quiet hope that unremitting work, trials, and compromises are usually qualified and sometimes overcome by knowledge of the accomplishments and sacrifices of those who have gone before, by reminders of the numinous beauty of nature around us, and by having a good laugh at the foibles of this species of featherless bipeds, labeled ironically *homo sapiens*.

Louie Attebery

Acknowledgements

For twenty years I have wanted to write something about Idaho, but the competition is fierce. True historians like Merle Wells and Arthur Hart have already done this to perfection. My literary interest began with the assassination of Gov. Frank Steunenberg in 1905, but this would entail tedious research, and I had lost my library card. So instead, I walked down to Fourteenth and Everett for an afternoon with George Crookham, a nephew of the governor. George had once been my scoutmaster when, Lord knows, I needed one. Well into his eighties, George was still rafting the Salmon River, and when he died at ninety-two he was planning another trip. His encyclopedic memory included not only details about his uncle's death but everything else about Idaho, including the Oregon Trail before stop-lights were installed.

He was too modest to tell me that his life-long participation had changed the course of Idaho politics from water rights to the sales tax. Accuracy was paramount to this quiet man who hesitated to comment on western geography unless he had been there at least four times...five would be better. To repay his kindness, I gave him an 8x1O print (only a fool would suggest cuff links) of the round barn near Frenchglen, which immediately evoked a litany of every detail of its construction in 1888 when an Old World master carpenter searched the reaches of Harney County to finally locate a twenty-six foot juniper for the center post. When he failed to find an archival sketch of the intricate umbrella rafters, he drew one from memory. I was so mesmerized by my old scoutmaster that I was tempted to abandon my original project in favor of a biography of George Crookham.

Anthony Lukas, a Pulitzer prize winner, also utilized George as an unimpeachable resource on Steunenberg's intervention during the mining strife in the Coeur d'Alene district. Lukas committed suicide just before publication of *Big Trouble*, which taught me that too much research can be downright risky.

For other local history, I turned to Lorene Bales Thurston, a classmate from long ago in Washington grade school. She and Elaine Lippert devoted countless unpaid hours to compile a delightful photo essay on Caldwell. About the same time, I was lucky enough to know Al McCluskey so I would have a life-long hunting companion and, from Wilder, met Bill Paulsen who would provide the pheasants. Bill left his farm just long enough to ferry supplies "over the hump" in the China-Burma-India Theater. The C.B.I. was an obscure component of World War-Two, from which Bill was one of the fortunate pilots to survive, and he got back just in time to fatten the pheasants who were failing fast without him. Bill's mother, Rachel, was such a persuasive Republican that she alone converted the entire state. She once forgave me for ground sluicing some quail which flocked to her feet when she was feeding the chickens. Since Republicans are obviously compassionate, I have been spreading the word ever since.

My salvation in high school was Erwin Schwiebert whose disciples enrolled in whatever he taught...which was everything. In a school that size, he filled every slot from track to baseball to math and finally (get this) public speaking. That very day, Dale Greeley and I became debate partners. Schwiebert did not smoke or drink so neither did we. That's what coaches do. We didn't even know there was a "j" in marijuana. He taught us to stand up before a crowd of strangers and pretend we knew what we were talking about, but none of us could ever emulate his

resonant baritone voice, me least of all. One sophisticated
senior told me that picturing the audience without clothes
reduced stage fright, but Schwiebert, who sang bass in the
Methodist choir, disapproved. Maybe I should join the
choir. During the next two years, Erwin clipped and saved
war-time headlines as air combat wiped out our team:
Dale went down over Holland, then Ernie Hickox in
Alaska and, finally, Buck Skinner, who flew the *milk route*
over Berlin once too often. These departed men were better friends than I deserved.

Among those who survived the war were my trail
mates, Bill Moore, the campfire's master story-teller who
really belonged on TV, and his appreciative cousin, R.C.
Pasley, whose contagious laugh could start an avalanche.
Annual mountain trips with others ended painfully soon.
Dr. Oakes Hoover could carry a sixty pound pack and
yours as well if you could not keep up. This intrepid
kayaker drowned during a sudden spring storm on a nearby lake while Bill Vandermeer, his boating companion,
survived in freezing water for two hours with that legendary toughness that God reserves for small men. His
core temperature was barely ninety-one degrees by the
time I saw him. Bill continued as our anesthesiologist (the
best in the valley) for another twenty years before he himself died along the shores of the Galapagos Islands. With
sardonic irony, water had joined them at last

Charles Krause divided his time between the hospital
and his church, and when one member of his Sunday
school class fell into a boat propeller, it was he who conducted the search for her body, consoled the family, sang at
her funeral, and began a scholarship in her memory.
Charlie never went half way. When my group ostracized
me for missing an elk at ten feet, only Charlie would vol-
unteer to travel with me next year. In his shirt pocket, he
carried raisins, peanuts and the New Testament, all of
which he willingly shared. Charles Krause, Bob Jensen,

and Jack Kennevick. belong to the highest echelon of loyalty. You cannot pry off such friends with a crow bar.

Working with doctors like Wilbur Waterman, Art Dole, Dick Roberge, Bob Taylor, Kent Kreuder, or George Wolff made long days shorter. It is not healthy to limit one's friends to doctors, so I was fortunate to know Bill Rankin, a world class musician, who still brings great jazz to our valley and keeps old men young, even though we stomp our feet one at a time. But it is women who make things click. When Sarah Ney's old hospital was demolished, she came over to run the new one and surrounded herself with magicians like Gene Hansen, Alice Bittick, Jo Anne Cayler, and Dorothy Basey. Chris Craig or Joan Truesdale could make any doctor look good (or bad if he misbehaved).

Idahoans are provincial folk, but at least one out-of-state friend is allowed. Since we must be selective, mine was Bob McClary, a medical school classmate who joined the psychiatric staff at Johns Hopkins and hoped no one would notice. Mac brought his camera every fall and exposed a dozen rolls on the same scenery that he had admired the year before. It took twenty years to get it right, just the way he planned it. Mac had been the top man in our class, so I always took his advice on photography, and anything medical...except psychiatry. Eventually, he evolved into a serious Lewis and Clark scholar because one can pursue this hobby from a car.

Every story needs some interesting characters and, around here, there is no shortage of these... all will be fictitious lest I do them some factual injustice. None of these folks ever said I should write a book. On the other hand, neither did they forbid it. Having spent half my life in school, I considered myself a superior linguist with no need for an editor, but friends (who had gone to school even longer) urged me to contact an emeritus professor of English at Albertson College of Idaho. As an Idaho native whose education began in a one room school house, Louie

Attebery was uniquely equipped to recognize and correct several errors in both geography and sequence of events. He is hard to fool when everything is all typed out. When one quotes Shakespeare, he felt that one should attempt to approximate the author's words (only a suggestion). Scriptures are especially risky because, chances are, somebody else has read that book. Writing is easy. Bring your own commas and Louie will do the rest. Because of a good editor, I was able to use eponymous not once, but twice.

Read on and see for yourself.

INTRODUCTION

In the first years of the nineteenth century, Lewis and Clark set out to see just how big our country really was, probably thinking that such a vast void could never be filled. Until this brand new continent was discovered, European writers were limited to repetitious fiction, with the Acropolis, Notre Dame, or the Tower of London providing the same monotonous background. For their darker literature, creative authors relied on the Black Plague (probably caused by some previous administration).

Queen Isabella pawned her jewels so Christopher Columbus could cross the Atlantic, and find something new for Spain to write about. As it turned out, our novel continent taxed even the poet's imagination.

Exhausted adjectives and exclamatory verbs were revived just to convey the splendor of the rugged Maine coast or an Appalachian autumn, but after the Louisiana Purchase, panoramic nouns had to be invented just to describe the endless western prairies and the relentless stream of Conestoga wagons when the West threatened to empty the East. Describing the Rockies depleted most of Meriwether's remaining prose, which may account for his creative spelling.

Once across the mountains, the expedition had run out of proper nouns, even though most of their rivers would be re-named later by prominent politicians. The expedition was fortunate in that California was already spoken for and had Spanish names, too romantic to change. With their supply of words exhausted, Lewis and Clark were forced to return to St. Louis, never dreaming that Jefferson had an untapped verbal supply back in Monticello.

Eventually, word got around that the Louisiana Purchase deserved serious exploitation. In their eagerness to settle Oregon, pioneers almost completely overshot Idaho, but eventually this void was filled by retrograde immigration once the Indians were thinned out. By then it was safe for my father to be born in 1889, just one year before Idaho achieved statehood, but Will had been much too young to notice and too poor to care.

By the turn of the century, he witnessed changes in a world that would never be the same. Before that, folks lived abbreviated lives within a tight, grudging radius and hauled their meager possessions with the same beasts of burden described in the Old Testament. While Will was growing up, the mare was sold to buy a truck, fertilizer became fashionable, and manure was never mentioned again.

Tractor treads obliterated hoof tracks. The ox left the farm. The mule left the farm. The farmer left the farm. The best way to see a horse was at the race track. After the Spanish-American fiasco, even our wars were sensibly spaced. America's battles could have been more frequent, but for some reason we don't fight the British any more.

Idaho is a nebulous hinterland which, despite a different zip code, is still confused with Iowa even though a recent National Geographic map places us fully five inches to the west. To further delineate these disparate states, Iowa is colored pink and Idaho is green. For reliable orientation, the Snake River is down at the bottom, the Salmon runs through the middle and there are lots of big lakes at the top. The rest is mountains.

This book contains several border tales and, by preordained proximity, adjacent states are necessarily mentioned, but with a little luck and devious writing, the story tries to cross the border and stay in Idaho where it belongs.

My own life has been quite dull, but I have known some interesting people. For reasons beyond my control, most of them were doctors, but reasonable people will overlook this.

Idaho Anthem

CHAPTER ONE

Conventional American history begins way back east, but Idahoans learn theirs retrograde by tracing Lewis and Clark from this end of the trail. We derive a vicarious pride from our geographical connection with their little Indian guide. She was born in Idaho but nobody knows exactly where Sacajawea died and—at risk of crude chauvinism—what did the girl look like?

The Hollywood answer can be found in an epic based on the arduous search for the Northwest Passage wherein the actors tried not to look foolish in coonskin hats and buckskin pants last worn at a studio costume party. Their quaint dialog hinted of southern California, but the mountains were authentic as were the long muskets which, to the relief of the viewing audience, were properly registered. This movie serves history well enough since they did find the right ocean, so it is reasonable to conclude that Sacajawea looked just like Donna Reed.

The captains were out west to count the bison, bribe some Indians, and keep a journal with creative spelling. Sacajawea was there to have a baby. Pregnant teenagers were not standard for government expeditions, but Thomas Jefferson wouldn't hear about it for two years.

At Fort Mandan, Captain Lewis attended the "labour which was tedious and the pain violent." In desperation, he consulted with Rene Jessaume who suggested "bits of rattle from a rattlesnake mixed in water." Lewis just hap-

Charbonneau Monument, a long way from the royal courts of Europe.

pened to have such a snake nearby: "She had not taken it more than ten minutes before she brought forth."

Oxytocics are unpredictable even today. Were uterine contractions augmented by pulverized rattles or—perhaps just as likely—muddy water from the Missouri? We shall never know.

Jean Baptiste Charbonneau was born in 1805 and soon became a footnote in history. This involuntary recruit in the *Corps of Discovery* hugged his mother's back while she struggled toward the setting sun. From North Dakota to Oregon there is no mention that any of the robust adventurers took turns carrying the papoose. Finally they ran out of land and found the Pacific though it was largely obscured by perpetual rain which enveloped Ft. Clatsop.

Ruins of 1863 Innskip Station. Sacajewea's son died here in 1866. A few rifle ports are still visible.

When they finally got back to St. Louis, the French-Shoshoni boy was two years old, and a favorite of William Clark who arranged for his education which included touring the royal courts of Europe where he became multilingual and looked very sharp in blue velvet. It may have been genetic predeterminism or just the urge to live in a teepee, but Jean Baptiste renounced cotillions and caviar and re-crossed the Atlantic. With the same inexplicable destiny that beckons the salmon from the largest of oceans to the smallest of streams, he returned to the wilderness where he was born.

In 1866, Sacajawea's son died at the Ruby Ranch near the Idaho-Oregon border. For another century, antelope and coyotes wandered over his forgotten grave. Then, one cowboy-historian cared enough to clear the sagebrush, mix his own cement, and erect a permanent monument to the memory of Jean Baptiste Charbonneau. Except for this one man, a priceless link with the Corps of Discovery would have been lost forever.

Three rivers are born in the deep snows of the Sawtooths. The Salmon, the Boise and the Payette monopolize the scenery after which the Snake borrows the water to gouge a mile-deep canyon intimidating enough to keep Oregon on the other side. Without Idaho's contribution, the Columbia is nothing, but Washington and Oregon—they have more congressmen—will confiscate every drop to spin their turbines. Beyond Hanford, it's radioactive.

This predilection for the Pacific has something to do with the continental divide where Lewis and Clark first made journal entries about the westward flow of the Salmon. Before the captains wandered by, nobody knows where the water went.

Once upon a time, Chief Tendoy stood at Lemhi Pass and urged Lewis and Clark to detour North and try the trail along the Clearwater. The Lemhis had never seen the Pacific but knew for damn-sure that the seething Salmon was not the way to get there. Sign language can be tedious, and Tendoy soon developed painful hand cramps trying to convey this admonition:

Too steep. Bad water. Break bones. Lose many horses. Your men really won't like it. Oh rats! What's the word for impassable?

Edmundsen Cabin, French Creek Canyon. Unskilled neighbors learned nothing from this master English carpenter because he talked funny.

In desperation, the chief pointed to the grave of a recently departed Indian brave, Aha-Oh-Oh-whoopee-GLUB which means "Hot damn! I'm unsinkable."

But the white men knew better—one of them had spent time in Washington D.C.—and wasted a few days probing the Salmon but it went badly. Battered men were soon trapped against vertical walls and barely escaped drowning. Horses murmured mutiny. It all evolved into a cacophony of Caucasian screams and Indian derision.

Enemy tribes declared a truce and streamed in from miles around just to watch the show. Squaws served sage brush tea and begged Meriwether to do it all again tomorrow. This can really hurt.

Here's an original thought: Why not abandon this hellish river, back track into Montana on State Highway 324 and follow the signs to the Lolo trail? The expedition could always pretend it was their idea and, if bribed with a few trinkets, the Lemhis would never squeal.

Toxaway Lake is a sequestered jewel, proud to serve as the headwaters of the Salmon whose flow is soon augmented by a dozen other Sawtooth watersheds. And all worth seeing. Dominating a 6000 foot valley, the clearest of water wanders eastward from Stanley to Challis where, in deference to the continental divide, it runs parallel to Montana and then on to the village of North Fork near the border where kayakers with a death wish line the shore. Downstream they can expect to encounter a few twisted canoes abandoned on some unforgiving rock, but even less welcome are helicopters guarding some president and his harem. All is not lost. Pretend you voted for him. Make for the shore. Hide the women. Fake an accent from some country enjoying Most Favored Nation Status.

The river begins wide, deep, and dark but its fickle flow conceals the varied spectacle ahead: Violent as a fire hose. Calm as a tranquilized nun. It twists and grinds and deepens for four hundred and twenty miles westward to Whitebird, a town that began as a dozen Nez Perce teepees until recently modernized with tar paper.

In a final convulsive torrent, the Salmon cleaves the Snake like some Pleistocene plow, roaring its deafening entry into Hell's Canyon where there is no one to hear. This mile deep gorge shames all others in this hemisphere and decisively separates Idaho from lesser places like Oregon.

Longhorns near Whitebird summit. Nothing enhances docility like castration.

As if ashamed of such vast emptiness, maps around here include abandoned mines, ghost towns, even solitary cabins, just to fill the space. Now, at least on paper, there is enough print to resemble places like New Jersey. If all this vertical geography were ironed out it would be larger than Texas. And, with a little luck, without any Texans.

The configuration of the West was described by Thomas Wolfe as out where the states are square. Were it not for all those haphazard mountains, Idaho would be square too. Ever since high school, four lads, whose parents considered them normal, had hiked or floated much of it and we never got lost down in the square part. Today's rafters on the main Salmon are limited by Fish and Game

Warren Post Office. They made up their own zip code.

drawings which reduce congestion at campsites although there is still occasional bloodshed.

The shore is patrolled by men with badges wearing funny hats and belts that get tighter every year. But it's not all glamour since government boats must also collect exotic garbage including syringes from San Francisco.

The Salmon's most remote tributary, the incomparable Middle Fork, happily retains much of its seminal uniqueness where humans look up to marvel at mountain goats which in turn smile down at the spectacle of a capsizing boat. Yes, mountain goats do smile, though if they eat tin cans like their city cousins, it could just be gas. The Middle Fork clearly ranks first in the world, though occasional historians confer some significance to the Tigris and Euphrates. Due to an inexcusable Biblical oversight,

Idaho's river is not mentioned in the Old Testament, and we have hired an unemployed monk to re-interpret the original Greek scrolls.

It's OK to give your kid a nickname but don't mess with your rivers. There were days when sturdy wooden boats with long sweeps fore and aft plunged on a one-way trip from North Fork to Riggins where they were dismantled for the lumber. North Forkers planning a second trip had to build another boat even though they would never see it again. Ideally, these white water scows should be salvaged at the end of the float, *not during.*

The Salmon River was doing just fine until it came to be called *The River Of No Return.* Certainly descriptive, and harmless enough, but some folks don't know where to stop. As proof of this we now have THE FRANK CHURCH RIVER OF NO RETURN WILDERNESS which has replaced historical accuracy with a self-serving declarative sentence, three inches long on my map. Devoted cartographers have somehow managed to compress this immodest nomenclature between Oregon to Montana.

Since these states have their own political agendas, none of the Idaho print has been allowed to cross the border, forcing liberal zealots to abandon: *Frank Church, Keynote Speaker for the Democratic Convention, Chairman of the Senate Foreign Relations Committee, steadfast patriot, and wonderful human being.* Idaho's Mt. Borah is still named after a Republican but it's not as high as it used to be.

After the Louisiana Purchase the Northwest was still contested land. Jefferson hoped the French would stay put in Europe and be content just to stomp on their grapes, but as the *Corps of Discovery*

probed westward two other nations tried to spy on the interlopers but could never keep track of them. This is not to belittle their efforts because thirty-three men wandering amongst a million square miles of wilderness are hard to locate even if they bathe.

The British worried about American encroachment into Canada—and with good reason. The Spanish were holed up in Santa Fe fretting over dwindling bullion and a crumbling Mexican empire. We can all rejoice that Lewis and Clark planted the U.S. flag first, because when the English move in, everybody drives on the wrong side of the road. On the other hand, were it not for the British we would all be Spanish.

About thirty years after the American expedition, Prince Maximillian of Wied and the Swiss artist Karl Bodmer cornered William Clark in St. Louis. Bill must have been impressed with those patent leather shoes and lace shirts because he loaned them his maps. European royalty can out-borrow anybody, and no mention is made of their return. Fortunately, there was a historical bonus for the rest of us. Maximillian's detailed diary and Bodmer's watercolors recall the forgotten life of the plains tribes before white acculturation, before small pox exterminated the Mandans in 1837, before the Army Corps of Engineers inundated what was left of Indian lands.

When Meriwether Lewis first saw Idaho, he was pretty excited about it. Today the rest of us can share that same exhilaration without all those uncivil pioneer discomforts such as starving or losing a scalp. There are many ways to retrace the route of 1805, but the easiest is to use a car. Start at Salmon (a wide place in the road) then motor south to Tendoy (a narrow place in the road) and proceed to no road.

Tendoy was a Lemhi chief and Salmon City was named after a fish. Now try your luck to the east by releasing the steering wheel and relaxing while ancient ruts lead your dusty car up to the Lemhi pass. Wrong ruts. Wrong pass.

At the continental divide one can't escape the feeling that Montana is downright proud to touch Idaho. In a confusion of currents some hapless water flows eastward to dilute the Missouri and brighten its mud but the lucky creeks gurgle to the west. The *Corps of Discovery* crossed this very spot and tried not to trample the wild flowers since there are plenty left.

As if preparing for a monumental coincidence, this colorful carpet paved the way to the white man's first contact with the Shoshonis and a surprise encounter with Sacajawea's brother. She recognized Cameahwait immediately, so apparently all Indians do not look alike. Sego lilies, camas and bitter root were only part of the botanical bonanza which seized the captains in a scientific frenzy of Linnean nomenclature. A thousand years ago observant Indians had already identified every tree and bush, but Caucasian tongues trip over those interminable vowels and Latin is so classy. Jefferson had sent Meriwether to Philadelphia for a crash course in science. Clark missed this but was a naturalist by instinct. Both men made liberal use of six packages of ink powder which was mixed with western water to scribble and sketch in field journals as they described a world, wondrous and untouched.

It had to be frustrating to depict the colorful western tanager in black and white. From the Mississippi to the Pacific should be about two thousand miles but this became eight thousand for men who had to struggle up, down and sideways with a few detours to bag a bison and still keep notes about the whole thing.

They described everything they saw and most of it was new. Among the flora and fauna, hundreds were unknown to science. The expedition's hunters chased sage grouse, invariably airborne just out of gun range, and marveled at sprinting pronghorns who left them in the

The Island of Unintentional Landings. The end of the trip for careless kayakers.

dust . . . and there was plenty of that too. They discovered what would become three state flowers: Montana's bitter root, Idaho's syringa, and the Oregon grape. They did waste one afternoon pouring gallons of water down a burrow though any Indian kid could tell them the prairie dog would never come out.

Along its Idaho component, the trail of Lewis and Clark is still identifiable. Cafes and motels proclaim their name—L & C is used where spelling is a problem—and to patronize any other is to compromise your patriotism. Road side signs may offer curious hybrids:

LEWIS & CLARK & SAM - CARBURETOR REPAIR

On the Montana side of the pass, less evidence remains of their trek up the Missouri where the once Great Falls hides its shame behind a Great Dam built by a Great Government. Much of the route is obscured by withered towns and occasional monuments, badly blurred when glimpsed from a high speed interstate.

The historical marker at Lemhi Pass has suffered the usual stigma of western manhood—three bullet holes. From the exit wounds they were obviously fired from Montana. Furthermore Idahoans shoot a much tighter group. The perforated printing laconically tells about the *Corps of Discovery* which represented all seventeen sovereign states, back when America was proud of genuine heroes who, after revisions by eastern historians and west coast screen writers, are no longer recognizable.

Reading from left to right:

Hoping for an easy trip to the Pacific, Clark explored the first few miles of the rugged canyon of the Salmon River below here late in August 1805. His small advance party camped near here with poor but friendly Indians. Clark reported that the Salmon is almost one continued rapid and passage with canoes is entirely impossible. So the expedition had to buy pack horses and go one hundred and ten miles North to an Indian trail across the mountains.

Scratching in the dust, the Lemhis sketched a wild and tortuous river and, with a flair for the dramatic, included a Caucasian skull and cross bones. Lewis and Clark got the idea. Now it was obvious to even the most obtuse white man that THE RIVER OF NO RETURN was more than picturesque hyperbole. Thus, in September of 1805, the myth of the red savage faded into affability. Anthropologists have since determined that it was Idaho's salubrious climate that made these Lemhis so generous and lovable.

Little Salmon River, frantically trying to look like the Big Salmon river . . .and often succeeding.

DON'T INVENT SOMETHING NOBODY WANTS
~ Thomas Edison

The Lolo Trail is two thousand feet lower than Lemhi Pass, but this was only a seasonal advantage because when Lewis and Clark arrived, the Bitter Roots were obliterated with snow. For a thousand years—give or take a century—the Nez Perce crossed the Lolo to hunt buffalo. These shaggy beasts are not as dangerous as they look but Blackfeet are. If they could not steal an appaloosa they would settle for the owner's scalp. This was the risk of bringing some red meat back to the Weippe valley to supplement a diet of salmon and camas bulbs. And animal hides make better teepees than fish skins. In the vast greenery between the Salmon and the Kootenai, civilized Nez Perce cherished the dense forests and ancient cedars.

The Nez Perce had endeared themselves with Lewis and Clark, but the white men who followed soon discovered that these unique Indians had a lot worth stealing. The towns may be called Lapwai, Kamiah, and Kooskia, but the banks are named after Chase and Morgan.

Hiking Nez Perce country today evokes memories when camp fires penetrate the blackness and nineteenth century ghosts rise in a shroud of pine smoke. (For historical reference you can learn all about the cast of characters from an adventure movie with Fred MacMurray, Charlton Heston, and Donna Reed.)

Kindly indulge me as we turn back the clock and join the original *Corps of Discovery* . . . a party of thirty-three unbathed *voyageurs*. This phantom assembly includes one black and one female. Unfortunately, both were slaves. Several are crowded around the fire, but many are out in their tents—probably laid up with gonorrhea.

Clark: "As I see it, the round trip will take twenty-eight months. When do the rest of you have to be back?"

Lewis: "Jefferson said to take all the time I need. (Lewis was a great name-dropper.) I don't know about you, Bill, but I can't wait to see Idaho."

Sacajawea: "Dear captain, by Idaho perhaps you really mean Ahtee-ooaakako-hooyeeee."

Meriwether: "Sorry, Sac, I thought that was Montana."

The little Indian guide had explained this a dozen times: "Try to get it right, Mer."

Since John Coulter hauled the wood for the fire, he was allowed to speak: "It is fortunate that Cruzatte can play the fiddle, but a one-eyed Frenchman with a gun is a menace. Some day he'll shoot Clark in the butt and say it was an accident."

This drew a big laugh until the day it came true.

After surviving what would kill most men, Coulter made it back to the Mandan village, turned around and did it all over again.

John would later discover Yellowstone Park so, obviously, he always thought big.

Since Lewis had grown lax with his journal, John Ordway and Pat Gass were keeping diaries of their own and two figures scribbled by the fire light. "We'll pre-empt the captain, get a Jewish agent and write a best seller."

Pat could see this as a movie: "Gary Cooper could play me." Gass lived to age ninety-nine but not quite long enough to meet Cooper.

While they were arguing over top billing, George Drouillard began to grumble about their last portage: "L and C said it was seventeen miles and supposed to take five days. I am half Shawnee and a good judge of terrain. What Indian would be surprised when the portage took a damned month? I think I slipped a disc (probably L4 on L5) lugging their collapsible boat before the idiotic scheme was abandoned. I hope they build a dam and obliterate the entire place." Thus, this very night there was invoked the Shawnee curse on Great Falls while Cruzatte played back up with a plaintive violin.

The Indian maiden frowned. The violin stopped. The drums began. "You men bitch about trifles. Now let's talk about real trouble. I was just another carefree kid in the Lemhi valley, weaving baskets, smoking venison over a sagebrush fire, and waiting for my first period. Then, when I was only eleven, I was kidnapped by the Blackfeet and auctioned off to Charbonneau, a sniveling braggart who even dickered for a 10% discount."

This was overheard by Ordway who had never been to a slave auction so this was good to know.

"My white owner was uncouth, unwashed and obviously French. While my captors dined on filet of buffalo, I

Salmon River relic. The barn collapsed, the house burned down. Only the outhouse remains. There is a reason for this.

survived on raw ravens. Why do you think they call me the Bird Woman?" Ever since Fort Benton the men had wondered about that black feather sticking out of her teeth. "I was beaten and starved and pregnant at fifteen. Then I had to nurse a new born as well as a deadbeat husband.

This can give marriage a bad name. Now I am walking across the continent with a squirming papoose clawing my back. What I resent more than any of this was being hauled off to a place like North Dakota. You've all seen it. I have my pride."

Clark jumped up, scattering hot coals over the entire group: "Sac, you've been one helluva good sport."

Screams from painful burns were mistaken for support since nobody crossed Clark.

The Bird Woman chirped on: "The French fancy themselves as great lovers—perverts like Charbonneau keep a mirror on the ceiling of his wigwam—but don't send up any smoke signals about their sexual prowess. Beaver ignore him because he is usually impaled in his own traps. Hearing him yell is what I live for."

For the men, these were hilarious diversions, and they dashed to the trap whenever they heard a scream or spied a beaver with a smile . . . and with those incisors, this is a smile to remember. Wholesome entertainment in the woods is hard to come by.

"His real specialty is capsizing canoes. He swims just like he makes love and watching him do either is not a pretty sight."

Meanwhile, Sacajawea was smitten by Clark's red hair, and her voice adopted a husky, sensual tone. Cupid was lurking in the Idaho ponderosa and launched his arrow with a compound bow. Or maybe it was Cruzatte's violin.

"If ever we reach the Columbia I can tell you exactly how BRAVES got that name."

These celibate mountaineers were a long way from St. Louis, and tonight Sacajawea's resemblance to Donna Reed was uncanny. Secretly she prayed to the Great Spirit of Deodorants that the snow would melt and the men could bathe.

While all this was going on, somewhere back East, Aaron Burr and Alexander Hamilton were fighting a duel, after which one of them would get his portrait on a ten dollar bill.

When things were tough—this would be all the time—weary men were cheered by Sacajawean philosophy: "White men worry about getting lost. Indians call this Getting to Know the Country. It's a question of attitude."

Toussaint Charbonneau stayed on the payroll as an indispensable link in the tedious sequence of interpretation. His wife translated Shoshoni to Hidatsa. So far, so good. Then Toussaint relayed this in French to Labiche who—with a little luck—passed it on in English. By then everybody lost interest and it took less time just to steal the horses.

Charbonneau had arrogance to match his indolence. His forte was abusing blacks and York was the only one around. The group had to keep the Frenchman, but since York was a slave he had the ultimate job security. Every camp fire deserves a good songfest, and York led the group with that great African beat which was so infectious that even wolves could be heard singing an eerie harmony.

Who's in the sac
With Sacajawea
When Mr. Jawea
Is away?

York's catchy tune resounded down the Clearwater and on to the Columbia where Umatilla Indians repeated the chant as they netted salmon. Clark's black slave contributed mightily to the expedition's success and saved several white scalps. He was easily the best dancer west of St. Louis and made a hit with the Indians who were only two shades lighter than he. The Shoshonis made him a chief, and his first edict was that minorities would no longer ride in the back of the travois. Clark intended to free his slave, but not today when York was more popular than his owner.

A thousand leagues to the east—a safe distance for the man who dreamed up this trip—Jefferson had just mailed twenty seven million dollars to Paris where Talleyrand waited for the check to clear. It is not every day you can buy Louisiana.

Before he could savor this sweet deal, he was pestered by an erythematous senator from some Northeastern Commonwealth. He had recently survived a terrible accident in which his girlfriend had drowned. Now he offered a bribe—dad had plenty of money—if the expedition would bring back a brace of comely Shoshoni maidens. Blackfoot or Nez Perce would be OK. The president had to tell the disappointed senator that most virgins never remain so beyond Nebraska. An exasperated Jefferson slammed his Monticello door which he himself had designed to sustain such executive trauma. Tom knew there would be days like this.

He was also concerned if Meriwether would ever make it back. As the president's secretary, Lewis had been indoors most of the time and could not be in the best of shape.

CHAPTER TWO

ALWAYS BE SINCERE
EVEN IF YOU HAVE TO FAKE IT.
~ Groucho Marx

Idaho was a territory prior to 1890 at which time it was urged to join the Union in an attempt to upgrade the quality of the entire nation. Lewiston was the designated capital until Boise stole the official seal and escaped in a high speed row boat.

Mining equipment on Columbia River barges was transferred at Umatilla and distributed at about six hundred pounds per mule. After a few level miles they left the river for the tortuous mountain grind to Pierce or the old Magruder Trail to Elk City.

North Idaho gold petered out just as a lot more was discovered farther south where endless pack strings struggled over steep trails between Boise and Idaho City where mines eventually out-produced all of Alaska.

With so many big rivers, people with no particular destination always wanted to get to the other side. Ferry operators proliferated, and their quaint names have endured on modern highway maps, but only after cartographers had already borrowed every Indian name under twelve syllables. These maps are beautifully printed in three colors and at least show the way to Highway 95 and give a general idea of how much land we stole from the natives.

Idaho extends from Canada where miles become kilometers so you can drive forever. Its southern border offers a choice between Utah, home of the Mormon Tabernacle Choir, or Nevada, which sells the sin that Mormons occasionally buy. Pioneer ferries were gradually replaced by bridges so vagrants would have some place to sleep. From this dry sanctuary they beckoned their brethren, and together they brewed White Lightning which fortified courage enough to rob an occasional stage.

Seattle was achieving notoriety with its Skid Row while San Francisco's coastal barbarians specialized in sexual deviants which evolved into the world's queerest monopoly and ultimately the pride of California. With this concentration of perverts, other western states were badly outclassed but managed to cultivate a handful of child molesters. Transvestites actually shunned Idaho because they could never find a thing to wear. A few moved to Portland where they entered their own queen in the Rose Festival Parade.

Territorial denizens pursued the usual frontier activities where men swung the axe, followed the plow and learned to write. Wives fed farm hands in shifts and delivered babies in the same kitchen—occasionally on the same day.

Methodists didn't drink. Catholics just a little. Kids didn't carry spray paint. Everybody said *shucks* and folks in general were quite picturesque. Every town had its own kiln which was cheaper than freighting bricks from Weiser. Next to every livery stable was a brewery since beer is good for horses.

When not clearing sagebrush, men looked for gold on some Indian's property. Southern secessionists were everywhere. Most had deserted the Confederacy when the shooting started but were still capable of pushing the red man around since there were no blacks out here. Several Yankees joined them in this sport.

Social activities were largely limited to the church and grangehall, but for outdoor excitement town folks gathered on the village green. But here citizens found every seat pre-empted by grizzled blue and gray veterans who mustered daily unless bugled away for secret maneuvers.

One constipated soldier failed to report after overdosing on Cascara sagrada. One rebel boasted that he once rode with Nathan Bedford Forrest, but derisive Yankees on the opposite bench screamed that if he rode at all it was in a buggy.

Bayonets often miss but barbs in the park always hit the mark. The spectators had actually built these benches but were willing to stand because these garrulous gladiators were the best show in town. Courteous citizens considered the outside possibility that one of these uniformed curiosities had actually fought in the Civil War.

The miscreants and mendicants were rarely employed because the heroism of imaginary battles had consumed every ounce of energy. If subsequent community performance was any measure of earlier military action, nobody would have won the war. So many battles. So few scars.

Working just half a day in the mill had left one veteran so exhausted that he could barely hold his bench from a group of small children who were planning a picnic. Bearded reserves arrived just in time to secure the bench and capture the entire park. Furthermore, if the pesky brats tried to use the swing, another battalion would be summoned from Boise. And the little cowards backed off.

Civil War caps and buckles, purchased at the local Waldorf tavern, identified the ersatz warriors as CSA or USA. Most of the scabbards were bent from prolonged sitting, so these generals were mighty slow on the draw. If a

saber conferred rank, both armies were top heavy with
brass.

Beyond the histrionics of the village green were those
genuine veterans who paid the taxes that built the park.
They tolerated the sedentary soldiers whose glorious fabrications of Antietam pulled in most of the county. This
was good for business. Eventually, spontaneity yielded to
predictability. This was show biz. The first and second battle of Bull Run always drew a good crowd, but when they
tried to fictionalize a third the town rebelled. The insulted
audience boycotted the entire event until they were
allowed to vote and decide which side should win. History
has always yielded to entertainment.

Despite ample documentation, the Southern bench
denied every Union victory, but none of the Federals had a
fifty dollar bill to prove that General Grant ever existed.
Battles were so entertaining that the drama of Vicksburg
was ignored. Nothing is quite so boring as a siege.

Every Wednesday they re-fought the Battle of
Chancellorsville, which was apparently located somewhere between Twin Falls and Pocatello. Folks weren't
sure because nobody traveled much. Through the dust and
din one bent and bearded Union man tried to force himself
upright but his venerable vertebrae were now molded to
the curve of a bench. He attempted a pathetic yell—the
rebels had a patent on this and he damn well knew it—
and brandished a cane with gnarled knuckles that probably never gripped a musket. Frenetic beyond his tolerance,
he self-inflicted a minor laceration which he encouraged to
bleed. Whereupon he was captured by the Confederates
who threatened to whisk him off to Andersonville prison
unless he promised never again to brag about his war
wound.

School children hoped for more blood and had not forgotten when their picnic was driven from green grass to

sulk in dry weeds. Would there ever come the day for revenge? There would.

They heard a rumor that one of the combatants had been a deserter. One of the children had a grandfather who was an expert on the Civil War in general, and the Falls City contingent in particular. If only the oracle would disclose who had been the infamous deserter, then one lowly second-grader could be the hero of the class. Such a chance never comes twice. The old man would allow the expectant hero just two questions and no more.

Hopeful peers huddled to deliberate on how best to ration these inquiries:

"Grandad, could one be a deserter?"

"Yes." So far so good.

"Really? Which army?"

"Both."

And the crestfallen lad said "RATS" and was disciplined for swearing.

The whitest, indeed the purest, church in Falls City dominated its finest hill from which alert Methodists could spot any late comers. This enviable site had been selected years earlier when an immigrant wagon debarked the founding brethren who promptly took the high ground. As always happens, this monopoly was disrupted when an Italian contingent wheeled into town and a long train it was, for these were fecund folk.

Staging a second assault, they erected a Catholic church every bit as white but, at least to the Protestant eye, on a slightly lower hill. Near the edge of town they shared an acre of cattails with red-winged blackbirds, but the Catholics misinterpreted their melodies as a breeding song. Methodist spirits sank when the priest whispered that expansion plans were already on the drawing board. Most of the denizens spoke with some accent and carried bibles in various languages, but there was a hopeful glimmer of compromise when one day some Protestant Scot was heard singing a Verdi aria to a sonorous accompaniment of bag pipes.

But apparently this town harbored more sin than two churches could handle. Spies reported that a battalion of German Lutherans was on its way from Minnesota. They were said to be Protestant, but their minister dressed like a priest with a congregation that brewed beer in the kitchen. Zounds!!! That's exactly where those pesky Catholics bottled their wine.

Migration west was often mandated by hopes already failed in the east. People like the du Ponts were so comfortable in Delaware that there was no pressing reason to leave. German loggers were overjoyed to discover New World forests covered with Old World snow but memories of Europe persisted.

Teutonic towns like Genesee, Keuterville, Hauser and Mohler soon sprinkled North Idaho. Incongruous as it seems, even Moscow was dedicated, not by Russians but nostalgic Germans. With the inducement of land grants, the Czar had once aspired to infuse his country's primitive agriculture with industrious Germans, and after a generation, Moscow became the equivalent of Berlin. Since Idaho's Moscow began as an anomaly, what better site for a university? Boise owed these folks something ever since they stole the state seal and moved the capital (and the treasury) farther south.

Not every town up north has a German name. In pathetic proximity to the University of Idaho there is one Harvard and one Princeton. Their glittering eastern aura never rubbed off, and all the U of I has in common with Harvard and Princeton is a lousy football team. Coeur d' Alene was never altered, since retaining at least one

A sign with this many German names belongs in Berlin. This one is on the Camas Prairie where French must wait for their mail (assuming they can read).

French name maintains cordiality with the Canadians who are close enough to invade us.

The Lutheran exodus of the nineteenth century did not go unnoticed. Fresh off the reservation, during an unauthorized absence, a renegade Cheyenne brave extem-

porized a smoke signal though—and this seems curious—
no record remains: *Pale faces rolling STOP Heavily armed
with axes STOP Too dangerous to attack the wagons STOP
Hold up the stage instead STOP Chief says OK to use the
same warpaint.* With matadorean grace he swept his tele-
graphic blanket over the green fire: *These cheap government shorts are chaffing my loins STOP Don't* (apostro-
phes are tough in smoke) *start massacre without me END
OF SMOKE.*

His bellicose exhortations were ignored. All the
Cheyenne were mesmerized by high flying Valkyries
(based in Minneapolis) riding through the clouds, beckoning the wagon train westward across the plains. It was
evident that in only a few months the Methodists of Falls
City could be relegated to second place.

Maybe even third.

CHILL PENURY REPRESSED THEIR NOBLE
RAGE AND FROZE THE GENIAL CURRENT OF THE
SOUL

~ Thomas Gray

The old man's flowing beard could identify him even
from the next farm, emphasizing the menacing vis-
age of an old world prophet. Gripping a shovel, a
maul or a scythe, Hugh's callused hands had molded to
anything with an ash handle. His posture was regal or
rigid depending on which crop had just failed.

Irish skin lacked the requisite pigmentation to withstand the relentless hazards of his trade. A face like
stitched leather was rarely strained by a smile so most of
the sutures were still holding beneath which one could
count the bones.

Stoic and silent, the last time Will's grandad raised his voice was when he saw a buggy try to stop a train. Every gesture was rationed with an economy of emotion that excluded even basic animation which is inherent in human communication. Hugh was never heard to groan or even sigh. Brave children approached cautiously just to touch his beard, behind which they perceived the gruff generosity of an old man willing to help a neighbor just so he himself was not expected to smile. Hollow promises, exhausted mines and failed mills had stripped away all feelings. His strength was already wrung dry when tuberculosis wiped out his own sons, and now withering crops barely sustained his adopted grandchildren.

By never displaying anger, joy or grief, he became unapproachable to all the world . . . except one boy who was growing up beside him. And to Will, he silently conveyed what most men seek forever—approval.

A grim countenance was not unique around Falls City, one of those towns that had not changed—or couldn't. Grandad owned one hundred and sixty acres which owned him. It was all out there waiting in the rain, struggling to grow or more likely wash away.

In a few years, Falls City's son of poverty attended a college only slightly less destitute than its ragged students to whom the Greek tragedies were like a letter from home. Thomas Gray's allusion to chill penury captured the reality of despair by an author who spoke from experience and Grandad haunted every stanza.

Fortunately, there was one gifted Irish writer who could temper cynicism with humor. During his sophomore year, Will encountered a discarded portrait of George Bernard Shaw encased within a tarnished frame, peering sternly through cracked glass. G.B.S. bore an uncanny, almost twinly, resemblance to his grandfather. There were no extant pictures of Hugh (and probably no one else in Falls City), so Will polished the frame and carried this portrait of Shaw. In time he replaced the glass but the face never smiled. Close enough . . . and a profound compliment to both Irishmen.

It was two generations later when Will's own son learned about that substitute portrait. By then it was too late for me to revise a long established concept of my great grandfather as the Grim Reaper. Perhaps it was that scythe. It had been a harmless deception especially on faces that were mostly beard but it exemplified the change from days when there were no family photos to when there are entirely too many.

Only one of these Irish skeptics became famous. Hugh was never published but his words have endured on a page in the family Bible:

I have lived many years.

I have seen many changes.

I have been against every one.

ONLY CANCER IS MORE DESPISED THAN THE CALORIE.

After the death of his first wife, Will's grandfather Hugh scouted the countryside to locate a new one. Hugh must have been a master salesman because most women would surely have heard about his two recently acquired orphans who were hardly an enticement to matrimony. I lived in the wrong century to know my great grandfather who must have been endowed with that enviable appeal which attracts women, that elusive animal magnetism which, as near as I can tell, is not inherited.

The new stepmother was introduced to an Idaho valley and the one farm which had faltered where others prospered. After hesitating at a door without hinges, she entered a room with a leaking roof. Her lasting memory would be that of Will and Edith crawling on a wet floor under a table with no food on it. Meat was never in abundance unless something died. When the food was blessed, meat was mentioned right after God. As an alternative to starvation, the family practiced involuntary vegetarianism before it became a fad. Hugh's first wife may well have overdosed on turnips. Food which could barely sustain two must now stretch across a pine table where eight elbows flanked four meager plates.

The innocent calorie began with the noble assignment of defining "that quantity of heat required to raise the temperature of one gram of water by one degree centigrade." Alas, this well intentioned unit of energy has fallen on bad times. Angry protesters, the fatter the madder, circulate petitions aimed at its extermination.

It is assaulted by TV professors whose mesmerizing voices outweigh their credentials. With the scientific authority of Madison Avenue, they malign the calorie while encouraging addiction to amphetamines. But there were even more dangerous times when the ultimate fat fighter hit the market in the 1930s: an expensive white pill with sugar on the outside and tapeworm eggs on the inside. And they really worked until some sore head exposed the scam after passing a ten foot white worm which struggled to swim out of the toilet. The sale of vermifuges soared as an accidental by-product of the perpetual profit in obesity. But quackery and gullibility are joined at the hip. Shrugging off momentary embarrassment, tapeworm breeders assumed new roles—sorcerers who hovered over cauldrons concocting some new cancer cure which rivalled the crystal ball and spinal manipulation.

But the calorie of 1900 was eagerly sought, highly respected, consumed fast and burned even faster. Woe to the worker who burned more than he ingested. A chronic shortage of calories we dignify as malnutrition which, at the turn of the century, conspired to stunt growth for the young and keep the old from getting much older.

After high school, a scrawny kid convinced a logging camp to hire him. Will grew eight inches and picked up forty pounds where, if you weren't killed, the twelve hours of sweat were rewarded with mountains of food.

Nor did he ever doubt that Idaho's tree business saved his life. Edith was not so lucky and even sharing his pay check was not enough. She taught school, never married and coughed her life away. Miliary tuberculosis deserved its crude but descriptive alias, galloping consumption. This relentless cough, when theatrically blended with loud music, became the inspiration for straining arias where captive patrons in tight tuxedos awaited the gasping demise of the soprano in the last act.

But when your best sister dies young, it's nothing to sing about.

Sharks and historians are drawn to blood. School text-books limit their coverage of Pasteur and Edison to allow more space for Caesar and Genghis. Violence and mayhem will hold the child's attention in the class room and prepare him for television, politics, and marriage.

Battle hymns glorify the hero felled by an enemy bullet, but when the killer is microscopic there are no ballads about victims languishing in military hospitals. Even with a catchy tune, most lyricists can't rhyme anything with clostridial gangrene.

Hippocrates was first to describe a devastating catastrophe when many of his philosophy pals down at the Acropolis slumped in their chitons and forsook mortality with Greek finality. He called it influenza, derived from influence to convey its widespread lethal behavior. Greek derivations eventually make sense. By 1610 this disease was better documented and they began to keep score. Influenza probably killed more than the better publicized Black Death. ("Forever Amber" was a movie about the Black Death, but with the propriety of Hollywood censors in those days no one could understand exactly how Linda Darnell got pregnant.)

For the next two hundred years, these epidemics were periodic but mercifully localized. As the speed of travel increased so did the spread of the virus culminating in a world-wide pandemic. Starting in Siberia in 1889, influenza swept inexorably over Europe leaving a swath of corpses and too few wagons to carry them. Within two months this lethal alien crossed the Atlantic and soon the New World was seized with Old World panic. Theaters were closed along the east coast. Spontaneous public gatherings were discouraged, voluntary at first, but soon enforced. Those restaurants not already closed revealed diners in white muslin masks—a pitiful prophylaxis.

When Pacific ships anchored in San Francisco, the pestilence established a second beachhead. Invisible stowaways debarked and decimated the bay, then exploded inland, gaining virulence along the way. No town was spared.

Cemeteries ran out of monuments. Grim granite was replaced by wood which, though less lasting, was intensely personal when carved by the family. Two such improvised markers guarded both parents of an infant who was born just in time to become an instant orphan. Theirs were of pine and they leaned a bit . . . as if listening. Will never considered himself an orphan, never even heard the word, until his older sister figured it out because most of her school friends had parents who were about fifty years younger than the folks at her house.

Grandad had already raised and lost his own children and also buried a wife who was just plain worn out taking care of them. This was common among women, many under thirty, though the cause on death certificates was usually something in Latin.

At the turn of the century, diphtheria choked infants by the score; boys big enough to hold the reins were crushed in runaways, while typhoid and influenza lurked to ambush any survivors. Tuberculosis was prevalent but dying took longer.

Will's grandad had observed the coughing death of galloping consumption and buried those who got too close. And now, despite the crush of poverty, he did not hesitate to do it all over again. With a little luck, Will and Edith might even live.

The catastrophic pandemic of 1889 revisited the world with familiar vengeance during the Great War. By then, Will was a physician trained to conquer disease . . . but not this one. His frustration was shared by doctors on both sides of the war as German doctors watched thousands die until the Kaiser's trenches were reinforced by child-soldiers. Influenza mortality was even higher this time because in 1918 the world had more people to kill. When the war ended, he came to Idaho where he practiced for fifty-five years with devotion and gratitude. Will personified a grand, forgotten era when prescriptions were in Latin, handwriting was elegant and no word was ever misspelled.

Never yielding to common medical slang, he spoke of influenza with almost reverent respect.

It was never the THE FLU.

FULL MANY A FLOWER IS BORN TO BLUSH UNSEEN AND WASTE ITS SWEETNESS ON THE DESERT AIR.

~ Thomas Gray

They didn't have an illegal still in the barn nor a family skeleton in the closet, but there was a pinochle deck hidden in Grandad's kitchen. As an infant, Edith had crawled across the floor and found them quite by accident. One quick shuffle with stubby fingers and she never played with her rattle again.

Few church-goers admitted to playing cards, and it was a shameful secret that little Edith could beat any adult in town, a sure sign of a misspent youth and for Methodists the gateway to big time sin. Only a green visor separates pinochle from poker, the game of the devil himself, in which he deals off the bottom, rarely needs to bluff, and bets with coins too hot to handle.

Her brother remembered her as a scrawny six-year-old with uncanny card sense who could crush any opponent though once a boy with a cute smile beat her. But not twice. A smile could go just so far.

The entire family was genetically taciturn, but Edith's poker face became permanent. Folks remembered when her cough was merely a nuisance, but the occasional hack became persistent, causing her entire body to recoil. Now episodes were triggered merely by talking. So she didn't talk. No wonder teachers were crazy about her.

It was during the pledge of allegiance that her worst bout began, barely audible above the monotonous mumbling. Then, as the class unisoned "one nation indivisible" she turned cyanotic with one uncontrollable paroxysm.

Seized with patriotism, Will raised his voice in a camouflaging crescendo. Together they made it through, but he began wondering if she would ever get well.

Learning is an unexplored ocean. First grade is a wading pool where even imaginary sharks are real enough to keep many kids from ever reaching the sea.

Will was lucky he had an older sister to shoo the sharks. He had devoted the first five years of his life to tormenting Edith but that's what brothers do. Now he would stop it and torment someone else.

Last year she carried a delicate white handkerchief, but sheer lace could no longer conceal frequent stains of red. Now she clutched a less feminine but more absorbent bandanna. Ordinary people sleep in bedrooms though some beguiling ladies have changed the course of history by calling it a boudoir. (French conveys decadence better than most languages.)

Edith never made history but her bedroom concealed its own secrets. Pillows muffled her cough and after ominous night sweats she quietly changed bedding. A few stitches tightened her home made dress to conceal her alarming weight loss but it was hard to overlook that tightened face. *Galloping Consumption* was an archaic but eloquently descriptive diagnosis that left little doubt as to her plight.

Such terms so assaulted our fragile sensibilities that social architects hastened to replace the graphic (tell it like it is) with the delicate (tell it like it ain't). Convulsions (archaic) are now seizures (modern) and while this meaningless change might make the spectator feel better, it won't do a thing for the victim.

Will's grandmother was also losing weight. Maybe it was something she ate—or didn't.

Both grandma and Edith had always been picky eaters and could never choose between turnips and dandelion greens. Meanwhile, unknown sisters in unknown places were also coughing blood and all were doomed. Tuberculosis killed these girls but it was in no hurry.

Will was drawn to medicine hoping to fit the pieces of a deadly family puzzle but lived to see an honorable profession suffocate under a mountain of oppressive governmental directives, interminable, inconsistent, but always arbitrary.

Fraudandabuse (that's one word) became such a catchy accusation that it was quickly embraced by the press in a crusade of class envy. Only the imperfect are qualified to demand perfection. The judge and jury were sulking appointees who had failed to be accepted by any medical school.

Under the banner of fraudandabuse (still one word) arrogant bureaucrats could even investigate any hapless doctor who accidentally mis-dialed a phone number.

Through misguided compassion we subsidized the world and opened our shores to a tidal wave of disease. The sicker the immigrant the more he evoked our sympathy, and instead of effectively treating the world's afflictions we imported the causative organisms. The objective logic of quarantine has been overwhelmed by subjective feelings. The memory of Edith deserves better.

Through a series of mutations, we have created new and improved acid-fast bacilli, virulent enough to decimate the world. Morality itself has undergone a mutation just as devastating. Children starve on spawning continents with parents too ignorant to cover a sewer or ligate a vas deferens. It's their religion.

And, by God, doctors should do something about this.

Curiosity over eastern mysticism evoked western experimentation until we modified our own beliefs to embrace the ugliest aspects of theirs. Science and logic must swim upstream against the torrent of animal sacrifice, cymbals, and incense, led by a bearded cultist with copper bracelets on his wrist and magnets in his shoes.

The white lab coat has been replaced by a stained toga. Green parks have yielded to weeds and pungent communes where free love flourishes with the cacophony of amplified guitars while parasitic offspring write home for money. Superstition breeds with California cults to produce a hideous hybrid which, now and then, delivers prematurely but never aborts. Pampered students march armpit to armpit with activist professors in a parade of the unwashed, the unemployed and the unashamed. In sandaled feet, they storm the chancellor's office, demanding socialized medicine and with stolen bull horns, clamor for Asian aphrodisiacs.

Berkeley teachers, about the same age as those they teach, vilify all western pharmaceuticals except a few antibiotics which still come in handy for venereal disease which they caught from some student.

After four years of Marxist indoctrination, the enlightened graduate culminates his academic legacy by urinating in the campus fountain.

In the evil days of Sodom and Gomorrah such egregious behavior could turn godless folks into a pillar of salt but this is now regarded as obscure symbolism. The TV generation is immune to special effects, and the FDA interprets the pillar of salt as God's confirmation that too much sodium is not good for you.

But our Creator, ever adaptable, now distributes retributive pathogens to educate 20th century transgressors. For the old fashioned, He offers an upgrade of Edith's tuberculosis. For the more fashionable there is always AIDS.

Freshmen begin med school looking at microscopic organisms and shudder at exotic curiosities that actually look back. These were never to be seen again. Or so they thought.

Some of the ugliest parasites were perfectly happy in the Nile or Ganges but are now here for a special engagement. In today's spirit of liberal generosity we dare not send them back where they came from. To do so would be inhospitable. What kind of a nation are we? In some countries, dogs are a delicacy though when your gut harbors a ten foot tape worm and you are half blind from trachoma all pets look alike.

After intense and costly deliberation, The United Nations has decreed that those sagacious dog-eaters can be the salvation of the decadent west.

ONE WORLD really means THEIR WORLD.

America has been shamed into supporting any culture that is anathema to our own.

And not over there but right here.

Meanwhile, let's bring back leprosy.

OFTEN HUMILIATED.NEVER EMBARRASSED

Hugh's farm was not the saddest in Idaho. The adjacent homestead was mismanaged by a sanctimonious Methodist deacon who prayed more than he plowed: "God will provide. Disturbing the soil would only interrupt His plan."

God was crazy about weeds and His Will included fallow fields and an army of creditors, including the Methodist choir director and one Catholic priest. Agrarian ineptitude crowded under an umbrella of platitudes while malnourished cattle awaited heavenly intervention.

The same closed mind that never grew a crop also had strong opinions on medicine. Better a child choke to death with diphtheria than allow a tracheostomy: "All doctors ever want to do is cut somebody's throat. The Bible says so."

Nothing ripened in the fields but the bedroom had produced seven uncouth offspring. They had to be his. They were that ugly.

Their last bath had been to wash away the meconium the day they delivered. Alas, his alacrity was limited to reproduction, and the education of this pathetic litter was relegated to watching daddy tend the farm at which he was slower than eating soup with a fork.

He reminded other farmers of the three-toed sloth, and Hugh hoped to catch his neighbor barefooted just to count his digits. He never removed his boots (or his rotting sox), but The Salmon River Grangehall nicknamed him Three Toes just the same.

It was as if the deacon was put next door just to exasperate Hugh and test his tolerance. The intervening fence collapsed every year not because the posts were buried less than six inches but because it was God's Will.

Grandad could take no more: "Surely, not Him again."

Hugh also read the Bible but covered other bases with the Farmer's Almanac. The correlation between confidence and ability escaped the deacon: "School is a waste of time. Confidence is everything."

His family did not walk on all fours. That was enough.

One of his grubby kids cautiously tried a job at the mill, but the noise assaulted his delicate nervous system, and nobody told him there would be so much sawdust. Once he came to work early, but that was only to steal the payroll before the foreman arrived. Work ain't fun but crime don't pay. Nobody told him there would be even more sawdust on the jail house floor.

For several years Grandad marveled at this paradox of confidence and failure, but even with the Lord doing most of the chores, Three Toes was finally overwhelmed, and a sympathetic warden paroled his son with one proviso: "I, too, am a Methodist and will agree to release the prisoner only if you all switch to another church."

Side by side, father and son accomplished together what neither could do alone. They lost the whole damned farm.

Verily, now they were stuck with all that confidence.

MAN IS THE ONLY ANIMAL THAT BLUSHES . . .
OR NEEDS TO
~ Mark Twain

First Come, First Saved. This axiom prompted many of the congregation to skip breakfast just to qualify. Good for the soul meant hard on the stomach, and God's message was often obscured by heretical intestinal rumbling.

On the other hand, the evening service could be risky in quite another way. After a heavy supper, drowsy druids succumbed to that audible digestion and somnolence which has plagued the faithful since Antioch. Ptosis can pass for prayer only as long as your head stays on. The sonorous might be obscured by a cooperative choir, but all hymns must end when no snore can be ignored. This demands a well directed elbow, preferably by some family member.

These are stoic folk, able to shrug off a child screaming with his third tantrum as easily as they can pass an empty palm over the collection plate. For the truly steadfast these growls and snores are too trivial to empty a church.

But there is one sound which can. I speak reluctantly of an odious disruption almost too embarrassing to mention but too common to disregard: that tasteless disaster which obtunds Christian brotherhood, that sphincter betrayal which transcends propriety, that indelicate

whimsy of nature where the bolus meets the bowel . . .
FLATUS. Like a blind man bitten by his seeing eye dog, so
can a faithful colon turn on its owner.

And all the while, flatus skulks behind crude aliases
proving that all the four letter expletives are not reserved
for pleasurable functions. There is no choir, no sermon, no
elbow and, alas, no prayer to mitigate the Olfactory
Salute. Panic seizes the perpetrator who has only seconds
to shift the blame to some hapless victim in an adjacent
pew. The native reflex is to turn to anyone behind you . . .
the time honored Stare and Share technique.

This carries some risk, when frightened eyes fall on
the banker who holds the mortgage on your farm. He has
no sense of humor and is stubborn as a yeast infection.
When stare meets glare, transfer your fragrant challenge
to another innocent victim or you can lose your home.

God admires a quick-witted Methodist.

The decrepit ladder had uneven legs, a few rungs
missing, and fell short of the eave line by about a
yard. It was probably last used by Indians to storm
some cavalry fort and brought out of retirement to shingle
the barn roof. This can happen when a kid complains too
much about bucking bales.

His first appeal for sympathy failed when Will showed
his battered hands to an indifferent grandfather whose
calluses were at least sixty years older.

Finally he went too far by whining about the dust and
was banished to the barn which was covered with dust-
free moss but needed new shingles in case the moss
leaked. And if he did sneeze from such a frightening height
nobody on the ground would hear it.

He had watched real carpenters store nails in their mouths and wondered if they ever swallowed them. Carpentry was a risky business.

Will took a sandwich and all the tools he could carry since one trip up the ladder was all he cared to risk.

He looked longingly at the bales of hay far below, as he struggled to the crest and hammered his first row, which was noticeably straighter than the second. Only when Will was admiring the finished job did Grandad explain that the boy should have worked from the bottom to the top so the shingles would properly overlap to shed the water. Staying on the job was more important than good technique and such a steep roof would never leak anyway.

June was Grandad's favorite month. One can accomplish so much more with all that extra daylight. Will disliked it for the same reason. His aversion was counter to the mainstream as brides homed in on the sixth month to don the white gown of virginity while her family celebrated the acquisition of an unemployed son-in-law. Eventually, June weddings became popular for bored eighth graders since it was something they hadn't done before. Other months were optional as dictated by the stage of gestation.

As if to confirm his Junophobia, Will lived to marvel at the proliferation of wedding rental shops, the *sine qua non* of the American mall which offered a wide array of veils to cover the bride's acne and cummerbunds to conceal the groom's erection. Realistically, what the world needed was a Divorce Shop:

BUY THE TUX. RENT THE RING.

Way back when Will was still shingling the barn roof Grandad had attended a tragic wedding which was the ultimate of poor planning:

"No sensible groom would ever get married on the 21st of June.

"This means that the honeymoon begins on the short-est night of the year."

YOU CAN LEAD A COW TO SLAUGHTER BUT YOU CAN'T MAKE HER LIKE IT.

Summer finally ended with a deserved diversion from farm chores, and in the 1890s this meant boisterous festivity when the threshing crew rolled into town.

Kids jockeyed for position on what would be the curb if the town had one.

Leading the parade was a recently polished tractor-engine pulling the separator which was liberally adorned with pennants totally unrelated to the job ahead.

Adding to the harvest pageantry, was the clanging chuck wagon where a Chinese cook fried onions with a tantalizing aroma that made every gallbladder contract with anticipation. With studied panache he tossed an occasional fire cracker into the stove which impressed children who had never seen an oriental, and they begged to go home with him, thinking he did this sort of thing all the time. This never worked out because he spoke no English. For another month the folks on the farm seemed mighty dull.

The parade continued with seven boarding wagons with colorful canvas tops, each bearing the name of some local farmer and modified just for this occasion.

Flattery and crass commercialism worked even then, and Will burst with pride to see Grandad Hugh glorified in letters a foot high. Will had always thought you had to die to get your name in print. The itinerant cast of about thirty included steam mechanics, cooks, and a roustie whose chores included unsolicited food sampling. Red and yellow grain separators declared that Idahoans approached the 20th century eager to replace primitive techniques unchanged since Moses (though flailing, winnowing, and stomping on grapes are still more picturesque and put women in their place).

Bundles of grain were tied by dollar-a-day binders and hauled alongside the threshing machine. Feeder-engineers earned the most, and a man with a team was worth $2.50 a day which was pure profit if he never fed his horses.

In descending order of pay came the separator tenders and sack sewers. To put everything in gastronomical perspective, the last to be paid were the cooks who were lucky to get a dollar. The criterion for a French chef: "How well can you bake?" For a thresher's cook: "How much can you lift?" These parade participants were the migrating nucleus which was then expanded locally by The Recruiter, a mesmerizing con man who was smoother than his starched shirt and whose already ample waist was further augmented by a money belt. On his extravagant promise of profit most farmers wound up working for nothing. He'd be back to fleece them again next year unless he violated his parole.

As a grand finale, the wagon foreman opened the stove and ceremoniously tossed in a pound of sulfur from which the billowing yellow smoke was well worth the lasting odor of rotten eggs.

In a town starved for entertainment this brought cheers from all except Grandad who had also frowned at last year's frivolity. Grandad correlated sulfur with brimstone, easily validated by a stream of parables, and from here it was a short trip to even more specific allegories about the devil. This was Hugh's area of expertise. Nobody knew more about the ecology of Hades. Every earthly event carried a moral and Hugh's grandson was expected to make the correct biblical inference—brimstone, locusts, floods, bank failures, or a squirrel with a heart attack.

Big city implement dealers came to display their wares which all of Falls City envied with the one exception already noted. Gleaming equipment rolled past—and in a sense rolled over—pioneer spectators who still worked with machinery about the same age as the prairie schooner which brought them here in the first place and had been converted to a manure spreader.

The twentieth century trumpeted down the street while anachronisms in homemade clothes stood by as their world submerged in an immiscible brew of wonder and resentment.

And it all happened so fast.

After 1910 the hand-fed stationary threshers were gradually replaced by steam driven automatic feeders and straw blowers, powerful evidence of the burgeoning technology when Yankee ingenuity was admired and engines worshipped.

The thresher's grand parade only made four lads restless and begging for more. Their wish would be answered the next day with the county fair: a cornucopia of prize hogs, elaborate quilts, painted women, and the road to ruin.

Admission was gratis, the usual seduction for depravity, but inside the tents lurked a fast talker with a limber cane and a straw hat who was even slicker than the thresher's recruiter.

Each youngster had saved a dime from salvaging a mile or so of baling twine and gleaning a few bushels of wheat carelessly spilled as only machinery can.

Buxom ladies in bloomers were friendly enough, but the timid boys could not hold up their end of the conversation. After much giggling by one group and blushing from the other, one girl offered to expose part of one breast for a quarter. Damn! This was way over budget. Only the lack of a measly two bits had separated these lads from hell and damnation.

It was that close.

Then suddenly appeared an arresting sign with red letters, not crayon on butcher's paper, but professional printing and probably from Boise.

TALK TO THE WISE MAN - FIVE CENTS.

With those piercing eyes, he did look mighty smart. For today only, and because he really liked them, the oracle would share the wisdom of the ages but hurry before the sun goes down. Maybe he wasn't so wise after dark.

One nickel later, and comfortably seated on separate barrels, they listened attentively. Johnny Flynn took notes.

After a theatrical delay the curtain parted and a robe staggered into view surmounted with mesmerizing eyes which by now were a little bloodshot. The head was mostly Adam's Apple which began to vibrate under a slurred tongue. The voice was mysterious and his accent was distinctly foreign—maybe Seattle:

"I have lived three score and ten.

My life has been full.

Attend thou to the words of the wise man."

Johnny scribbled furiously but it didn't take long for the punch line.

"BOYS, NEVER WHITTLE TOWARD YOURSELF."

That was it! The sun went down with a thud. With an adhesive blend of anger and cotton candy their fists remained clenched until they bolted the tent. Silent for hours, sullen for days, they grew wiser by the week as proof of which they crafted next year's strategy. They would save enough dimes to check out the friendly lady in the bloomers, someone a lad could trust.

Meanwhile, they would whittle as they damn well pleased.

CHAPTER THREE

A FLOWER FOR EVERY GIRL
AND FOR EVERY BOY, A FROG

The trauma of September was palliated when one fortunate first grader walked with his sister, she of third grade status and this day a goddess. To allay his apprehension they traveled a trail of shale along the Salmon River, once trod by ten thousand moccasins and now deepened by small Caucasian boots. This riparian route was the long way to school, but surely any stream that siphons away the cares of childhood must be a shortcut to somewhere. They could rely on the Salmon's wise counsel.

Tranquil pools diluted the burden of poverty, and small people with big worries saw it washed away in its roaring rapids. Nobody walked the shores of this noble river without feeling better. What's more, there were fish in there. Because of Edith's tranquillity, Will's secret admiration surfaced when he realized that she had started school alone, walking this same path without sibling support. He even noticed her new dress, a tribute actually to her in-house seamstress. Most children (93.6%) wore homemade clothing, but talent varied amongst their mothers. Brother and sister paused to propitiate the gods of stitchery. Suddenly without warning a grim reality loomed before them.

The schoolhouse, surrounded by slouching forms, had been there all the time, hiding behind an enormous spruce. Had these neighbor kids grown or had he shrunk? What if you advanced by size instead of merit? Will might remain in school forever.

A few youngsters established an ephemeral independence by maintaining a manly distance from their mothers. One was emboldened to whistle, cheerless and dry. Another affected a pathetic swagger but his eyes were unmanfully moist. Mothers eat this up.

Falls City's forlorn playground boasted a solitary swing which strained its ropes to attain a terrifying arc and was supported by twin ponderosa . . . its only reliable components. The frayed ropes should have been discarded but were, instead, donated by an outlying farmer who had no kids apt to use the swing. Awaiting their turn, an impatient ground crew pushed many a screaming occupant to new altitude records and an occasional wrist fracture. Directly beneath the swing was an eroded chasm which deepened daily, correctly maligned by mothers distraught over shoes rendered prematurely toeless.

To bless abrasions, quench thirst, or wash tears there was the ubiquitous schoolyard pump. Three first graders struggled with the rusted handle, having been told that there was water down there. Probably some adult had lied about this just as they misrepresented everything else about school. Later they conscripted some heavier kids to lean on the handle before they died of thirst. Dangling from a bent nail was a battered cup, once bright but now suspiciously green with something that belonged under a microscope. This notorious receptacle was the chief northwest distributor of contagious gingivitis or its colloquial equivalent, trench mouth.

Will learned to drink with both lips inside the cup, a persistent habit that bothered his wife years later when they dined in fancy Boise restaurants. There were two.

"Why can't you drink like other people?" To which he peered over his cup with the omniscient grin of a man who never caught trench mouth.

Before the bell's last reverberation all pupils stood by pre-initialed desks. For their predecessors, these crude carvings would prove the only lasting mark they would ever make. They pledged their solemn allegiance facing an old "Kansas" flag with thirty-four stars though to be properly patriotic in 1894 the canton could use a few more stars. The teacher came from Wichita and got the job because she brought her own flag. It was Edith who stitched on two more stars so it would look just like flags back East. The pledge was serious business and the mumblers were admonished to *think* about the flag. Otherwise Miss Lane would know. Thoughts were supposed to be entirely private, but this bunch had never dealt with anyone from Kansas.

After the ceremony two lads, disciplined for some non-capital offense, beat dusty erasers into submission as both disappeared in a cloud of talc. Now sufficiently repentant, they were paroled to their seats, but the clemency was ephemeral as the braids ahead were once more baptized in the ink well behind. The erasers could take just so much pounding, so this time the parolees were condemned to recite the story behind each star.

When the threat of war became a reality, West Virginia was created to become the thirty-fifth state, separated from her sister who remained to bleed with the Confederacy. Next emerged an unlikely candidate for statehood: 110,540 square miles of desolation separated from the Arizona territory by the Colorado River and from the rest of the world by alkali, lava, and scorpions. Who would make a state out of this? Even Indians rode around it.

Now let us speak of GOLD. This rare element can be relied upon to punctuate history (usually dull) with a smattering of greed, intrigue, and murder (always exciting). Caesars and Pharaohs hoarded this stuff and not because it was so malleable. Patient rocks, badly ignored for thirty million years, revealed their latent beauty and by pick and pan came to glow with nature's most seductive hue of yellow. Virginia City mushroomed and even had its own newspaper where Mark Twain, who always liked to exaggerate, saw no need to.

On October 31, 1864, Nevada was welcomed with an auric embrace as the thirty-sixth state, and the Comstock Lode bore the ore that could win a war. Coyotes rejoiced, knowing miners discarded great garbage. Their only other source of food was rabbits and most had already left for California. Nevada mines filled federal coffers until it became a habit. Civil War reparations are still accepted in Las Vegas. To those first graders in 1894, every star on the flag meant history. We are deprived of this pride a century later because you can't learn what isn't taught. Will sat secure at his desk with a premonition that Idaho's star would be firmly anchored to the canton in another six years.

He returned to Falls City after World War One and checked on his flag, a corny thing to do but, after that particular war, the stars and stripes signified history, not combustibility. Having first waved in relentless Kansas winds, it was well worn when Will returned to Idaho, and he guessed that by now it was (in Lincolnesque) about three score and four. Reciting the history of every star in a one-room school launched Will's sustained interest in vexillology. Most of his hobbies had odd names. He collected common flags bearing Fleurs-de-lis, Turkish Crescents, Maple Leaves and Rising Suns while forever searching for the unusual. This flag collector almost acquired a real prize. Johnny Flynn had a guidon once flown by Custer's doomed Seventh Cavalry which he offered Will in return for help with multiplication tables. Alas, Will's math was no better than John's so he had to give it back. Encyclopedic research disclosed that the battle pennant of one pharaoh incongruously displayed a PLACENTA. Not even a mummy could endure this long but Will never stopped hunting.

He was inspired by the vexilla of Roman legions marching into glory but then reflected sadly on his own ancestors, when Irish harps played out of tune and the bright green of the shamrock faded. Gaelic banners drooped at half mast, and Ireland limped into poverty and famine.

❦

E ducation prepares children for life where one of the first lessons is the duplicity of adults. On the first day, pupils discovered that the playground was only an inducement to herd the trusting flock from the swing outside to the desk indoors. The conspiracy only worsened by allowing innocent children to believe parents would be waiting near the pump where they left them. With a resolute twist of a sticky porcelain knob, the schoolhouse door opened grudgingly into a solitary room and slammed decisively against the child's world outside. Inside, darkness prevailed as was appropriate to the somber business of school.

The educational budget did not include kerosene, because young healthy eyes should not need a lantern, and whenever necessary, a whack with a ruler seemed to enhance visual acuity.

The blackboard set the scene, which was severely reinforced by Miss Lane wearing exactly the same color; and a sinister blend it was. Above the black stove was an even blacker ceiling to which was precariously pulleyed an almost spheroidal globe. The real world may be round but this one wasn't. When not lowered during geography, it hovered overhead as a menacing reminder of their own insignificance.

During winter, the mica window of the cast iron stove bestowed a reassuring flame, but this was hardly central heating unless you, too, were central. Thermal favors extended concentrically from the favored inner circle out to huddled blue figures at the periphery where even youthful joints moved with reluctance. Pens stood upright in ink wells to validate the viscosity of December. But by April, the windows of the outer zone shed their frost and became the best seats in the house. During the passing weeks the scene exploded with chokecherries, dogwood and camas. Will and Edith would always remember when spring was invented, somewhere along the Salmon River. Even Miss Lane moved from her blackboard to the window, still gripping her chalk but with nothing to write on. Against such a background her silhouette softened.

WOULD EDGAR ALLAN POE WRITE ABOUT BELLS IF THEY WEREN'T IMPORTANT?

The custodian of the school bell did more than yank a rope. Duties for this exalted position included winding the Regulator clock, and the Sacred Key was necklaced securely to the trustee who never took it off. The Regulator relentlessly dictated every chore.

Those relentless hands barely moved during geography and it was dangerous for drowsy students to dwell on its mesmerizing pendulum. During the last hour it seemed to stop completely. Of course, the hands accelerated rapidly during recess, but nobody stayed inside to check this out. Just like the clock, Miss Lane operated with hidden cogs and was twice as punctual.

The clock-winder enjoyed more prestige, but the bell-ringer had all the fun. Both positions were determined by appointment tainted with favoritism and—say it isn't so—even nepotism. In this village there was not enough money floating around to consider bribery.

There is only one way to wind a clock, but with a bell kids can be creative. By delaying release of the rope—it's all in the wrist—there could be imparted a mournful toll like muffled drums at a military funeral. The debut performance lamented the first day of school: The Dirge of Autumn. But this opus was eclipsed a few months later when school ended with the joyous Salute to Summer. A sophisticated bell critic (who just happened to be passing through) compared this resounding classic with the triumphant peal from St. Peter's on Easter. And remember, the Vatican has more than one bell. Despite these occasional improvisations, the sanctity of the bell was always appreciated until one uninhibited fifth-grader, dizzy with power, succumbed to syncopation.

The town was not ready for this. Deacons frowned. Horses bolted. Bankers called in loans. The perpetrator was summarily defrocked and banished to a segregated desk where she sulked and resisted rehabilitation. Falls City should have known that syncopation was only a precursor to greater sins . . . like dancing. A few years later she left town pregnant, became an actress, and made millions. Pulpits throughout the valley decried this gravid departure and, even worse, her unsavory profession on the stage. However, on learning of her fortune, one prudent preacher urged forgiveness. The actress could donate to the church now and recant later.

Miss Lane quietly tolerated most adolescent provocation because, more than most, she suffered the mores and hypocrisy of those days. Male-dominated school boards contracted only single female teachers who must absolutely conform to the schoolmarm caricature, an outrageous intrusion into any private life. Sanctimonious elders presumed that unmarried also implied unattached. By sneering inference this also meant unwanted. The repressive judgments of 1906 were renounced on the 4th of July. While the nation celebrated Independence Day, Miss Lane declared an independence of her very own. That summer the schoolmarm became personally involved and—several times a week—ATTACHED.

Will was in school to learn and wrongly assumed everybody was. On the first day, adult perfidy had lured innocent children into Miss Lane's room where they were imprisoned until 4:00 pm, after which the day was shot anyway. He was no smarter when he escaped and, as near as he could tell, neither were the other captives. Grandad had drilled him since the cradle so he knew all about proper respect toward flag and teacher. To enhance this indoctrination, Edith took notes on his behavior which she would submit to Grandad that evening. Everybody in town was grading him. Earlier that day, Will had slouched his way to school, but now he returned along the Salmon with a confident stride. In another week he might not even need his sister. But alas, Edith had not yet prepared this whistling first grader for the menace just beyond the schoolyard.

Dominating the river bank loomed the tyrant who terrorized the entire school and half the board members, and prudent town folk always sent out a scout before traveling this route. Edith had been so busy lecturing on good manners that she forgot to tell her brother that not everybody observes the social graces.

A frothing giant straddled the trail and Will approached to introduce himself, but his ingratiating smile was greeted with a hairy fist. This is what Edith meant to tell him. Until then Will thought his nose bled only if he picked it.

Billy was half muscle, half anger, and either half could kill you. His forehead sloped back as if anxious to escape the narrow eyes. Quail could hide in those eyebrows and live on the lice. Hair sprouted between randomly spaced yellow fangs which effectively enhanced his snarl. His guttural growls were incomprehensible, but those gestures were quite eloquent. This belching behemoth was rarely seen inside the classroom, not actually a drop-out because he had never dropped in. Billy had left home after beating up both parents and a sheriff. Since then he skulked behind trees where he clawed his mark and strangled grizzly bears every time he needed fresh meat. Damp spots in the woods from salivation (or something) would have made him easy to track—most unlikely since nobody wanted to find him.

Will's nosebleed was actually a manifestation of vicarious revenge. The true object of Billy's animus was Edith, who had thoughtlessly advanced a grade and left Billy behind—for the *second* time. No question about it: Will's civil rights had been trampled and he limped home to consult with his omniscient grandfather. He paused on the doorstep just long enough to restart his nosebleed.

Yes, the old man did know the hirsute antagonist and was proud that his grandson had held his temper and did not retaliate. This had not crossed Will's mind. The wise counselor did not mention that he had once seen Billy tangle with a powerful lumberjack and left him unconscious. Big Foot and the Abominable Snow Man were probably myths, but the Neanderthal of Falls City lived right here on the Salmon River.

Grandad slowly stroked his beard. This was always the prelude to impending sagacity: "Son, my plan is two-fold. You can protect yourself and bring salvation to the bully." He selected a sure-fire passage from Ecclesiastes and during a test reading, the nosebleed miraculously stopped.

Alas, the second confrontation with the Beast came before this was completely memorized. Scripture poured from his terrified lips as a disorganized stammer which ended with traumatic abruptness. That tooth was loose anyway. The Old Testament was always more persuasive when it came from Grandad. If the sinner was not responding to Ecclesiastes, he could adjust his beard and down-shift to Psalms without grinding a gear.

The rules of the school were posted near the black-board, and next Monday a line had been added in bold red crayon: "Every first-grader must leave the conversion of heathens to others."

THE IRISH BELIEVE IN LEPRECHAUNS
ONLY BECAUSE THEY EXIST.

For her battered brother, Edith had her own advice, a blend of cowardice and discretion: "Run like the devil but get a good head start. Billy is mighty big but he's not slow." Sympathetic friends surrounded the boy with the fat lip, allies of necessity, and themselves in peril. They volunteered as scouts to check the brush for movement and trees for claw marks. Johnny Flynn had the confidence of a bodyguard, but lacked the weight requisites, and when the frothing giant reappeared, both Will and his protector made their breathless escape.

The next words would give life a new meaning as John gasped: "We don't have to put up with this. Let's talk to my brother." Will wondered:

"Would that be the one with red hair?" They all had red hair: "Yea, that's the one."

"Maybe later. I'm late for chores." Of the two boys, John had more sense.

"You are too bruised to lift hay and fractures can't be far away."

And Will went with John and, verily, he was glad.

Patrick Flynn was about fifteen and not much bigger than John though his hair was even redder. When the clan all stood together it hurt your eyes. John called the meeting to order, dispensed with the reading of last month's minutes, and launched into the new business at hand: "Pat has figured out some interesting things about leverage. He can toss me over ten feet and you even farther, since you're not family."

A few centuries earlier, leverage attained status in the Far East and they named it Judo. Since the Flynns read very little oriental history, it was up to Pat to re-introduce it to the Occident as controlled mayhem though he called it "teaching good manners." After a few weeks of soft straw landings, the neophyte listened gratefully during the graduation ceremony. With solemnity befitting the occasion, the Flynns had even prepared a genuine sheepskin diploma plus a few lamb chops that were left over: "Today you are officially a Flynn, so allow me to review the finer points of self defense: 1) Turn your back to Billy; grab his wrist with both hands. 2) DO NOT LET GO no matter what. 3) Then bend forward real sharp. 4) If you look straight up that's where he'll be. 5) Just landing on the rocks should do it but there is one extra trick in case you don't want to see him again . . . EVER." Pat detected a shudder but all reluctance faded as the instructor recounted loosened teeth (Will's), blackened eyes (John's), and rearranged noses (Will's and John's). Much more than a specialist in concussion, Patrick was a motivational speaker. Will was attentive to the instructor's final advice: "When he's about two feet from the ground stop the momentum by yanking his wrist in the opposite direction."

"But Pat, won't that break his arm?" There was a thoughtful Gaelic pause: "Every time."

There is a far off voice that commands a chosen few: "You must fish." The common man has been spared this distant discourse but obsessed anglers confirm that they are rendered helpless by a mesmerizing baritone much like Charlton Heston doing Moses. The lesson this Sunday may have carried a more adult message but the basic theme for Will was that everybody was fishing on the Sea of Galilee and doing very well. Like Jacob wrestling an angel, he struggled to escape these diabolical distractions but even the scuffed leather of his Bible somehow resembled fish scales.

What a forceful message!

A cramped hour with restless kids can give anyone a headache so the teacher suggested that the class step outside for a brief intermission. But how long is brief? What's an intermission? The latent little Christians obeyed immediately, leaving only a few skid marks. Splashing reverberations came from the mill pond where hungry trout sounded desperate. How long were headaches supposed to last?

He understood temptation since they had studied it only last Sunday, but Satan's grip was tightening. Resolutely he turned his back on the pond and, seeking a sign from above, faced the church steeple, ever a source of strength.

And one of the louvers winked.

He was back in thirty-four minutes which, as God willed it, was the precise duration of this particular headache.

And Heston spake: " That was a close call."

The essence of fishing is deception. Intelligent men pit their minds against something with scales and a much smaller brain. Landing a big fish had been compared to bull fighting though a matador can't fake his results with all those people watching. For this reason many devoted nimrods carry a camera not to photograph mountain scenery but to compound their duplicitous hobby with the insidious pursuit of —we must whisper the word —perspective.

Field and Stream sold more magazines when their cover displayed a glistening rainbow beside a rod and reel. In succeeding issues the fish came from the same refrigerator but the reel kept getting smaller. When subscribers rebelled, the editors switched to the pseudo-science of actual measurement and tried a ruler. Centimeters are better because there are more of them. Frying trout over a studio campfire was another ploy to magnify the fish and even imply that they are edible, but perspective became truly ugly when one unscrupulous sportsman borrowed a miniature frying pan from his daughter's doll house. Such a comparison would flatter a gold fish. Outraged purists shunned him in public but, behind the scenes, they secretly tried to borrow that pan.

Fishermen share many qualities with normal people but guilt is not one of them. Will and Edith had no need for a camera, since they had yet to catch a fish. Brother and sister continued on into high school for the last few years they would enjoy together, during which one particular pursuit cemented their sibling alliance. Together they created flies which came to be known as the Royal Coachman and Queen of the Waters, a regal allusion that is by no means exaggerated.

Fishing is a sinister game and there could be no creativity without secrecy. This furtive team tied flies only after dark by the glow of a lantern with high test kerosene. When grandma lost a spool of sea green thread, she never thought to look in the attic where Edith, as chief of quality control, scrutinized every strand for strength and hue. Ceremony is paramount. Not just any feathers will do but must be analyzed from the fish's point of view. Domestic chicken feathers project an insulting docility, whereas the pheasant is wild like the trout. Because this makes absolutely no sense, it fits perfectly with the rest of the angler's ritual.

Occasionally, man's finest creation fails to entice, probably because it was so spectacular that the fish simply did not deserve it. In a moment of desperation, this Falls City team briefly abandoned flies and resorted to a lure resembling a minnow with a smile on its seductive face and a hook in its wooden belly. They mentioned this to no one though years later, quite by accident, their descendants learned of this family shame. Will and Edith were basically decent people and never part of that worm and cheese crowd.

Fly-tying is high art where paranoid purists worry about contamination, thievery, or commercial imitation. It begins as a childhood hobby that wanes briefly during puberty until the fisherman discovers that women are more perfidious than trout, more expensive to catch . . . and spoil faster.

In later years when eyes fail from too much sex, or the wrong kind, the craftsman wears a green visor and increases his magnifying glass by one diopter. He is no longer a fly-tying amateur but an Insect Engineer, whose personalized flies are a treasured gift and the gratitude of the recipient endures beyond the grave. You can grow old with this hobby—but not as fast a you would without it.

O ver the fence, across the road and just a sprint away was Falls City's mill pond with its teeming treasure of trout. The polished surface quickly forgave the momentary turmoil of a six pound rainbow and soon resumed its undisturbed reflection of consenting trees and a sky which was never indifferent to the spectacle. During the autumn competition, just when aspen were stealing the show with their shimmering yellow, towering tamaracks superimposed a vivid October orange. Here was the seminal scene that a century ago inspired landscape artists to paint those nostalgic calendars still hanging in kitchens long after the dates have expired.

THIS WAS THE POND.

You have endured fishing hyperbole which bent credibility more than the pole. Now you deserve the truth.

THIS WAS THE FISH.

After hours of serenity, these waters splashed to life at sunrise with piscene pirouettes. This was only the overture to a dance of deception which diverted human attention away from a behemoth which—at least until Will managed to catch him—was more legend than fact. Here dwelt the patriarch of the Salmon River who rarely dined on the surface but instead devoured those who did. Camouflaged near the bottom, this monarch could pass for a branch—or a log—like the elusive queen bee which is rarely seen but said to be very large.

THIS WAS THE QUARRY.

The pond itself was not visible from the field but its distracting turbulence was inescapable to acute young ears that could hear a trout if it merely moved its gills. Will had learned to disregard most such sounds but still recoiled at an occasional low register THUD, the declaration of a truculent trout so huge that he didn't much care how he landed. This can work on a boy's mind until he was forced to open a one-sided conversation with his old partner-in-harvest: " Grandad, did you hear that?"

"NO, son and I didn't hear it last time." Most of their conversations were even shorter because an age disparity was a door too heavy for a small boy to budge. To ask again would be pestering, and full grown men, even church deacons, had learned never to pester Grandad. Despite a practiced deafness, Will suddenly dropped his end of the bale at a resounding splash which no man could ignore. The old man's ears were not all that bad and he yielded by answering an unasked question: "Son, that sounded like a tree may have fallen into the stream. Why don't you run down and see what happened?" Silence overwhelmed him at the pond until he was suddenly hypnotized by a huge dorsal fin which left a wake like an Evinrude. Grandad's reprieve allowed time only to stand and watch, as silence became reverence.

These would be his last free moments while exhausting farm work wrung the hours dry. Throughout the summer no hook touched the water, nor did he own a hook. Wondering what was attached to that fin was enough to sustain him, nourishing as bread and rejuvenating as sleep when both were in short supply. Each evening Grandad blessed the day's bread while Will parenthetically put in a few good words for his fish. Edith had once eaten trout and added a silent Amen. The family continued to share all they had, poverty and faith. Poverty didn't do much for Will, but faith was honing an inchoate talent from which would emerge a master fisherman. As a neophyte, Will knew nothing about fishing. He had never seen a reel, a creel or a ferrule so he began with the basics:

A) You don't chase fish with a club. He had tried that.

B) Trout ate insects and each other.

C) He should reject A and research B.

D) He will not be hampered by adult supervision. Time favored the fish as farm chores ever encroached on the long postponed mission, and Will worried that his adversary might succumb to old age.

Then on the nineteenth of October, in the year of our Lord, one thousand eight hundred and ninety seven (and of the fish, nine) there came to pass a miracle. The teacher and half the class were ill.

Anxious to report this medical mishap to Grandad, Will raced along his familiar riparian route but was suddenly and forgivably diverted. The millpond was quiet and the trout were fasting, probably observing some piscene holy day. Surrounded by autumn's yellow and orange, he crouched motionless amongst willow and alder, looking much like them though perhaps thinner. The King of the World rose from his shadowy palace, swept near the bank and devoured a school of minnows. Such crude cannibalism seemed unworthy of one so regal. No insects were flying so the boy on the bank anticipated the next hatch when he could offer a tantalizing creation of his own. Then the king would no longer need to eat his own family. The concept of a fake fly was a brilliant discovery which he would secretly share only with his sister, to which Edith repeated the standard oath but only after he tied her hand to the Bible.

A willow rod has never forsaken any lad. Bamboo enjoyed some popularity, but probably in the orient, where the poor devils may not have willow. A pole without a line won't get a boy very far unless he has a sister with a basket of thread and a mind like a trout. Wool was rejected because, when wet, its odor was repugnant to humans and discriminating pond-dwellers were no different. Fish found her waxed cotton enticing, but its tensile strength was inadequate for the monster they had in mind. Finally she braided a few strands of undyed silk, strong, supple, irresistible.

Who invented the leader? Edith, that's who. Without a reel, the line often sawed Will's index finger. Once it bled for an hour but it felt GOOD! To improvise hooks he needed wire of which there was no shortage because it was wire that held the entire farm together. With a jeweler's precision he hammered out hooks and filed the barb. All the signs were right. God was in his heaven. The moon was full. Saturn and Mars were aligned. Ordinary fishermen rely on superstition but this was pure science. Will and Edith were in business and that trout was in trouble.

CATCH AND RELEASE APPLIES ONLY TO THE FISHERMAN, NOT THE FISH.

Despite harsh daily demands, no farm feels obliged to repay your efforts. Hiding among eighty acres of stumps there had to be something edible and it was Will's job to find it, dig it up and haul it home. Philosophically, he was resigned to this after visiting with one neighbor whose only harvest back in Maine had been rocks. Actually Grandad had homesteaded one hundred and sixty acres but only half was cultivated. The rest was unexplored territory but no one could tell one half from the other.

The property was bordered by a river, the trout from which could feed the family better than the stingy land ever could. Throughout their lives fish never stop growing, especially those in the Salmon which gained a lot of weight by stealing Will's bait. During his early worm era, rainbows gurgled their thanks for nourishment contributed when ravenous strikes left homemade hooks woefully naked. To avoid this, he deftly withdrew the lure from any trout under a pound but this was analogous to *coitus interruptus* and caused some to become neurotic. But in retaliation, the behemoth disdained all offerings. Will imagined he saw an aquatic aristocrat with a lorgnette under his pectoral fin, surveying the shore with theatrical arrogance. Overtures were increasingly appetizing, adroitly cast, jiggled with troutly realism, but met with contempt. The quarry would bump the hook, smirk at the angler, and then show a clear preference for other flies not nearly as beautiful as Will's.

There were several spectacular strikes which snapped leaders and straightened hooks. Now the fisherman must again temper the attenuated wire, already weakened under the strain of baling last year's hay. Edith re-worked the silk and braided three strands into four. She yanked it hard. It did not break. Edith smiled. Had he known about this concerted sibling plot The Sultan of the Salmon would stop horsing around and give up now.

All equipment was readied the night before and sequestered in a corner of the field. From the kitchen, Edith served as sentinel because it took two sneaky kids to keep track of one old man who equated fishing with frivolity. During brief intervals between wagon loads, Will sprinted to the stream where his cast was air born before his feet touched the bank. When he was in the fourth grade, there was one day when the chores and daylight came out even. One cast, one strike and the pole bent double. He knew it was the leviathan who in turn knew it was Will. The fish had been perfecting jumps just for the main event. Will set the hook but landing him would take a block and tackle. Sportsmanship, or in this case lousy equipment, demands playing the fish to exhaustion. This assumes both parties to be of equal strength, but this beast didn't seem to know it was only a game and was actually on the attack.

After ten minutes, it was a draw until the trout took a wrong turn. He should have known better since this was his pond. The line snagged on a branch with a double half hitch, triple square, quadruple bowline, one of those knots they use to keep battleships from leaving the dock. Neither antagonist could budge the log. Worse yet, the line threatened to saw off several fingers. Through long, impatient months the boy on the bank had prepared for this moment and anticipated every possibility—except this one. This aquatic impasse demanded calm, mature deliberation. So he dropped the pole and jumped in after the fish.

Back on the shore he had been in charge of his own destiny but down here things were different. He expected to be wet but not this cold, the first of many surprises.

The hook, and for that matter the teeth, were at the other end so perhaps he could wrestle the fish into submission by grabbing the tail with both hands. Locked together in five feet of water the fisherman—if he could still be called a fisherman—appeared to be smiling but this was actually the rigid face of anoxia.

Now all he needed was a plan.

The monster held him immobilized in a crouch, analogous to trapping a monkey that reaches through a small hole in a coconut to grab the rice, whereupon a narrow hand becomes a thick fist which locks him inside until he releases the prize. But monkeys have more time to solve their dilemma than a short kid in tall water.

He tried to stand but his nostrils barely surfaced. Why hadn't he grown two inches last year like his cousin Arch? He began to regret all those years he had thoughtlessly squandered oxygen, but the thrashing giant permitted only an occasional glance up to where the air was.

Working up from the tail, he wrapped his aching arms around the fish's waist (or whatever). If you have never done it, this is slippery work. Even the gills looked menacing as he dislodged the hook and awaited results which more than ever included drowning. Frantic stern-driven kicks propelled both into shallower water where the jockey surfaced and the trout thrashed onto the shore. Triumph and admiration faded to sympathy and remorse. Here writhed his valiant antagonist, caught not fairly but by a fluke, struggling for life and wondering what was going to happen, exactly like Will only moments before. Fishing was supposed to be more fun than this. He cradled his trophy and guessed its weight which, thereafter, fluctuated as necessary, depending on other fisherman who might tell their story first. They had a little chat and then his adversary of four years was gently returned to the water's edge where he seemed to know the way home. This had been quite a day and he had a lot to tell his family. God only knows how big that fish is today.

Eventually Will fished Idaho wherever there was water and there was plenty of it. He outwitted fish of every hue: Rainbow, Cutthroat, Native, Golden, or Brown and, though many deserved it, none was ever weighed. For him, it was as if none dared to be greater than the Emperor of the Salmon River which he once fought to a draw when the fisherman was no bigger than the fish. On that memorable day a blue ribbon was awarded to a great and wondrous trophy whose position would be secure forever. Because fishermen cannot avoid hyperbole, you deserve a more reliable source.

The above story was told by the fish.

When Will first gripped an axe he was about six. By the time he was big enough to get paid for it logging was at its zenith when western forests promised easier wealth than grubbing for gold and equaled railroads in creating millionaires.

America's tree business began in Maine which later stamped its ligneous legacy on northwest maps with names like Bangor. The loyal Maine native acknowledged only one Portland but tolerated its sister city in Oregon since it was 3000 miles away, a pitiful counterfeit near a second class ocean where lobsters must be imported. In 1820 the District of Maine, not yet a state, offered timber at 12 cents an acre; lush forests untouched for eons by more than a stone tomahawk. Six years earlier Benjamin Cummings invented the circular saw which soon grew to terrifying diameters under the specialized care of the *Saw Filers*. This secretive cult took orders from no one but sequestered themselves behind locked doors and whispered in the occult language of freshets and droughts. By exhausting the inexhaustible, those Maine forests were leveled so houses could replace teepees and soon caulked boots stomped westward to the Lake States where a white pine colossus, already auctioned, stood at attention, awaiting execution. After this assault, mountains of Michigan sawdust remained as a fragrant memorial to insatiable demand.

While loggers died violently in the woods, Scandinavian replacements were debarking on Ellis Island. They were homesick for trees and brought their own axes, eager to take a job with a life expectancy of seven years. By 1905 Minnesota and Wisconsin were pretty well scalped when some irresponsible reporter leaked the story about two billion board feet in the Northwest but because it rained so much nobody wanted it. Talk about luck!!

Tales of Douglas fir 300 feet high and 14 feet at the base seemed preposterous until Fred Weyerhaeuser took the trip to see for himself. It must have been true because he moved his entire operation from St. Paul almost before the saws stopped spinning. At six Weyerhaeuser dollars an acre, timber was costlier, but these monarchs grew denser and faster than anywhere else on the continent, and with a little German luck Fred just might turn a profit. He and a few cronies soon controlled two million acres in Idaho, Washington and Oregon. And Fred said *"Wunderbar!"* Oregon soon dedicated a second Saginaw in grateful memory of its bounteous counterpart back in Michigan, and both towns were devoted to horizontal trees. Finally the Northwest had borrowed so many names from Maine and the Lake States that they had to rely on picturesque Indians or French trappers, a cartographer's nightmare and always mispronounced. Humboldt Bay was already notorious for shipwrecks, but the nearby California redwoods did not escape notice. Some of the men who joined this new frenzy of timber claims had gambled earlier in the gold rush of 1849. This time they might get lucky and the insanity of Sutter's Mill was repeated.

Competing to set up the first sawmill, one outfit beached the side-wheeler *Santa Clara*, hitched long belts to her main shaft and drove four saws on the shore. It all went slicker than skid grease and was the only camp in America where workers dined aboard ship.

Even then, California had panache. Once man discovered tools, his first task was to convert trees into logs, but it took either slaves or oxen to move them. This increased the overhead. Both had to be fed and one became illegal. It was in 1882, during the Humboldt boom, when John Dolbeer patented his donkey engine and steam moved what muscle couldn't. Oxen rejoiced! Dolbeer's genius would not be equaled for another sixty years when McCulloch's chain saw further revolutionized logging.

William Carson's ornate Victorian home in Eureka still attests to the fortunes to be made from trees and boasts a sixty-eight foot tower bristling with lattice work. Of the eight garish gables there are no two alike. Beyond stained glass doors, beveled English mirrors reflect a dining room copied after Chapultepec Castle. Such imported opulence was possible because Bill got his redwood wholesale, and his mansion in Eureka rivaled any of those in San Francisco built by railroads, Comstock gold or embezzlement.

Log rolling, or birling, endured as a colorful vestige from early camps where hobnailed agility evolved into high art and heavy betting. The greater hazard lurked on the shore where drunken spectators supported their favorite with money they didn't have and axes which they did. These were violent camps, but work in the woods was merely dangerous while Saturday nights in a bar were often fatal. Merely raising the champion's arm suggested a victory less than total so it was considered good form to stomp on your opponent's face. The idea began in Europe where Heidelberg dueling scars were the badge of courage —not too many and not too deep—proving to the world that this was a macho German.

In American lumber camps the imprint of a boot was the mark of a real man. Occasionally, smallpox scars might resemble nail marks, but that edentulous grin implied something more traumatic and demanded respect. Will's college tuition was earned in one of these camps where at two dollars a day he still mailed money home to his sister who was frail and failing with a cough that would soon turn bloody. Tuberculosis was the devil's opportunist ready to add finality to debilitating malnutrition. Orphaned during the world-wide influenza pandemic of 1889, Will and his three sisters were scattered among elderly relatives from Oregon to Pennsylvania. Consumption manifests many deadly variants including pulmonary, renal and osseous and the sisters succumbed to the full spectrum. Edith died a cachectic spinster, but the other two lived long enough to cough on their children. Their only brother who had always left the table hungry found salvation in forest food where one breakfast would feed the folks back home for a week. This was the fuel that ran the saws and would save his life.

Ham, steak and eggs were stacked to eye level. A small army of beloved cooks bore corn bread on heavy trays and ceremoniously divided it into one foot squares. Corn bread tends to crumble but these fastidious diners held theirs together with a pound of butter. Men rose to the triangular clang of the Gut Hammer, but in fancier camps dawn was announced by tooting the Gaberel, a degradation of Gabriel. These were tin dinner horns, the bigger the better, that competed in lengths up to eight feet.

Jammed along one damp wall were triple-tiered bunks that could be entered only from the end. Twice a day, but always in the dark, ravenous loggers slouched on a long halved log, the Deacon's Seat. Not to be confused with etiquette, elbows were kept off the table to avoid splinters. Veterans wielded a huge spoon to shovel in the calories, but their fork was poised to defend against marauders and an impaled hand was more than a casual threat.

Speed was paramount as they chewed and spewed and burped and slurped along a table of a rived spruce sealed with tallow. This surface reduced friction and though food was never passed it occasionally slithered by when a quick hand might manage a lucky interception.

French profanity was always admired, easily mistaken for elegance but invaluable when demanding larger servings. These Cannuks still axed the smoothest kerf and sang the dirtiest songs. French glory peaked in New England camps but some migrated to the west where they were gradually relegated to obscurity until their colorful attire and phony accents resurfaced as the essence of today's television.

In one recent episode, toqued Quebecers are still logging in Peru. A few went into politics and their descendants in Montreal are today demanding separation of French Quebec from the rest of Canada, not with the usual benign political bumper stickers but metal license plates permanently stamped with *je me souviens,* the provocative promise that they remember their roots while conveniently forgetting that they lost their last battle to the British at Louisburg in 1758. These profligates of the pines lived only for the next paycheck, their down payment for a Saturday of sin though the company store already held most of them in hock up to their 19 inch necks. It took two months of accumulated wages (unless it was company scrip) to allow the ultimate: a night in Portland. Idaho City and Silver City dominated Idaho mining, but only from Portland could millions of logs float down to California, the land of conspicuous consumption.

From 245 North Burnside, a landmark beckoned the entire Northwest: Ericksen's Cafe and Concert Hall. This was not a bar but THE BAR: Six hundred and eighty four linear feet of imported mahogany was fastidiously polished by fifty uniformed bartenders who changed aprons every two hours. August Ericksen's presence dominated the chandeliered expanse with a portrait framed by rosewood and gold and barely wide enough to contain his mustache. August was better known and more respected than any face engraved on U.S. currency. Spittoons were so numerous that there was no excuse to miss though the aim falters as frivolity graduates into oblivion and the brass foot rail becomes a headrest. There were two loggers who never saw Ericksen's.

Illiteracy skulked behind the transparent shield of profanity but not for one abstemious Finn who kept his caulks on the log, his mind out of the gutter and his heart in Helsinki. He already spoke several languages of no use to him now but yearned to learn English, the official language of the paymaster. Will happily obliged, threw in a little Latin and picked up some Finnish in return. The Finn, of course, was called "Swede." Both read the same Bible in different languages and became lifelong friends where life wasn't very long.

Throughout the Northwest one logger died every other day. The foreman kept these vital statistics sealed at the head office in Portland but most of the timber beasts could not read such a report anyway. Friendship was tenuous. They recoiled when a sawyer was crushed but it was nothing a jug of whiskey couldn't handle. A death in the camp meant little more than one less plate at breakfast and bigger servings for the survivors. Swede sent half his check to Finland where his sister, just like Will's, suffered from consumption. Will and Swede may have missed Ericksen's bar, but they could still hit a tree when hungover loggers could barely lift an axe.

Will and the Finn trudged a wet half mile in dim light to their designated tree. One lugged the axes, springboard and wedges while the other shouldered an ungainly ten foot saw, that unmanageable monster designed for those awesome diameters seen only here. Some workers sought better paying jobs such as operating the donkey engine. These fortunate men were called engineers but were actually the owner's relatives. But there were other ways to earn an extra dollar. The top of the tallest tree was rigged with pulleys and cables to serve as a spar from which they could derrick logs out of the forest. But first somebody had to climb it, usually some unmarried kid with a death wish.

With axe, spurs and rope the High Climber drew a modest bonus for preparing the Spar Tree which he scaled, lopping off limbs on his way up. About 30 feet from the top (and 150 feet from the ground) he dug in his spurs, belted himself precariously and chopped off the crown. It was

important that the top segment swing *away from* and
never *toward* the topper so he didn't ride it back down.
Furthermore an errant swing of the axe had been known
to chop a leg which was bad or sever the safety belt which
was even worse. Either way it came out of your pay. With
Scandinavian sagacity Swede observed: "There are more
climbing spurs than climbers and some spurs have blood
on them. We have all the excitement we need right here on
the ground."

The veteran Finn had cut his way through countless
trees on two continents, but when first light struck Idaho's
giant ponderosas both man and boy stood in awe. No one
pretended to stay dry in this constant rain, but an oil cloth
reliably protected their mid-morning snack: two enormous
loaves of sourdough bread, split lengthwise and stuffed
until it extruded cheese, bacon grease and, perhaps for
color, brown sugar. About ten minutes after a 10,000 calorie breakfast they were hungry again, and the trick was
not to wolf down their six pound sandwich before 9 a.m.
Will was lucky to have a partner who owned a watch since
stomachs and peristalsis are so unreliable.

Because the base of a Douglas Fir flares out greater
than the width of the saw, metal tipped springboards were
jammed into deep notches six to eight feet above the
ground. Working at this height reduced the diameter of
the tree but compounded the risk for the sawyers. They
yelled "TIMBER" just like in the movies but master
woodsmen always hit their mark so the trunk itself was
rarely a menace. Not so the snagged high branches, themselves larger than most trees. These were called Widow
Makers for the best of reasons and often hung up unnoticed, waiting to crash later whenever they pleased. One
such snag waited for a week before plummeting toward
Will. The Finn saw it just in time to yell "YUMP," probably losing the two seconds he needed to get himself out of
the way.

Carson Mansion, Eureka, California. You can have a house like this if you control a forest.

Will jumped free as the deadly missile struck the spring board and catapulted his partner about thirty feet. The floor of a damp forest usually offers a soft landing but this unlucky Finn found the only spot hard enough to fracture his skull.

He was carried back to camp by friends with unguarded tears and just before he died they saw him smile at the kindest words ever spoken: "He was a good sawyer and his English was better than anybody's."

Everything this unselfish man owned was wrapped in an oil cloth beneath his plank bed and the inventory didn't take long:

1) A Helsinki address.

2) A watch.

3) A letter from his sister.

Will used the first to mail the second to the third and penned a few lines in clumsy Finnish which he always knew would come in handy.

His Baltic correspondence continued for many years until eventually his son grew curious about a shoe box packed with yellowing envelopes postmarked *Soumen Tasavalta*—and there were plenty of them. I became a philatelist before I could spell the word.

The man who saved my father's life deserved to be remembered by his real name. But I never knew what it was.

I'VE BEEN RICH AND I'VE BEEN POOR.
RICH IS BETTER.

~ Pearl Bailey

For the next four years Will alternated college with logging; books he tried to remember, woods he would never forget.

School's penury dictated two part-time jobs and one meal a day which found him gaunt when he returned to the lumber camp each spring. During his seasonal returns to the deep woods he traded the pen for an ax and English for profanity. When bleeding blisters became meaningful calluses he was ready for a full day on the long saw from which he derived enough muscle to live off his own protein when he returned to school.

Will witnessed the apogee of an American epoch after which logging would never be the same. With a paradoxical mix of triumph and remorse, he felled some of the largest trees that ever grew. On June 16, 1911, he graduated with a Latin diploma with no wall to hang it on because the walls and even the ceilings of the old homestead showed evidence of decay hastened by deep snow and shallow neglect. Greek had been a hobby, albeit a strange one, self-taught from childhood until he helped teach it in college where he was known to classmates as Willopolis, a dubious compliment.

As a language instructor he was paid in ham sandwiches worth 20 cents each on the open market. (With ham, 25 cents. Bread, 5 cents extra.) But the master linguist's first experience was brief and humbling: teaching German in a German community. "All the kids' parents had been born north of the Rhine - **and not too long ago.**" He appealed to the school board who were expecting him and had already found an escape clause in his contract. This town was not for him and they tactfully suggested that he try Athens. For severance pay he was offered a ham sandwich.

Der Deutscheskinder held a touching farewell for their teacher whose only shortcoming was a peculiar English accent. He was astonished at the big turnout because on regular school days his class had never been this large. After a Teutonic feast of schnitzel and strudel the entertainment featured a tuba-zither duet with your choice of finales:

A) *The Star Spangled Banner* for those who liked to strain on high notes.

B) *Deutschland Uber Alles* for those who liked to march.

Still reluctant to renounce German, he returned to the logging camp where, as luck would have it, he teamed up with an immigrant from Munich because Will's verbs needed a little work. They anchored their springboards, sawed for a year and most of the money went to his protective sister who had walked him to school, walloped bullies with her lunch pail and would never get well. Her tuberculosis motivated him to medical school. Don't *see* a doctor . . . *be* one. His driving hope was to help her but she died before he graduated; and certainly long before the discovery of Streptomycin which might have saved her.

Will was accepted at the University of Oregon Medical School when it was still located in downtown Portland on Lovejoy St. close to the tenements and indigent patients. Five threadbare students shared one room which they named La Boheme, after Puccini's penniless artists who sang about starving together in Paris. But for some reason, French garrets seemed more picturesque than American attics and if this was an opera nobody paid to see it. Portland was a big city with electricity, at least enough for two bare bulbs and one hot plate which perpetually nursed a simmering stew. They were spared washing dishes since they had none. This saved on hot water which they also didn't have. Every man kept a never-washed spoon in his pocket where other folks carry money. They never sat to eat but ladled directly from soup to mouth as they filed past the caring cauldron.

Under a gentlemen's agreement each man must add *something* to the stew every week. If this happened to be meat, all five tried to be there just to see it splash and sink because meat doesn't float. This had actually happened only last month when an engineering student—he was the only one who owned two pair of shoes—lucked onto something attached to a bone. Will was pre-med and thus qualified to confirm its animal origin. The dental student told everybody to floss and handed out a foot-long section to be shared by all.

One sad day the soup became transparent and obviously too hypocaloric to sustain life. Somebody was not contributing. The attic was in crisis. No one came forward. Then after forty-eight hours the dental student cracked. At first the miscreant protested that he had in fact contributed something to the stew but eventually confessed that this additive was *WATER*. The jury applauded this ingenious technicality and admired the devious mind which contrived it. Dentistry was not for him. Was he not perfect for the law?

The remaining four dwelt together in the attic and the pot simmered on. They tried to joke about school (the grind of it), sleep (the lack of it), and food (the memory of it). They all felt guilty about their banished comrade, a gracious gentleman who accepted a painful decision as vital to their common survival. Will got a job as the night watchman in an office near the Heathman Hotel where solitary nights were spent with Gray's Anatomy, a flashlight and a rusty gun. The pawnbroker had included bullets of the wrong caliber but just looking at the shell box was reassuring. With his obsession for saving electricity, the entire building was black enough to hold off any burglar who was afraid of the dark.

Back in the attic, his relinquished cot was subsequently occupied by a recruit who heard about the kettle and gained admission with a bundle of withered carrots. Downtown Portland was never in better hands and thievery dropped to zero. Most of the crooks lurked along Burnside where he spread the word that he had nothing worth stealing. He lost the flashlight and rust locked the cylinder on the revolver. After safely passing anatomy he pawned the book because, unlike Greek, anatomy can get boring. Bill Shakespeare's words nudged him at 2 a.m.

and recommended "Sleep that knits up the ravel'd sleeve of care."

After graduation to the rigors of medicine he fondly remembered the easiest job he ever had when he pretended to guard the City of Roses.

On Sixth and Yamhill, during his junior year, he heard the familiar voice of his banished old comrade-in-famine. He was now back in dental school having worked in a Beaverton pharmacy for two years and driving ambulance on weekends. Will had noticed other Portland men in new white shirts but now was actually talking to one and this one suggested dinner:

"I'd like to accept but have Biochem Lab until five and then an appointment every night at eight."

"You look like an underpaid Greek-reading night watchman to me. I have a car and can pick you up at the lab."

Will was no hick. He had seen cars but still wondered what made the wheels go around.

"Would dinner include meat?"

"Absolutely. We'll dine at the Benson but they like to keep their table cloths clean so wash your elbows."

So people really did eat at the Benson. He had always thought those were mannequins inside. That evening Will learned the difference between eating and dining but while counting forks and keeping his elbows off the table he had to wonder what had propelled his benefactor from poverty to prosperity by working in a drug store. "I won't make you ask. I married the owner's daughter." Did she have a sister? "Only a brother. How desperate are you?"

CHAPTER FOUR

SANTA CLAUS IS A MYTH.
THE TOOTH FAIRY, MAYBE

My father was among the thousands dislocated by the Great War and when he returned to Idaho in 1919 he was surrounded by a sportsman's paradise. Thinning out the fish was considered a civic duty because trout had been known to attack children. There was also the feathered menace—enormous pheasants that killed cats and even drove cattle from the fields. Geese blackened the skies and never bothered to migrate since they were crazy about Idaho. To give the game a fighting chance, Will carried an awkward weapon that was hard to lift and reluctant to fire. This robust 10 gauge was a *man's* gun with well-rusted Damascus barrels, twin hammers and a crowbar to cock them. The date was engraved in Roman numerals because Latin was the prevalent language when the gun was built.

The Caldwell city council had recently ordained that the owner must file a public notice before he fired it. Both barrels had a full choke and despite separate triggers usually fired together. This opened a wide swath through the brush, enough to expose terrified birds as Will blew their cover. Any pheasant dropped under seventy yards could be identified only by the feathers. Wild shots occasionally rattled off the patina roof of the Dewey Palace in Nampa whose citizens were already sulking because Caldwell was the designated county seat. Nampa probably deserved it, but they already had the Union Pacific roundhouse. But Nampa has always wanted more, more, more. Flames escaped from a loose breech and the lateral blast had tattooed Will's thumb, verily, the proud mark of a true hunter. This museum piece was in lieu of payment for delivering a series of quasi-legitimate kids of some riparian homesteaders whose descendants are still spawning along the Snake River.

The chambers of this formidable weapon accepted archaic brass casings which were reloaded with black powder. This was never measured. Once when the price of lead shot soared, Will almost substituted ground glass but realized this would be hard to pick out of the meat and dentists advised against it. Its colonial predecessor was the venerable Miles Standish model which was supported by a tripod. All Will lacked was a gun bearer and this job was reserved the day his son was born and soon perambulator wheels were removed to build a caisson.

No bird in North America is more colorful than the China rooster, but Will's pheasants were monochronous due to a rust tattoo which also imparted a distinct flavor which the family came to prefer. Iron deficiency anemia was unheard of among Caldwell's pheasant eaters. The jolting recoil would make a sensible man think twice before pulling the trigger, especially since he was already gorging on pheasant three times a day with quail on Sunday. Old friends avoided him when anybody with a truck was urged to take a few loads. One competing doctor—you know how petty they can be—threatened to spike both barrels but Will discovered the plot and retaliated with a late night deposit of a dozen birds on his doorstep. Cats dispersed the entrails but the door mat was bloody for months. Then he discovered Tabasco Sauce —a powerful rust inhibitor—and hosted a dinner for the entire town but nobody came. A desperate Will ran a full page ad, but even under an alias everybody knew who this guy was. Always inventive, he urged creative fishermen to use his colorful feathers to make flies with real style, because it is gauche to ask a noble trout to gobble a bare hook. But nothing fails like success. Now the doctor had to peddle fish.

Will owned another gun almost as heavy, a lever-action 30-30 with a long octagonal barrel. Only one weapon in the West was older, but it was stolen by Crazy Horse at the Little Big Horn. The rear sight was missing but its owner learned to aim two feet high and exactly twelve yards to the left, a secret he never shared. Now he had five hundred pounds of venison which is even harder to peddle than fish. So he learned to make jerky which keeps for years, so durable it can easily out-last your friends. It was rumored that Will put the jerk in jerky. In those days it was but a short walk to country teeming with upland game, but elk lived up where a man needed an automobile. When finally he could afford a car (by now the town had five) it boasted a Ruchstell gear to climb roads where there were none. What was an option in Detroit was in Idaho a necessity.

Because reverse was the strongest gear, it was standard to back up the steepest grades though after a few miles this strained eyes, neck and disposition. Downhill was even tougher. The frightening drop from Grimes Creek Pass down to the South Fork of the Payette required two disciplined men and a survival plan. At the summit they would drop a tree, cut a six foot length and chain it to the rear axle, never the bumper which they pulled off on the last trip. Dragging a Ponderosa controlled the descent which brakes and gears could never withstand. Even with the Life Log, veteran mountain drivers removed both doors to expedite a quick exit.

Log control was tricky and on hairpin turns it had to be re-aligned . . . and FAST.

The steepest inclines demanded even more drag but sections longer than six feet were so unmanageable that they could slip over the edge and pull the car along with them. At the base of the cliff were two twisted derelicts whose drivers forgot this. Next to them was an abandoned transfer wagon, fractured evidence that a vertical catastrophe could befall even experienced mountain mules. At the end of the descent was a pile of discarded logs with curious chain marks, and each testified that another hero had made it all the way from the top. This was not Idaho's worst road, but the rest were above the tree line where there was nothing to drag and even mules rebelled.

Grimes Creek was named after a prospector who was killed by Indians just before the big gold strike in Idaho City. Since he was the first known fatality, Grimes got his name on the map but if murder deserved remembrance most of the mountains would have Chinese names.

In addition to a Ruchstell Gear, Will's car had a trunk deep enough for a medical grip and wide enough for a fly rod. Response time to house calls depended on the severity of the illness and the proximity of a good stream. Not unexpectedly, old timers surveyed each catch with covetous derision and compared them to those "really big fish we caught before the War." This has been the loser's mantra for a thousand years. Only the war changes. In truth, they could not out-fish this doctor if they used grenades. Most fisherman were no more than imposters holding a pole. When Will got his line in the water they became spectators.

Bounteous throughout the twenties, western waters grew more grudging as the word spread east. Hoosiers, Hawkeyes or Hindus could fish forever for a couple of dollars. Idaho Fish and Game coasted for years on that paradise reputation and blew their hatchery budget by touring mountain lakes with congressmen who camped in heated tents and gigged trout without limit. Rainbows were sauteed by an aide in a three piece suit and washed down with champagne.

But one doctor never forgot the legendary fishing of 1919. Somewhere there must be one last undiscovered lake, so inaccessible that only he could find it. In fact, there did exist such a remote piscatorial haven, but it would be another twenty years before Will would blaze his own trail into Enos Lake.

DOCTOR, DOCTOR, IS THIS GONNA HURT?
BILLY, IT WILL HURT PLENTY.

One of his early patients had been so garrulous that Will was compelled to excuse himself under creative pretexts. Unfortunately, he left so many times that the old biddy started a rumor about the doctor's prostate. Neurotic bores can make other people sick until the wrong person must leave the room. The solution came the next day when he went to the secondhand store, where for six bits, he purchased a regal chair whose padded arms invited the occupant to lean back and stay forever. Then with a bone saw he shortened both front legs by one diabolical inch.

Just enough! Will had just created the Fabled Chair of Brevity. Its forward slant was imperceptible but soon a vague uneasiness discouraged even the most loquacious. Mysteriously the most persistent motor mouth surrendered to an aching back.

As a backup there was an escape button under the rug which only the doctor's educated toe could find and unexpectedly an urgent buzzer called him away. Sometimes he never came back. Nobody died. Buzzer patients were not sick in the first place. In a litigious society discerning complainers are encouraged to cross examine doctors, not for edification but a chance to use big words. Welfare patients prefer Latin terms culminating in Carpal Tunnel Syndrome. Ordinary diarrhea becomes Schistosomiasis except Monday, Wednesday, and Friday when it's Shigellosis. Not to worry. The government buys their toilet paper.

Critical patients frowned at a bottle of new pills, expecting a recitation from the Merck Manual or at least the PDR. Will's brevity was not limited to his chair: "That's medicine. It's good for you. Take it."

An orthodox chair was reserved for fishing companions who deserved a little time to display the flies they tied last winter. Here he enthroned ranchers who fed Canyon County pheasants. Each bird could have his own corn field and a lucky few were even allowed to dine with the chickens . . . until opening day in October.

The ritual was always the same. Will unlimbered his antique shotgun with its engraved Damascus barrels, fired into the air to clear the rust, and the hunt began. He usually had his limit by noon, but one year the flock scattered when most of the town came to see if the doctor could still lift the mammoth weapon. Pheasants sought relief and a new game bird was introduced. Will urged (some say bribed) Idaho Fish and Game to import chukkar from Turkey where they were called *keklik*. Turks carried a few guns but saved ammunition by beating pans to drive the *keklik* into box canyons where the women waited with nets. Within minutes, the birds were frying in olive oil and, after doing the dishes, the ladies served refreshments. Americans really don't know how to hunt. Chukkar proliferated in Leslie Gulch and Succor Creek Canyon where there are no Anatolian women with nets. These crafty birds have a knack for staying just beyond the range of any gun (from .410 to 12 gauge to canon) with a derisive cackle that sounds exactly like *Heart Attack. Heart Attack.* Chase one and you'll see why.

Will's longhand notes were in classic Jeffersonian script worthy of framing and uncharacteristic for a physician. These were faded but elegantly legible when his son admired them years later. Some records included sketches to pinpoint the prime hunting in Greenleaf or New Plymouth and even across the Snake River where he was always welcome in Oregon. One note was in code as if to conceal the true route to a bird haven east of Cambridge but even an amateur cryptographer could interpret: CHUKKAR in the canyons. QUAIL along the creek. GROUSE in every tree

In the margin of his office records was penned a grateful discount where the game had been bountiful. Some bills were erased completely. All farms were graded with one to four stars. Symms' orchard in Sunny Slope crawled with pheasants but ranked low because "there were too many trees between the barrel and the bird."

Caldwell's two cars ran into each other and Will's first patient was carried upstairs where he worked in the hall. His office would not be available until the rent check cleared. Even before the iodine was dry there came a far off irritating voice that would hound him for the next fifty-five years: "What about the paper work?"

After marveling at his superb work, spectators begged him to go downstairs and check the car but he couldn't do a thing for it. When cavemen chased nubile women with a mating club, they often were so blinded by love that they stumbled and tried to break their fall with an extended hand to which they exclaimed: "Oh rats! I have a Colles fracture." Eventually cars replaced clubs to catch women (though clubs are still popular in Nampa). If girls were not attracted to a roaring muffler, they would surely succumb to a fox tail on the antenna.

Detroit produced their first autos with only the driving essentials: an inner tube repair kit and a crank. Cranking entailed a vigorous clockwise motion while the wife offered tips from the back seat. Frequently the crank shaft rebelled and a sudden counterclockwise backfire forced the wrist into hyperflexion before the radius and ulna were ready. Automobiles thereby changed the extension fracture of the cave man into a *reverse* Colles fracture.

During those years, other clinical entities went into reverse and even hip dislocations changed directions. For centuries these were anterior (forward) and known poetically as Gondolier's Socket Injury when one leg went with the boat and the other one stayed on the dock. Their high pitched Venetian screams have motivated Italian tenors ever since. But the socket goes both ways, at least in American cars, where high speed trauma caused the knee to crash into the dashboard and introduced the driving world to posterior hip dislocations.

Cars were very good to Will. His old office records illuminate the gradation from the run-away wagon where a soft landing was possible to the automobile where steel and concrete were less forgiving. His first clinical notes were hurriedly entered on a handy 4x6 index card and these became the standard record thereafter. Gradations of yellow indicated the passage of time and there was no need to file these cards by the year because to him they were already color coded.

Like too many small towns, Caldwell's Main Street was gradually vacated until the lumber business was confined to selling plywood to board up windows. Will's new office was just a hundred yards from the third green which he had leveled and planted when both he and the town were young. The fourth fairway ended in cattails where duck hunters claimed lost balls and golfers soon learned never to argue with a man who carries a gun.

Popular in those days was the rambling edifice with big windows and even bigger heat bills. Architects touted this as the ranch style and they were seen everywhere except on ranches. Will kept looking for cows in the parking lot. The doctor questioned the extravagance of space but forgave the architect who may have been preoccupied:

"He still owed for his wife's last two babies. And one wasn't his."

He missed his old office, only recently remodeled with new linoleum, and was now lost in the uneasy opulence of thick carpets, pastel instrument cabinets and potted palms where wary patients could hide for hours. Nurses with long diplomas and short skirts demanded their personal pop machine which dispensed Coke by the cup and gossip by the gallon. Will worked alone, answered his own phone and kept all records in longhand. Since he was also the receptionist, he called in the patients he liked best. Impartiality was the myth created back in Washington.

After those fourteen foot ceilings on Main street, Will still fumbled for the pull chain but soon mastered the wall switch. As light filled the room he invariably glanced gratefully at the bulb to propitiate the spirit of Thomas Edison.

At the grand opening he was presented a monogrammed leather appointment book. It graced his desk unopened for fifty years. Appointments were for lawyers or Beverly Hills abortionists.

Some adjacent states, motivated no doubt by envy, simply that Idahoans are uneducated dolts who usually vote Republican. Anybody can check one of those free highway maps and quickly identify these detractors since we are bordered by just six states. This does not count Canada, our chief source of gray wolves.

When Will opened his office, many of his early patients paid with potatoes, corn or, failing that, a promise. This included two of his contemporaries who began at the bottom of the educational ladder but soon climbed to the top rung. Neither of these inchoate entrepreneurs had attended high school—going to work at twelve will do this—but Ray and Harry proved that an eighth grade education could do wonders just by paying attention. By persistent self-education they pursued the American dream from rags to riches. Both wisely married school teachers to improve their grammar in return for a promise of an elegant house and came to learn that a private tutor would have been cheaper. They borrowed the *Wall Street Journal* from the Carnegie public library and memorized a fundamental lesson: *It is better to receive interest than to pay it.*

Ray and Harry must have written quite well because their signatures were honored from Boise to San Francisco. It would be many years before I mowed Harry's lawn and requested a seventy-five cent check just to see his signature. That check is still around here somewhere. It would be foolish to frame any check that can still be cashed.

These two prevailed against three Jews, two Orientals and several college graduates—some of whom had actually been fraternity men. Ray's father had been a Methodist minister in Oletha, Kansas, where his meager salary was severely strained to feed eleven children. Many Sundays the preacher himself was invited to gorge on fried chicken while the kids stayed home. The congregation was not so eager to get into heaven as to include an overwhelming family that ate in shifts.

As an adolescent swain, Ray had courted the prettiest soprano in the church choir. He borrowed dad's buggy and whitewashed the mare's rump so the object of his affection might think his family had more than one horse. But a sudden Kansas rain exposed the ruse resulting in a monochrome chestnut horse and a drowned romance. Now the entire choir would know that Ray came from a one-horse family.

Next Sunday's sermon dealt with honesty. It must have worked because when he came to Idaho in 1910 he had packed honesty into an otherwise empty suitcase. C.C. Anderson owned the biggest store in Weiser and hesitated to hire some inexperienced kid with an eighth grade education and whitewash on his hands. It had been Ray's hope that this tale of shame would never leave Kansas. Fortunately, his father had also preached on perseverance so Ray offered to work the first six weeks for nothing. If C.C. could make everybody work free he would be bigger than J.C. Penny who recently opened his first store not far away in Kemmerer, Wyoming, and was doing very well. Sears and Roebuck even took notice.

By 1913, Ray was promoted from Weiser to the flagship store in Caldwell. Within a few years the kid who had once worked six weeks for nothing, bought both stores and eventually owned ten more. Even J.C. Penny noticed. Ray's grim countenance worried every kid on Dearborn Street, but he did smile once when I agreed to catch his son if he missed a limb playing Tarzan. And this kid missed plenty. I came to learn that beneath that granite face was a man of deceptive benevolence. Christ introduced Christmas. Ray invented the bonus. One employee played poker at the Elks just one night too often and had to sell his car. He walked to work for only a week, after which he was driving a new green car. Green was Ray's favorite color. Next Saturday found Ray at the Elks. The subject was poker. Ray was the instructor. His visor was green. Everyone at the table learned a lot.

When a shoe salesman died unexpectedly, his employer sent the man's son through college though Ray's own son—along with the rest of the town—would be drafted before he was so lucky. Despite their profound political polarity, Will and Ray became lifelong friends, and the merchant who never smiled was the only man who could make my father laugh out loud. All Ray wanted in return was anonymity, but grateful recipients could never keep a secret. He died in a car wreck in 1948 and even today legends of his generosity continue to surface. You may hear one tomorrow. This man survived the Great Depression and was soon transformed into the impeccable Merchant Prince of Idaho with grammar beyond reproach, thanks to his wife. Ray was smooth and urbane. He wore a three piece suit, had a weekly haircut and mingled with governors and senators.

Harry followed quite a different route to success as the shaggy-haired country hick with lousy syntax and creative spelling. Harry was the guy who *elected* governors and senators. He inherited buck teeth from his parents and deafness from a fox glove that penetrated his ear drum when he was bucking bales. Harry tried not to shout but those teeth made him spit when he didn't mean to. Careful folks decided that three feet was about right for conversation.

Caldwell warned Portland and San Francisco to stand back. Boiseans could figure it out for themselves. Supercilious competitors openly pitied this hayseed who took this as a compliment and played it to the hilt. If Hollywood needed another Andy Devine they could find him counting his cash up in Idaho where he was out-smarting corporate lawyers . . . and even one patent attorney.

His basic education began by driving the mail stage from Jordan Valley and he never lost a letter. When someone put tires on wheels he noticed that rubber wears out so he began a tire business. Most cars require four. Houses seemed to be popular so he opened a lumber company. He out-bid competitors by shingling the roof himself. Lumber comes from trees so to eliminate the middle man he bought a forest. I'm sure you can follow the theme here. Folks buy tires about once a year and a house only once in a lifetime. But they eat all the time. Food makes people happy. His restaurant flourished because instinct told him the difference between Boise and Caldwell. You can't sell prime rib in a roast beef town. Gravy makes anything better but French sauce scares people.

During the Depression, rabbit replaced chicken and if this offended fastidious patrons the defense was simple. Rabbits nibble healthful vegetables. Chickens eat earwigs. When the mayor ran for re-election, he promised to cut all that red tape. Harry won on the assurance that there would be none to cut. He was Caldwell's mayor when Jack Simplot, on his way to becoming Idaho's first billionaire, hesitated to open his potato dehydrator just outside the city limits. His concern was fire protection. Harry quickly disposed of this problem: "Don't call the Fire Department. Call me." My kids loved to eat at Harry's cafe because he gave each one a roll of Life Savers in the flavor of their choice. Then one sad day the candy display was empty. Life Savers had recently soared from a nickel to a dime. Idaho was not ready for this. Harry would not carry them for another month. During that time some competitor could spread the bad news and catch all the hell.

SOMEWHERE A BABY IS BORN EVERY FOUR
SECONDS.
WE MUST FIND THAT WOMAN AND STOP HER.
~ Sam Levinson

Soup kitchens in Detroit exemplified the Great
Depression but bread lines were shorter in Idaho
because it was blessed with the diversification of irri-
gated desert, canyons with silver ore and forests with an
elk behind every tree. A buck with a big rack may look
majestic but fawns are just as nutritious and certainly
more tender. Even kids bagged a few since the Bambi generation was yet unborn. As a bonus this selective poaching
spared cattle from excessive rustling.

Will had been in town just ten years when construction everywhere had ground to a stop. In an atmosphere of
nationwide despair, and against all advise, he managed to
take out a building loan at 12% interest. In 1929 his
Memorial Park Hospital was wired, plumbed and bedded
for patients too sick to leave outdoors. Rusty saws attest-
ed to the duration of the depression as unemployed carpenters lugged lumber from local mills and hammered
nails which back then were not imported from Japan.
Folks rejoiced briefly when Adm. Richard Byrd adven-
tured heroically over the South Pole to distract the country from its misery but bread lines only lengthened. Their
doldrums were ameliorated by a Caldwell architect who
had never designed a hospital. Harold owed on a cholecys-
tectomy, leaving the surgeon with only a jar full of drab
green gallstones. Will thought this color would go well in
the lobby but Caldwell Paint and Glass refused to mix it.

The designer only knew that you had to be in bad
shape to be in a hospital—like when his brother was run
down by a tractor. He would have made it but the tractor
was pulling a plow. They didn't even have to bury him. A
hospital roof must be secure because rain can hamper

healing, and the floors should be a neutral color so you could throw up anywhere.

He began by modifying residential plans from the *Good Housekeeping* which obliged him to retain that ubiquitous stucco exterior. Even an outhouse could not escape stucco. Harold was a Greek whose ancestors had done the Parthenon and even his service stations retained that authentic Hellenistic style:

"Fill 'er up but take your time so I can drink in the wonder of it all."

With this background, Harold created a curious hybrid which became a hospital but the Corinthian columns went over budget and were the first to go. Right after The Great War, Dr. Cole had converted the magnificent Dorman mansion at Kimball and Logan and now had two columns left over. But who wants to borrow from a competitor? Before going into debt for the rest of his life, Will consulted the scriptures. In his epistle to the Corinthians, Paul implies —at least in the original Greek—that columns belong in Corinth, not Caldwell.

The Memorial Park Hospital was lucky to have stairs, and elevators were a sure sign of a pampered populace, an unreliable contrivance seen mainly on the decadent east coast. Rooms were two dollars a day, or a dollar and a half if you did your own laundry.

There was a new wash board right down the hall and scrubbing sheets was great physical therapy. One new mother wondered how soon she could get pregnant again:

"That depends. Are you in a ward or a private room?"

Caldwell had one Jewish mother (has three now) who was contracted for her chicken soup. For therapeutic efficacy a single Kosher bowl rivaled the U.S. Pharmacopoeia and for love, surpassed it. In fact, all of the food was sumptuous since the kitchen was operated by a lady who lived to eat and, unlike many of circus proportions, was willing to share. Will's son always mowed the lawn during meal times where he could rest his grass-stained elbows on the table and pretend he was a doctor.

Canyon county patients were hard to kill, tough homesteaders whose vitamins were derived from brewing dandelion tea, quite tasty with lemon juice in case a lemon happened to roll into Idaho. Epitomizing this toughness was a tight colony of Basques whose speech was not quite Latin, not quite French and a far cry from English. The best way to comprehend this tongue was to be born a Basque and to get along with these proud people don't ever call them Spaniards.

The hospital staff of about five included Dr. Walter Jones whose office was sixty miles away in Jordan Valley, southeastern Oregon's heart of Basquedom, though a few of them spilled over into Nevada. He admired his Pioneers from the Pyrenees but no more than they deserved:

"If a Basque beats you out of a bill, he lied about his nationality."

It was his huge practice that helped to pay off that 12% hospital loan. Basques paid cash for every baby and among Catholics, volume really counts. On the down side were those polysyllabic names on the birth certificate which Jones offered to shorten at no extra charge. It was pointless to list them alphabetically since of the 26 letters only two were needed.

"Y" took care of all the Yzaguirres and since most daughters were named Maria the rest were under "M." The omniscient Jones confided: "If Jordan Valley ever gets a phone book, we're ready."

Basques confided everything with Jones except how they made chorizos . . . but some secrets are better kept. The non-Basque intestine can expect to suffer hyperperistalsis, known as The Amateur Bowel Syndrome. Walt's specialty was rattlesnake bites and he once had to treat himself when a set of fangs sank in his own calf: "I've sure had better patients. This one was a real whiner."

Will's Memorial Park Hospital was named after the park across the street where magnificent elms shaded vast green lawns that were never littered. Pure artesian fountains washed down venerated recipes from Nebraska (cleverly spelled backwards as Aksarben). Iowa and Missouri were also well represented and midwesterners were so numerous that if they all went home it would empty the entire valley. On this lush greenery softball games had no losers, and Sen. Wm. E. Borah, the Lion of Idaho, spoke from the bandstand just for practice since he was always re-elected.

He died in 1940 so The Lion did not live to agonize while the town surrendered its park to greasy gangs. With rings dangling from every appendage, pungent punks parked stolen hot rods on the manicured lawn and dying grass easily confirmed an incontinent transmission.

Petunia beds retained imprints of the female form as crushed floral evidence of last night's love and abandon. Some buttocks—these were good sized girls—were stamped deeper than others, testifying to a determined stud whose prodigious drive was limited, alas, to this single endeavor. Couples in heat, like salmon but not as bright, migrated up the Boise River just to spawn in Caldwell's park. Patients at the nearby hospital rose from their beds and, with unsteady legs, braced themselves against the window for a better view. Fevers dropped. Pneumonia subsided. Fractures knitted overnight. The ardor generated by group orgies actually de-thorned rose bushes while they savaged foliage and each other.

This phallic ritual ended about 4:00 a.m. when rigidity succumbed to flaccidity. Beer-laden bladders sought relief and the crystal waters of the great granite fountain turned to amber. Sen. Borah missed all of this.

DELIVERING BABIES IS EASY.
IT TAKES A GOOD MAN TO STOP THEM.

A twisted green cord dangled from a fourteen foot ceiling, dribbling electricity to an incandescent bulb, probably blown by Edison himself. With a pull on the chain it pretended to glow but a dim light is quite sufficient to diagnose a pregnancy since most conception begins in total darkness.

Somebody here was going to have a baby and the doctor got thirty-five dollars just to be there when it happened. The hard part was eliciting a routine prepartum history which was awkward for this restrained physician. Excessive modesty was ingrained from early childhood by his grandfather who knew sin when he saw it and he saw plenty. Will had learned all the right questions in medical school but visions of his scripture-quoting Grandad could still override science enough to make him hesitate. Sex is such a crude thing.

For centuries there has been some mysterious correlation between menstrual periods and pregnancy so a few questions were unavoidable. The grinning groom sat cross-legged with well manured boots, obviously savoring the doctor's discomfort which was almost more fun than getting the girl pregnant.

The bride made frequent trips to the bathroom far down the hall until she finally lost the key. Alone with the smirking cowboy, Will considered choking him with a few twists of his stethoscope but this would be bad form for a new doctor in town. Word would get around.

She was third trimester, maybe more, and they couldn't sit around all day. Only one awkward question remained. It was time for the reluctant physician to adroitly craft such words as would somehow mix the immiscible. With a blend of medicine, restrictive theology,

Victorian demeanor and vagueness Will formulated a question that seemed safe enough:

"How many times have you missed?" With downcast eyes the bride turned coyly to her husband:

"I don't believe we've missed a night, have we dear?"

A splendid office building had been built by Ancil K. Steunenberg, a brother of the assassinated gover- nor. At the entry, a peripheral vastness of beige tile surrounded A.K.S. which was emphasized in dark brown. Quite unnecessary, since ownership was never in doubt and the rent check went directly to Ancil. Two stories and all brick, this building testified to all that was modern except an elevator. Mr. Otis's eastern contraption was lit- tle more than a long chain and a couple of pulleys but it was rejected out West as decadent and unreliable though one seemed to work down at Vassar's Feed and Grain. A bright green arrow directed patients to steep, shallow steps where a ladder would work just as well. The doctor came downstairs if you were really sick where, of course, lawyers were already waiting on the curb.

The waiting room linoleum was recently imported from Boise and there were separate chairs for everybody with a plethora of educational literature: *Field and Stream* for the men, *Collier's* for the ladies and in one cor- ner a column of *National Geographics*, so high that they may have supported the ceiling. Those issues on Africa were always popular but for some reason sections which displayed bare-breasted native girls had several pages missing.

On the wall was a sepia-toned panorama of the Roman coliseum, jammed with bloodthirsty citizens in wine-stained togas, a few lions and one emperor holding thumbs down. There was a rest room somewhere but the doctor kept the key which he loaned only to fishing buddies and men with three pound prostates. The coliseum was expropriated from the Ernst Coal and Wood calendar and while their picture changed annually, this one of downtown Rome during the rush hour was too educational to take down.

Hat racks bristled around an oak-framed mirror which reflected to assure patients that they always looked better after seeing the doctor. To its left was the sphinx guarding a pyramid which had probably been vacated some time ago. These Egyptian scenes were not ordinary oil paintings, but real photographs which proved that somebody had actually been there. But it was the Ishihara eye chart which reminded thinking people that this was not some lawyer's office. Were these not the most educational walls in town?

From the waiting room it was not by accident that you passed a 1934 model X -Ray, an impressive and barely ethical form of advertising. After another 120 payments, more or less, Will would own this radiating monster, a confusion of switches, tubes and cables that filled an entire room. As a bonus, it emitted the exotic odor of ozone which most folks in Idaho had never smelled.

Courteous patients stared at the machine and extended perfunctory curiosity but immediately directed the discussion to their favorite subject. *That would be SEX* . By the time Will had delivered the second generation, this physician decided to get out of the baby business hoping that women would get the idea and stop having them. This never worked nor did his admonitions on the graceless practice of adultery which was quite popular in decadent towns like Nampa but certainly had no business in Caldwell.

One patient with undisguised pride, spewed forth unsolicited and disgusting details of his primal instincts which included a profound attraction to little girls. And this was only his first visit. The red-faced doctor struggled to change the subject but you know how persistent perverts can be. Previously, he had relied on one infallible, albeit cowardly, escape but even this was about to betray him: "Why don't you discuss this with your minister?"

"Doctor, I am a minister."

It was so easy to get to Curtis Park that nobody went there. It was further cursed with a dozen artesian wells which gushed water too pure to drink but by encouraging it to stagnate mosquitoes found a home. The wells went unclaimed and the park languished until a diabolical sport was imported from Scotland where the devil wore knickers and swung mysterious clubs with persimmon heads and hickory shafts. Some rich Caldwell merchant had vacationed in California and while posing for a picture in an orange grove spied a nearby golf course and came home speaking the strange tongue of *Brassies, Cleeks and Niblicks*. Skeptics suspected he hoped to develop a new Idaho market for sportswear since fishing and horseshoes required no special attire. He even started a Yellow Fever scare and blamed Curtis Park mosquitoes. The swamp must be drained and only an adjacent golf course could do it. Soon the town was shamed into building a links which could be watered by three laterals from Curtis Park.

Two weeks in California had created a monster. With subliminal P.R. he transformed a sports project into an unselfish humanitarian effort. The perpetrator recruited heavily in the local barber shop where Caldwell denizens congregated around the town's radio and admired themselves in beveled mirrors plastered with sartorial promis-

es by *Murine, Vitalis,* and *Lucky Tiger.* Radio reception
was limited to baseball games and the grateful Cincinnati
Reds had donated a poster including dates for games
which these fans could never ever hope to see. Broadcasts
were sponsored by *IPANA for the smile of beauty* and *SAL
HEPATICA for the smile of health*—promises unkept by
products long forgotten.

Behind the barber chair hung a 1932 calendar from
some auto parts outfit. That year would never come again,
but the blonde chick in shorts was timeless. One day the
barber's wife burned the salacious photo, forcing the proprietor to seek a new hobby. He became the first Idahoan
to renounce sex for golf. He locked his shop, grabbed a
shovel and joined the pioneers on the fairway. These volunteers were easily identified since they all needed a haircut. Everybody pitched in except the Western Union oper-
ator who, in those days, never locked his door and kept
Caldwell in touch with the outside world. There was also
one indispensable woman who played the organ during
Saturday matinees and without whom no movie could
begin. She was also contracted for weddings but her popularity for funerals plummeted when she accidentally confused Wagner with Offenbach and broke into the CAN
CAN. The corpse, before becoming one, had been a devoted womanizer and the grieving family feared such ener-
getic music might entice the lecher out of his coffin.

The John Deere dealer donated a plow but, since this
was the height of the Depression, it was a little rusty. The
mercantile wizard who dreamed up the whole thing
nudged reluctant husbands by working through their
wives. Women's hats, except those with feathers, were discounted ten percent. Men's knickers were eventually
marked down to half but with no takers. His store window
included a photo of St. Andrews where fashionable Scots
wore these peculiar pants but Caldwell was an overall

town. Eventually a gross of knickers was rejected even by the Salvation Army.

Eighty acres of wheat were sandwiched between Curtis Park and formidable lava buttes to the west. Six holes would be on the flat but three would demand a Crusader's scaling ladder to reach the top. In the days before electric carts, golfers were in better shape. A team and fresno leveled the greens which bore hoof marks for many months thereafter. To emulate California, score cards were printed but without a diagram of the holes since the sequence was never the same.

The flat land included a poorly framed house where the farmer's wife augmented her butter and egg money by converting her parlor into a club house. Adam's Gum and Tootsie Rolls sold out fast and an ice bucket on the porch was packed with daily donations from Aberdeen Coal & Ice. Beverages included Orange Crush, Delaware Punch and (only for the reckless) Coca Cola. Kids collected bottle caps and rare ones were worn as medals. After carefully prying the cork backing from the metal, any thin fabric could be interposed after which the cap and cork were snapped together. Thus an ordinary shirt became the envy of less bemedalled peers. Patient mothers stitched multiple perforations and collected creative adolescent alibis which Mom would share with her Canasta club.

Trembling planks traversed the ditches which were cautiously crossed lest the man ahead start enough vibration to catapult his opponent into the water which was artesian to be sure but cold nevertheless. The first dousing could be called an accident but subsequent immersions were viewed with increasing suspicion. At ten cents a hole, such drenching disasters were common if the first man on the bridge happened to be a sore loser. A jagged crater was dynamited half way up the cliff and balls which missed this green ricocheted straight back to the tee, hopelessly lacerated. A new ball cost two bits and one miserly merchant tried to play on with half a ball. A few shots made the green which was approached with a putter and crampons. A flour sack became my father's golf bag and I became a caddie.

Dad owned only four clubs so there was room for a single shot .22 rifle which could hold any kid's attention. Errant drives often soared deep into the sagebrush and, while the players searched and grumbled, the caddie guarded the foursome from rabbit attacks. I became only an average golfer but a very good shot. The greens were anything but. In the absence of grass, oiled sand was smoothed with a grader which was stored in the cup, pretending to be an orthodox flag stick. Golf etiquette demanded that only an opponent could tend the surface because unscrupulous golfers had learned to tilt the grader just enough to create a trough to guide the ball. When skillfully done this was inconspicuous but a low sun late in the day could cast a tell-tale shadow. Golf was a gentleman's game and the proof was in the grader.

Cups on the Curtis Park greens were buried tomato cans, but when they attracted too many crows, these were abandoned in favor of something less tasty—and just perhaps of greater diameter. The price of wheat went up. The farmer wanted his land back. Caldwell's seminal golf course was gradually abandoned to the jackrabbits whose burrows were filled with lost golf balls. The oiled sand greens were forgotten but NOT THE GAME.

When golf invades a decent community, gambling and prostitution are never far behind. This addictive game begins innocently with fresh air and fellowship but degenerates to an insidious infestation of the soul. Resolving this impasse is like asking Dracula to give up blood and stay in his coffin. A loose head or a bent shaft is OK for the beginner but if he breaks eighty—make that ninety—he demands customized Kenneth Smith woods. His children go hungry while the golfer puts mink head covers on layaway. The correspondent named in most American divorces is not sex but golf and the poorer the golfer the quicker the divorce. Deacons embezzle from the collection plate just to pay green fees. Scoutmasters, once idolized by trusting youngsters, award merit badges for stolen Titleists. Possessed by demons, the golfer collects putters because he is compelled to buy whatever model was used by the last man who beat him.

Baseball fans quote Yogi Bera and revere his incongruities but golfers have the incomparable Sam Snead who won his first tournament playing barefoot. He grew up in West Virginia hills where he trotted down country roads which "got littler and littler till they ran up a tree." He empathized with hackers: "Never go into a sand trap without a sandwich." Just like the four minute mile, a score of 60 was long considered golf's unbreakable barrier. Then one day Snead shot a 59 (that's fifty-nine) and the world trembled.

The sweltering locker room was packed with unbathed reporters who formed an oppressive circle and shouted moronic questions. How did this compare with an out-of-body-experience? Why didn't he wear a copper bracelet and magnets in his shoes like real golfers do? Sam knew how to handle the press:

"It shoulda been a 58." A generation later, Lee Trevino suffered similar interrogations after surviving a lightning strike that almost killed his foursome.

"Next time I'll hold up my one iron. Even God can't hit a one iron."

Golfers play every game twice. The one on the links is only a preliminary to the second round of armchair contemplation. Every stroke is reviewed, analyzed and dissected including club selection, ball selection and, yes, even tee selection. The grain of the green slopes away from the mountains and toward the ocean. Or is it the other way around? Does the wind blow for everybody?

Occasionally an errant drive—someone was talking on your back swing—may slice into the parking lot and kill somebody. Not to worry. Tomorrow the same shot could just as easily hit a bumper and ricochet onto the cup. These are not alibis. This is scientific stuff. The armchair game takes practice. If the golfer gets the feeling that his next game will be even worse, he must sit down and try again until he gets it right. Golf is a game like no other. When did you last hear a good tennis story?

The Table Rock quarry produced enough stone for the Idaho Penitentiary with plenty left over for several mansions on Warm Springs Avenue where prominent citizens already enjoyed free hot water. Shamelessly they offered the excess granite to the masses with a transparent generosity which by sheer coincidence cleaned debris from the lawn for their next garden party. But Boiseans are like that. Some of the rejected slabs were shipped to Caldwell to build a formidable fortress known as City Hall. In those days most municpal buildings were built right in the middle of the street so all traffic had to circle around them as befits their importance. Table Rock stone was a monotonous shade of intimidating gray which retained a distinct penal aura. City Hall's brooding walls kept the city fathers honest with images of prison. After fifty years, ivy clung desperately to conceal its origin but sometimes the windows cast revealing horizontal shadows and the entire council seemed to be wearing convict's stripes.

MONTHLY MEETING OF THE CALDWELL CITY COUNCIL, April 20th, 1936

Minutes of the last meeting were dispensed with because councilmen found the secretary's notes boring—or incriminating.

OLD BUSINESS

A) The iron hand rail of our outside stairwell is the favorite perch for vagrants. To discourage this, serrated strips have been welded to the top bar. These resemble dull mowing machine blades but, of course, could be sharpened just like they did in Boise.

B) Last year the Sebree family donated the marble fountain near the City Hall entrance. Every mule in Canyon county goes out of his way to drink here but manure discourages philanthropy.

Three previous committees have failed to appease the Sebrees so a fourth one will be appointed and, if necessary—a fifth.

NEW BUSINESS

Bill No. 17, Ordinance 534: "Construction of a Municipal Golf Course." This had been tabled in February and March so was hurriedly passed lest the voters perceived the council as indecisive. Thus began Caldwell's bold venture to build a links before Nampa did. It's not easy to propagandize a farming community and popularize the frivolous pursuit of a dainty, dimpled ball but is it not the shepherd's job to guide his flock? Success in the feed and grain business had taught the mayor that there was more than one way to sell the product. If the farmer himself wouldn't buy, he could always cajole the livestock. This master salesman observed the cattle's feeding schedule and dropped by when animals were hungry. Emery could make any animal smile and no one likes a surly cow. Poultry was even easier since chickens are flattered by the slightest attention. PURINA was not a chow. It was a way of life. Emery did not have to meet the challenge alone. Council members included Will who delivered babies at a special discount if the child was *not* named after Roosevelt.

Another councilman advertised: "Men can play in overalls but their wives will need a new outfit. Our sportswear is endorsed by Greta Garbo. You too, can look like a Swede. Buy ten. Get one free." Women's shorts were not mentioned . . . nor would they be for twenty years.

The old Curtis Park course was abandoned to a litter of feral cats who sniffed the oiled sand greens with feline disapproval. At Kimball and Grant, the inchoate Fairview Golf course began with three forlorn holes after Dorman pond was drained to wash away ankle-deep alkali. To avoid flooding the entire town, this phase was monitored by the park custodian who was borrowed, probably illegally, from the cemetery. In the excitement of the new project, few people found time to die. And then only by reservation. Mountains of alkali accumulated and while its destination was never known, Will was inclined to guess Nevada. The Work Projects Administration (WPA) was created during the Great Depression along with the CCC, the REA, and the NRA. Roosevelt introduced a maze of acronyms and initials but the president's personal favorite was FDR. Local citizen allied with the WPA to wrestle weeds, dig ditches and trap gophers. At the first hint of greenery the rabbits moved in but there were plenty of coyotes to handle these. There was no need to build sand traps which already pre-dated the links by a hundred years. Boys from the Civilian Conservation Corps. had been relocated from squalid shacks and tenements and now Idaho echoed with Yankee idioms and southern drawls. After street hockey in the Bronx, golf was just another game played with a stick so work on the first fairway proceeded with enthusiasm. There was no demand for cotton pickers but the versatile Confederates were soon swinging sickles and scythes through acres of cattails. In 1936, *Save the Wetlands* was a shout yet unborn. The project was imbued with a spirit of brotherhood comparable to an Amish barn raising. Tractors chugged in from Wilder and Parma and one John Deere with those new-fangled head lights volunteered for night duty. Workers grabbed their hoes with a professional interlocking grip that would simplify the transition to a real golf club. Levelling the ground proceeded without the city grader which was tied up downtown where they filled (or created) potholes. By the end of summer the first three holes were dedicated and only a hick town would be caught without a flag for every green even if the cup was a coffee can. The road department loaned some assorted yellow flags which made Caldwell look just like St. Andrews. Nobody read them and as long as they fluttered the letters were obscured.

Then one calm day their message could be read by all: The flag on the first green waved the news: ROAD EQUIPMENT. The second flag declared ONE WAY TRAFFIC. The road gang refused to loan MEN WORKING which they positioned strategically on the curb to perpetuate the myth of toil while they slipped into the Waldorf saloon.

So what was left for the third green? VOTE FOR HOOVER. Democrats saw Will's hand in this but couldn't prove a thing. They let is pass because the cup was a Chase and Sandborn coffee can which was of slightly greater diameter than the rest. The next annexation paralleled Bagley's pasture, *terra incognitus golfus*, where a bull in perpetual heat snorted fire behind a battered fence. A bad slice could put you in contested bovine territory, and Nampa players were encouraged to yank the ring in the bull's nose. Golf balls in the future came in assorted colors but somehow manure brown never caught on. The Bagleys were gracious folks who proffered fresh milk and cookies to anybody lost in the barnyard for more than an hour. Out of bounds was not too bad when you ate well.

The golf budget was squeezed as other fairways were carved along the ditch bank where Russian olives defied extermination just like real Russians. Thorns on these noxious trees resemble nails on a cross ready to crucify a careless back swing, most of which need to be shorter anyway. One might reason with Bagley's bull but not a Russian olive. But dedicated golfers pursue every ball, regardless of where it lands. The risk of this sport ranks with shark teasing and volcano diving.

It would be a while before the Sebrees donated a few more acres to finish the course but, by 1938, seven holes were plenty. The city fathers suspected nine was the minimum but kept this to themselves since it might affect green fees. Had they done the right thing? Was Caldwell ready for this game? Why was the ball so small? Local sports fans were already in a surly mood and Caldwell athletes were removing the gold "C" from football sweaters. A recent loss to Pocatello had been so humiliating that the bus driver refused to bring the team home. Boise was too big to beat and Nampa was so close that one could hear their incessant gloating just nine miles away. Then Caldwell's luck changed when they enrolled one spectacular athlete. One was enough. George was half Cherokee and that half was another Jim Thorpe. Basketball meant George plus four kids in shorts. Football was George plus ten. In fact, all George needed was a center to hike the ball which saved money on uniforms. George alone was a track team. During the Great George Era, pennants adorned the gym and silver cups crowded out the principal's bowling trophy which he had bought for himself. Caldwell swept every sport. Extra bleachers were added. Methodists started to gamble.

George quickly mastered golf when someone loaned him a few rusty clubs though half were left handed. After a few weeks George toured Fairview—the only course he had ever seen—in thirty-two strokes and townsfolk urged him to play in Nampa where even the best golfers rarely broke forty and, since this was a city of sin, they loved to gamble. Caldwell was a quiet Christian community but they did love their vengeance. Since these two towns rarely spoke, how was Caldwell to know that Nampa had nine holes? After putting out on the seventh green, the Great Hope of Caldwell started for the clubhouse (Caldwell's was a tent) but grew uneasy as the others prepared to play on. Cherokees know an ambush when they see one. This game was not over. Bad enough to embarrass his loyal sponsors but at 10 cents a hole his personal bankruptcy was quite possible. Ever since territorial days, Nampa had whispered that Caldwell was inhabited by jerks. George shot the last two holes birdie-eagle, won a fistful of dimes and saved his hometown from perpetual jerkdom.

Most of Idaho's early doctors rode west with the cavalry or were employed by the mines. With a name like John Wesley Gue it may be superfluous to mention that this pioneer doctor was the son of a Methodist minister who had been the youngest chaplain to serve in the Civil War. Dad must have been a good preacher since his side won. John belatedly celebrated the end of the war by being born 25 JULY 1870.

After graduating from Georgetown University, Dr. Gue became Surgeon in Charge of Mines at Hailey and Custer where ten thousand souls inhabited the hills but were hard to count because they were never above ground at the same time. He lectured on dynamite (the short fuse syndrome), how rotgut whiskey got its name and the perils of eating venison two weeks after the deer died without even being shot. For miners crushed beyond repair he offi-

ciated at memorable funeral services. The doctor's elo-
quence was without equal until one day the white men
heard the moving lament of an Indian as he buried his
brother. He set bones and sutured knife wounds until the
gold petered out after which he worked for the White Knob
Copper Mine at Mackay where they tried to pay him in
copper.

In September of 1909, he set up his civilian practice in
Caldwell where his wife always set the table for three. The
doctor always brought an unexpected guest, actually very
much expected. The Gues were childless but their home
became a children's Mecca. With more generosity than
prudence, the kindly doctor remembered to clothe and feed
his private orphanage but somehow always forgot to
charge for his medical services. Exasperated patients
stopped him on the street begging to pay, even waved their
money. His standard answer was "Call my nurse." Dr. Gue
had no nurse. He didn't even have a phone.

To lose money even faster he furnished an eighteen
bed hospital on the second floor of the Union Building on
Caldwell's Main Street, where he offered a snug bed to any
itinerant who was cold or hungry—or even pretended to
be. He searched every bar, looked under every bridge and
wondered why eighteen beds were never enough.

On the screened back porch he and Emma stored cribs
and high chairs which they loaned to new mothers . . . or
anyone who might be pregnant someday. Students at the
nearby College of Idaho—two lived free in their basement—usually forgot to return the borrowed typewriter so
they kept two on hand and were making payments on a
third.

In those days, the only requisite for football was
eleven men and the C of I played all comers on both sides
of the mountains. This even included giants like
Washington State in far away Pullman. The next day's

headlines ignored the 54 to 0 score and emphasized the real news: Dr. Gue had missed his first game.

His Model T, never too reliable even on level ground, had stalled on the Whitebird Hill and at this very moment a tractor was pulling Doc into Grangeville after farmers from Idaho and Washington fought for the privilege. Thereafter, he always rode with the team. Fair enough. He provided their leather helmets and rented the bus.

When Dr. Gue died 29 DEC 1930 his widow was left a pauper. For several years she lingered on at 1512 Cleveland still giving away her dwindling possessions. After years of unlimited hospitality her home was now an empty hovel. Will brought his medical kit and adjusted her digitalis while she was sustained by visits from Martha, a shrunken, bright-eyed pioneer who had delivered twelve children. One was ashamed to have been born beneath an Owyhee juniper but mother was thankful for the shade. Now none of the dozen bothered to see her but, in their defense, Mother's Day was a concept yet unborn and the town had no florist.

Martha recalled her early childhood in Silver City where she had witnessed the bloody mine dispute between the Golden Chariot and the Ida-Elmore. Claims were hard enough to delineate above ground, but chasing a rich vein a mile below was an excuse for tunnels to overlap. After all, it's dark down there. Both sides hired notorious gunfighters and on March 25, 1868, John C. Holgate was shot in the head. The tiny Martha was barely ten feet away.

Since Holgate was the owner of the Golden Chariot, his Board of Directors responded by hauling in a British made cannon (they were between wars) to which David Ballard, Idaho's Territorial Governor, dispatched a squad of cavalry from Fort Boise. In 1868, Silver City was better armed than anything in Boise but this was OK since the governor himself was not going.

Much to Martha's disappointment, the cannon was never fired—probably from fear it would collapse everybody's mine shafts—but Holgate was not the last to die. Marion More had brought his gold fortune over from Idaho City to speculate in the new bonanza. On April 1st while seated near the stage office at the Idaho Hotel he was shot through the left chest but managed to run fifty yards to the Oriental Restaurant where he collapsed. He died the next day after which every creek and peak in southern Idaho was named after him.

Today, as testimony to what the pioneers endured, you can still buy a rancid sandwich at the Idaho Hotel.

Anyone passing 1512 Cleveland could hear Emma and Martha singing hymns by the hundreds without ever repeating one. Will brought his son, ostensibly to carry the medical grip, but he actually needed an extra singer so Rock of Ages could become a quartette. Seniority was a factor. As a kid back in Falls City, Will had been the designated baritone but today his son got the part that was left over. Dad looked in on Emma every day and listened thoughtfully to her failing heart. His stethoscope was an artful diversion to preoccupy the patient while his son smuggled a sack of groceries onto the back porch. This was never discovered since I was sneaky by nature.

The Gue table was no longer set for that extra guest. The porch stored no high chairs for needy mothers, typewriters for students—or anything for anybody.

Smuggling groceries was a great game for a little kid. And I got pretty good at it.

DON'T LEAVE THE UTERUS ON THE WINDOW SILL. LAST TIME A DOG GOT IT.

The Memorial Park Hospital had a few design defects. After surgery and without an elevator, the stairs were too narrow for a Gurney. Thus the somnolent patient had to be carried to his bed. Will was forever looking for another doctor with a strong back.

Not every man could hold up his end of the patient but Elizabeth could. At six feet she was representative of a robust family which included four gigantic brothers all of whom were reluctant wrestlers who could have pinned the entire Northwest but they always worried about hurting an opponent. Any latent killer instincts were effectively repressed by an overwhelming compassion so these mesomorphs spent most of their time in the ring apologizing.

Even their employment was contingent on wrestling because the boss was just another little man who liked to see big men sweat. We also see this in the seven foot kid who doesn't care for basketball only to be kidnapped and awaken in a gymnasium with a number on his back and shorts that don't fit. But the brothers' intimidating mass was deceptive. Along with muscle, they inherited polycystic kidneys and all died young. Those funerals were attended by mourning wrestlers in size 52 suits where any one of the pallbearers could have carried the casket unassisted.

Elizabeth and her brothers were raised in Iowa where every farm was presumed prosperous but not this one. Iowa and Nebraska shared the same snow while a capricious wind distributed it between Hawkeyes and Cornhuskers. All snow began in the standard white but with each interstate transfer it picked up a little soot. Some blew in from South Dakota and Minnesota but it was all the same snow. Only the color changed.

The bus ride to school cost a nickel. Not everybody rode because you could buy food with the same nickel. Wading snow banks for three miles became a game where the brothers mushed ahead, pretending to be a locomotive, so their special sister could play the caboose. She grew tall only that she might see over midwestern drifts where something interesting might be happening but never was.

Polycystic kidneys were a genetic renal betrayal which struck the male descendents hardest but their sister was not spared. Idaho's best kept secret was Elizabeth's failing health though she concealed her own problems while solving yours. This caring doctor personally drove her patients to the hospital and stayed to tuck them in. The girl who always walked to school was determined that her patients would ride. Willingly she worked her way through high school, college, and finally medical school to which few women dared aspire in the 1930s.

"I was accepted only because the dean was afraid of my brothers." At the Mayo Clinic where Rochester winters reminded her of Iowa, she trained under surgery giants like A.B. Brown, E. Starr Judd and Virgil Counsellor. Judd was shot by an irate husband because his wife's uterus wound up in a bottle after which Elizabeth vowed to treat the womb with respect. In 1935, after four years in OB-GYN, she came to Idaho, probably better trained than any male counterpart in the Northwest.

At Main and Kimball she set up her office on the second floor of the Western Building (Caldwell had no three-story buildings). She paid the rent by delivering the landlord's babies which was a good deal until his wife hit the menopause. Elizabeth kept the placentas for catfish bait, a trick she learned along the Des Moines River. After attending a lengthy labor, sometimes the placenta was all she got.

Her boundless sympathy attracted young girls in trouble who even before they knew where babies came from were going to have one of their very own; menarchal maidens who had a couple of mysterious periods only to have them stop just as mysteriously.

Typical was a worried child in her second trimester who told a lacrimose tale of leaving the Middleton dance hall with her acned swain, the best dancer in Middleton, who drove her far out into the sagebrush to assault her innocence. After several rejected advances he delivered an ultimatum: "Get your clothes off or you can walk home in the snow." What could she do? The doctor's red eyes peered over a pile of wet handkerchiefs to ask: "You poor child. When did this happen?"

"Oh, lots of times."

The going rate for a delivery was thirty-five dollars, a euphemism for a side of beef, and even then she might get the bad side. Elizabeth saw medicine as her Christian duty but could never differentiate between Christianity and gullibility. Will agreed that caring for the poor was the first calling of medicine with one caveat: "I expect to do charity, but I hate surprises." Her next patient was a multiparous deadbeat who already owed for her last five kids and drove a better car than Elizabeth's. Will knew this family from painful experience and urged her to be resolute and collect her well-deserved fee. God would be proud of her. This motivational speaker extolled her generosity, and carefully avoided terms like sucker. She responded to this pep talk with:

"I'll even show you the money."

These fertile folk lived by the Snake River where, historically, labor begins after the sun goes down and twins delivered only during blizzards. In Owyhee County this is a matter of family pride and since children come from God they should be free. Her archaic home-delivery table belonged in a museum where in fact it now resides. Early medical catalogs touted it as portable, only because it had a handle, but the picture showed two robust men carrying it.

Part of the excitement of a home delivery is finding the home. This one was so remote that she asked the husband for specific directions but she was lost for a while because his sketch located the shack on the wrong side of the river.

Finally, a malodorous form grudgingly opened an unpainted door into a room badly in need of ventilation. His formidable gut was draped over a straining belt which was buckled somewhere near his knees. This would be the husband: "I didn't think you'd take this long. I should have gotten a man doctor."

In a chilly bedroom Elizabeth set about comforting the patient with blankets—Will advised her to bring these—while the inseminator remained by the stove in the kitchen with a slab of salami and a six pack of Lucky Lager. At first the doctor occasionally reported on mother's progress but was told to keep the door closed because this allowed frigid bedroom air to escape into his snug sanctuary.

After a few hours he announced impatiently:

"While you're wasting time I'm driving to Marsing for hamburgers."

What a guy! The famished obstetrician foolishly expected to be included. He returned with only two. At least enough for Mom and Dad. But Dad ate both. He did offer Elizabeth an uneaten pickle because they upset his stomach. He had intended for some time to talk to the doctor about this and, since she wasn't doing anything, he also had a few questions about a discharge from his penis. By dawn the babe delivered and the doctor smiled at the recently indebted bundle. Daddy frowned. This thing was too scrawny to be a boy.

After washing the sheets and emptying the kitchen of beer cans, the weary doctor finally got back to Caldwell where Will waited to unload the heavy delivery table. He patiently inquired about the unhappy details, none of which surprised him, but Elizabeth had been evasive about her thirty-five dollars. Had she contrived some crazy alibi Will had not heard? She had started to ask for the money but suddenly backed away.

The father wrapped the babe in swaddling clothes and laid him in a manger.

Only a handful of Boston doctors become famous but myriads hope that the mystique of a prestigious city will rub off if they just hang around. Already superfluous, they marry some wealthy heiress who will subsidize another year at Harvard while she shops at Filene's. Yes, she is unattractive but nothing new clothes can't fix. He is now seriously over-trained and still waiting for some careless patient to discover him. Ambition and talent are paralyzed by a mysterious apprehension. Terrible things might happen if ever he left New England's fountainhead of medicine. What's worse, he has an ugly wife and out west we notice those things. He has traded an unknown potential for a classy address on Commonwealth Avenue where a thousand doctors burrow in a warren of four story brownstones and surface by appointment only. Marble steps ascend to a carved mahogany door where this sequestrated surgeon is just another name on a polished bronze plaque which bears ominous similarity to the markers in Boston's Old Granary cemetery where they are not so frequently replaced. Almost every brownstone along Commonwealth Ave is packed with physicians. And this is a mighty long street. You know you are in Boston if every car is parked in a loading zone. The town swarms with Catholics, but a common religion is a poor reason for Irish and Italians to get along. Back in Falls City a family of Catholic Flynns had overlooked Will's Methodism, but this time he might not be so lucky. To a doctor raised in Idaho, Denver was way back East, and Boston was rumored to be somewhere East of that. On the other hand, Idahoans must contend with Boise. The Union Pacific originated in Omaha and Lord knows where that was. Any good map suggested that the Northeast was a puzzle of miniature states whose long names were probably misspelled. Massachusetts had been a benighted crown colony where folks dressed in black and burned witches. Wives accused them. Husbands struck the match. Children cheered. Verily, entertainment for the entire family. After a successful revolt against King George, the commonwealth came to deify some wealthy family on Cape Cod and began electing Kennedys. Mother Rose had ten of these and while Will was never invited to her many birthdays, he did celebrate her menopause.

He returned to the forests of Idaho where Scandinavian sawyers proclaimed that the climate would be perfect once they got rid of all those trees.

The Oregon Short Line steamed across the arid border where passengers passed the time by counting jackrabbits (one point) and coyotes (ten points). Scores over a thousand were fairly common and this included all animals scooped up by the engine's cowcatcher where an antelope (one hundred points) once broke a tie. The winner kept the horns. The loser got the meat. To count a horse and rider would be insensitive and passengers tried not to watch. Riding in a dusty clerestory coach a brand new doctor carried a canvas bag containing the last laundry his grandmother would ever iron for him. Caldwell was the first but also the last Idaho stop. The track did not yet extend to Boise and Will could hear them bitching thirty miles away.

But Caldwell was already tied up by Dr. Cole who had recently returned a hero from the battlefields of France. He guarded a deserved, but not necessarily permanent, monopoly on Caldwell's infirm. Dr. Cole's grim countenance suggested his war medals were fully deserved. Neighborhood kids said he kept them in a big trunk and there could be thousands. Will's ship never left the Bremerton Navy Yard because Cole had already won the war. Cole's first name was Fern so they called him Doctor.

Small town doctors are not supposed to get along, and even if the combatants called a truce their loyal patients would never tolerate it. Cole was army, Will was navy and the fight was on. During the sweltering summer of 1919 natives stared at the new doctor wearing heavy navy trousers. Comedians in cool overalls (Will recognized several of Cole's patients) suspected some woolen pretense at patriotism and self-promotion. Better this misapprehension than the awful truth: This was his only pair of pants. None of his shipmates had owned a shirt because official attire was limited to the rigid high-collared navy tunic which was designed by Napoleon and borrowed by some sadistic American admiral. Marines cursed the same restrictive collar until they actually became Leathernecks.

At Oakes Dry Goods, Will bought his first dress shirt and it almost fit. The proprietor should have mentioned that shirts came in different sizes but he had a gross of 15 1/2 x 32 and the doctor looked much too sharp to complain that the sleeves were short and the neck was tight. For the rest of his life he wore an unbuttoned 15 1/2 collar around his 16 neck. When I started college he bought the same size for me. Close enough. I also looked very sharp.

Like every small town with any pride, Caldwell supported a pair of everything. They had two bakeries; McClure's for the Scotch Protestants and Mueggler's for the Catholic Swiss. Jews—there were only three in the whole state—had to bake their own bagels. One of the two meat markets was called an abatoir, the only French word in town. Both theaters lied about when the next movie would arrive even though Hollywood sent only films nobody else wanted. But this was show-biz where deceit was implicit. Anything to keep you away from Boise. There were still two active livery stables but some upstart had sold three new-fangled automobiles just after the war. Many new owners with the necessary five hundred dollars took the Union Pacific to Detroit to save on FOB delivery and then drove back in a new (always black) Studebaker or Overland to brag about a cross country trip that their envious neighbor would never make.

Both of Caldwell's furniture stores advertised a funeral parlor in the rear. Nobody understood the connection unless it was that tables and coffins were both made of wood. Furniture sales were sporadic whereas dying was less seasonal and funerals were never sold at a discount. One of the morticians was a devout womanizer and his obsession with females caused suspicion when some embalming sessions took much longer than others.

A generation later, I pushed a lawnmower over the fastest growing grass on Dearborn Street with two exceptions, Dr. F. M. Cole, my father's nemesis, at 1708 Dearborn, and T. R. Walters at 1520. The former was the relentless, fire-breathing competitor who took food off the family table. The latter left dad's food alone but was a New Deal Democrat. Both owned corner lots which meant extra sickle work along the curbs which paid six bits but went to another kid whose work did not compare with mine. The *Caldwell News Tribune* persisted in printing Eleanor Roosevelt's MY DAY and soon after it arrived I could hear dad grinding his teeth in the next room:

"What do you expect from a woman who married her first cousin?" When Eleanor really hit a nerve he would cancel his subscription only to recant because the *Tribune* also printed hospital notices where he kept track of Dr. Cole's nefarious activities. They both kept score.

As an antidote, Calvin Cobb was a Republican and his *Idaho Statesman* proudly printed Westbrook Pegler, whose vitriolic pen creatively renamed the president's cabinet. Harry Hopkins became Bubblehead while others, especially Henry Wallace, suffered even more odious and delightful aliases. Pegler sustained the entire household until he became the first journalist to be successfully sued for libel.

I probably magnified the town feud which was an intense struggle between disparate personalities who actually concealed a reluctant respect. Cole was stubborn. This was bad. Dad was resolute. This was good. A distinction without a difference by a son forever loyal. Neither would win "Mr. Congeniality" or, for that matter, be allowed to enter the contest. Will could keep a secret. His son never knew that Fern Cole was chairman of the Idaho State Republican party. All those years I could have been mowing his lawn for six bits a week, even more in August when the grass really grew. After years of faithful party service, T. A. Walters was appointed Assistant Secretary of the Interior under Harold Ickes, until one day the man whose grass was always too long knocked at my door. His splendid coat—no doubt tailored in Washington, D.C.— was besmeared with blood, his eyes redder than his vest. He was cradling my dog which had just been killed at 16th and Dearborn by some motorist with undeclared political affiliations. We looked for a shovel and settled on a trowel. She wasn't a very big dog. We wept together and that day I learned to love Democrats. But, of course, this eventually passed. Another conversion was even more unexpected. When I left for medical school, Dr. Cole, to whom I nodded annually, gave me a twelve volume set of Waltman Walter's *General Surgery* plus a handsome leather-bound text by someone with a long German name who wrote in his mother tongue. Anticipating my father's astonishment, I waited to break the news from the train platform: "Look at the books Dr. Cole gave me. I thought you two didn't like each other." Dad never flinched:

"Whatever gave you that idea?"

It's 101 miles from McDermitt to Jordan Valley. Not everybody covers this stretch in one hour but it has been done. McDermitt—your last chance to grab your wallet and escape Nevada—is home to the Quinn River Reservation where one of the Indians sells gas. Do not ignore this Indian. For careless travelers who don't fill up it may be weeks before some cowboy stumbles across an abandoned car and not far away the hideous remains of the disoriented driver who has been trampled in a stampede. Don't let this happen to you. To escape the tedium of medicine, Will sought an occasional weekend of relaxation in Reno and this Sunday he was returning flushed with victory. His Methodist wife frowned on gambling but went along to criticize his driving. She never learned to drive so her qualifications were much like the literary critic who can't write. At McDermitt she reminded him to check the oil but both forgot an important detail: Do not leave the Shell station unless the hood is securely latched. Automobiles leave McDermitt faster than rockets leave Cape Canaveral but astronauts don't have to worry about the hood flying up.

Suddenly, where a windshield should be a large sheet of green metal completely obscured Will's view of the highway ahead. The car plummeting for a hundred yards on the wrong side of the road, careened blindly across the borrow pit and veered off into the sagebrush where a huge cloud of dust tried to conceal the shame of it all. Will's driving had often suffered uxorious derision but never like this. The hood was badly out of line but could be forced into position and anchored with barbed wire which, since he had just roared through a fence, was already wrapped around the bumper.

Twisting barbed wire without pliers can be quite traumatic but less bloody than a head-on collision leaving a head in Nevada and the torso in Oregon. He hobbled on to Floyd Acarregui's Chevron station where the Basque name confirmed that this was indeed Jordan Valley. The exhausted driver stumbled into the bathroom and, sure enough, the face in the mirror had definitely aged. The owner started to ask about Reno but suddenly noticed Will's tremor. Maybe he should change doctors:

"How did it go, Doc?" An unsteady voice replied:

"Floyd, I almost lost my hood." Floyd lapsed into his thoughtful Basque mood: "Good Lord, I like to gamble but I never bet part of my car."

When a fisherman neglects his wife, it may take a cruise to Acapulco to assuage his conscience. If he hasn't caught much all year, the guilt is proportionately less and an evening in Boise may suffice. For their penance, Will and Ray selected the Owyhee Hotel with its elegant paneled dining room which recalled a departed glory and a chef who proved it was still there. Just inside the foyer hung a huge sepia mural of The Finger of Fate, the most famous digit in the Sawtooths which more than once had beckoned Ray and Will on to Imogene Lake and their limit of rainbow. Beyond French doors of beveled glass they were greeted by Tom, a regal black waiter who had the good sense to travel to Caldwell for his medical care which explained his robust health.

With admonishing eyebrows or a tactful nod, Tom guided Will's napkin and helped select the right utensils. Back in Caldwell the rules of the table were simple enough: knife on the right, fork on the left, spoon on the floor. But during a six course meal in the big city you can't have too many friends. For this annual gala the wives had extracted an agreement from a doctor and a merchant to avoid the tedium of business. So far Will had not glorified medicine and reluctantly avoided belittling Eleanor Roosevelt since Ray was a New Dealer. But the treaty was about to be broken. Trouser sales had been down at the Idaho Department Store and Ray was a troubled man. Without warning, he switched from bland table talk to an incongruous declaration concerning the superiority of the zipper. Everybody within earshot already knew about zippers because realistic garment makers had introduced this revolutionary devise with back-up buttons for the cautious customer. This could boost sales among the more insecure men because flies were made bulkier than they needed to be, just like the lewd prosthesis that would bulge swimming trunks on gay beaches a generation later. Ray rose solemnly. He hired a lot of people and deserved respect:

"Actually these very trousers have a zipper." Tom dropped his tray which distracted Ray long enough for Will to challenge him: "The zipper was invented in 1893. What kept you?" Ray had prepared his response before they left Caldwell. "Progressive merchants are waiting for timid customers like you to show a little courage." Ray's barbs always made Will grab the wrong fork: "Zippers are a fad which will pass. The rest of us are here to eat, not listen to you tout some new fangled gadget and I'll bet the waiter agrees." Tom had already left.

"Will, to you new fangled gadgets include the light bulb and a cave with a door on it." Insults traded, wives mortified and Tom well-tipped for service (and bribed for silence) it was time for the five block stroll to see "It

Happened One Night," a title which proved to be painfully prophetic. After a good meal Ray was inclined to loosen his belt, the mark of a sensible man. Some say he did this even after a bad meal. Two notches were the ultimate culinary compliment. Entering the protective darkness of the Egyptian theater, he surreptitiously released his buckle to declare that the Owyhee had served a three notcher. Safely seated, he nudged his zipper down an inch or so and wallowed in expansive comfort. He repressed a belch. Why wake up Will?

In the 1930s even Idaho's hinterland emulated eastern fashions, especially the worst of them. The fox, that legendary predator already despised by chickens everywhere, had the further poor judgment to foolishly surround its insignificant body with highly coveted fur. The furrier's magic transformed this lowly scavenger from pelt to trendy female apparel and what began as beady eyes were now real beads. A silver chain passed from the fox's mandible to its former navel to accommodate any lady's neck from petite up to size 16—and a stunning fashion statement it was.

The more luxuriant furs were ranch grown. Cheaper ones had chicken feathers still stuck in their teeth. Tonight there were a dozen fox collars in this theater and a dozen more on layaway. Midway into the Movie Tone News the usher's flashlight flickered along the aisle in search of a seat for a late patron who never missed a Clark Gable film or a chance to wear her furs. The usher signaled and the entire row stood. Panic seized Ray who suddenly remembered his open fly as he fumbled for buttons which, alas, were not there. This wasted time proved critical because just as she passed, his gentlemanly instincts took over and he yanked the gapping zipper. An elegant silver fox was trapped for the second time. Extrication was impossible despite the illumination from the crimson glow of Ray's face. The newsreel droned on and Lowell Thomas watched impassively from the screen ahead. They had all come to see "It Happened One Night" but on this night the real entertainment was in the third row. The cartoon tried to avert the embarrassment but Mickey Mouse stopped mid-animation when the dancing rodent heard protestations of an innocent man who anchored one end of a badly stretched fox. The garbled quack of Donald Duck became suddenly understandable:

"Ray, you look ridiculous." Yes, he called him by name. Will woke up just in time to witness an ignominious procession which rivaled Prokovief's "Peter and the Wolf":

A) PATHETIC VICTIM: Depicted by a plaintive oboe.

B) JAMMED ZIPPER: Clarinet in a low register.

C) TRAPPED FOX: French horns.

D) MAD LADY: Cymbals, Kettle drums and lots of them.

E) USHER: Happy flutes. Blackmail would soon make this lad a manager.

F) FLASHLIGHT: Played by Ever-Ready.

In a distant corner of the lobby (thereafter known as Ray's corner) a dozen grinning spectators converged with pocket knives to sever the tedious tether. The main feature had started but nobody cared. Instead of a refund, many offered to pay double. None of them—perpetrator, patron, pants or pelt—would ever be the same. The woman's lip quivered over her desecrated fur. The usher wondered if glue would help. Ray could only mumble:

"Dear lady, please accept my sincere apology. I hope you have a sense of humor." And the usher said: "I know I do."

Boise's Egyptian theater later came to be listed among America's Historic Places.

And now you know why.

As Ray's business grew so did his wife's social prominence. Ruth's parties were punctuated with success stories featuring Daddy as the hero. Though shameless in her praise, Daddy could handle it. The hostess entertained dinner guests with delightful anecdotes but scrupulously avoided The Great Fox Caper. She even boycotted the Egyptian Theater where the usher called her husband by name. As a consequence, she and Daddy drove to Nampa (they still ate in Boise) to see second run movies at the Majestic (or even third runs at the Adelaide where no one wore fox furs).

Will's knowledge of all animals, especially foxes, was uncanny, and his vulpine recollections were a humbling restraint if Daddy's star soared too high. From the periphery of her parties, this doctor monitored Ruth's grandiosity and merely whispering "zipper" was enough to repress further deification.

One effusive evening Ray himself had to intervene during her compliments though, God knows, he deserved every one. Ray was one of few New Dealers who could boast a friendship with Sen. Wm. E. Borah, Idaho's most revered Republican since Lincoln. The Lion of Idaho was never indifferent to a few Democrat votes and skillfully directed conversation to the Idaho Department Stores, knowing that Ray already owned eleven. In one recent stock exchange, the Merchant Prince of the Boise Valley had also acquired a music store and a pharmacy. Before Borah could ask about this incongruous mix, Ruth interrupted with chiding pride: "Daddy, there is nothing you don't know about the mercantile business." True enough and all heads nodded.

"But, Daddy, why a music store?" All eyes turned to Ray:

"Because, Mother, I know how much you like music." Ruth should have stopped when she was ahead but she was on a roll:

"But Daddy, why, oh why, a drug store?" Even people in the street stopped to hear the answer:

"That's because I want to move my bowels at cost." All eyes left Ray, and the senator took the express train to Washington.

CHAPTER FIVE

WHEN ASSASSINATION ISN'T FUN ANYMORE

In 1899 violence erupted in North Idaho where owners refused to recognize the miner's union. Labor agitators high-jacked the Burke to Wallace train whose engine was designed to haul heavy loads over mountains which were part of the same chain that almost stopped Lewis and Clark. But this day, instead of silver ore it carried four hundred angry men and ninety boxes of explosives. On April 29th this was not too tough since the train engineer was a sympathizer; or at least decided to be when he saw all those shotguns.

The boss owned the mines but the miners had the dynamite.

All workers along the track were union except at the Sullivan and Bunker Hill and the train was coming to blow them up. Death and devastation paralyzed the entire Coeur d' Alene district and more was promised.

The five Steunenberg brothers, born of Dutch immigrant parents, were genetically endowed with that tenacity so characteristic for Dutchmen. The Nazis rediscovered this stubbornness when they tried to occupy Holland in 1940. It was Governor Frank Steunenberg who called for federal troops who came up from Texas. These were die-hard Confederate sympathizers who were sent about as far north as a Southerner could go. During the Civil War, sentiment leaned toward the South though not quite enough to go back and fight about it. Idaho even has its own Confederate river, the Sesech, whose contentious waters memorialize the secessionists and few Northerners catch any fish.

Twelve hundred miners with varying shades of complicity were herded into makeshift bull pens where the incarcerates screamed at the Texas guards with profanity usually heard only in mine shafts. Then, through a sudden conciliatory revelation they pretended to be Southerners. A long drawl beats invective every time and soon the troops were recalled.

Not every prisoner belonged in the stockade but Harry Orchard did. Most inmates renounced their phony dialect and grabbed a pick and a paycheck. But Harry had a private revelation of his very own: to make a career of dynamiting people, a special calling to become Alfred Nobel's devoted disciple of detonation. Once the gates were unlocked, disgruntled union leaders in Wallace and Kellogg organized the subversive "Inner Circle" and these assassins needed a persuasive advocate. At last Harry's life had meaning from which the governor would soon lose his.

Harry Orchard was born in 1866 and, after mastering dynamite, would live much longer than many who crossed his path. The first newspapers I ever read were about Harry who resurfaced periodically whenever editors were crusading for prison reform. The first articles invariably included the only available pictures, full face and profile with big numbers across his chest which didn't do much for him. Gradually he was de-demonized. Modern penologists and liberal journalists re-invented him, clean shaven and smiling in a flattering light just like an 8x10 glossy of Gary Cooper. How did Harry attain such notoriety?

The Inner Circle decided that quality murder needed a little practice and sent Orchard to intern out of state where there were lots of mines waiting to collapse by accident. The trick was to make sure the bomb went off while you were somewhere else.

At Cripple Creek, at the mine's sixth level, he rigged a cocked pistol a few feet from a box of powder caps with enough dynamite to teach Colorado the first of many lessons. With more anxiety than guilt he surfaced to watch. Waiting is the hardest part in the murder business with enough job-related stress to kill some men but not Harry. He lived eighty-eight years and became Idaho's most publicized psychopathic aberration. In Cripple Creek it was three days before some unlucky subterranean soul triggered the diabolical device. As the dust cleared Harry wandered by pretending to be new in town. To his dismay he had detonated the wrong shaft. The miners were working not at the sixth level but the seventh. Orchard had inadvertently wiped out several paid up members of his own Inner Circle. Probably embarrassed, he decided that the less said the better. The bomber failed again in an attempt on Colorado governor James H. Peabody but made it up in volume at Independence, killing thirteen and mangling twenty four. Prophetically, this train was pulling in for the *graveyard shift*.

At the Vindicator stampmill he left a stamp of his own when body parts flew one hundred and fifty feet. His old record had been about a hundred. Harry was learning.

Then with villainous versatility, he graduated from dynamite to poison. In San Francisco, Fred Bradley, the former manager of the Bunker Hill mine, swigged milk laced, actually underlaced, with strychnine. The poison did make the victim mighty sick but even had he died it somehow lacked something. For immediate satisfaction there is nothing like an explosion. Harry's devotion to milk began in Burke, Idaho, where he operated a small dairy which he burned down for the insurance.

The Hit Man should have held to his original plan, a bomb under Fred's chair or in the vernacular of the assas-

sin the BIG LIFTER. Their underworld lexicon embraced
other terms equally graphic but increasingly crude and to
include them here would only cheapen us all. After San
Francisco, some say Orchard went to Salt Lake City to
meditate among the Mormons and research future mayhem, but this is doubtful since no murders were reported
in Utah at that time. Meanwhile something really big was
planned and he hurried back to Idaho so fast that he completely forgot to bomb Nevada, almost an insult to the
Silver State.

During these revolutionary times when mine shafts
trembled across three states, my grandparents were
bound from Nebraska to Idaho, the land of milk and
honey—and IRRIGATION. Bill and Mary had been among
the dry farmers in the midwest who had been seduced
with slick ads describing miles of new canals which would
lovingly deliver clear mountain water to rich sandy loam.
Anything would grow. The promoters failed to mention
that the water was still somewhere up in the mountains,
perhaps a year away. Duplicitous developers instead
depicted luxuriant citrus groves with oranges and lemons
growing on the same tree. Even the weeds were green
enough to lure a Kennedy out of Boston.

Bill rode in the box car where he could pamper his
matched white mules with Nebraska hay. Mary offered to
ride the rods but Bill bought her a coach ticket. She could
pay him back by selling homemade bread once they got to
Caldwell. Whenever the locomotive stopped for water,
Grandad took his mules for a little stroll but once in
Wyoming the box car almost got away. They were oblivious
to the mining wars in North Idaho where occasional trains
were blown up in tunnels, some of which actually had silver linings.

Six years later these immigrants were living in
Caldwell while waiting for something wet to bless their
homestead a few miles away.

To make ends almost meet, Bill did the oddest of odd jobs while Mary operated an in- house bakery. Demand for her services exceeded his by three to one . . . always did.

Harry Orchard had honed his skills from the Coeur d' Alenes to Cripple Creek, and except for that abortive San Francisco fiasco (and some sputtering arson I forgot to mention) he was now a postgraduate assassin. He was still on the Inner Circle's payroll which today would include health insurance with a dental plan. The work was exciting. Harry got to travel. Harry would soon be far more famous than he ever dreamed.

In the fall of 1905, he and his dynamite (Orchard always traveled light) took a room close to Frank Steunenberg's in Boise's Idanha Hotel. Murderers get nervous (even in Boise) and Harry chickened out because the tick of his detonator-clock was too loud. The ominous scene moved thirty miles west to Caldwell and on to the doomed governor's valedictory. The bed in room 19 of the Saratoga Hotel sagged under lethal paraphernalia as detonators, fuses and associated purveyors of death were scrutinized and upgraded. Powder-stained notes were later discovered in room 19 which listed the governor's habits in murderous detail. Harry was ready.

Residing at 1602 Dearborn, Frank Steunenberg, now 44, was a private citizen, perhaps the best one in town if you count honor and generosity. Bill Lesley was living at 1716 Cleveland when one evening an explosion shattered his kitchen window. The governor had walked home (which he always did) from his dinner at the Saratoga (where he always ate) just as Bill was fixing his (he never dined out). It was 1905 and just two days before New Year's when Dutch punctuality brought Frank to his front gate right on time. At 5:30 pm the governor lifted the latch which pulled the fish line which lifted the cork which dripped the acid which ignited the caps which told the dynamite what to do. For blocks around neighbors guessed at what had happened but Bill instantly knew to whom . . . and why.

The victim was blown fifty feet from the gate and his daughter Frances ran for help. Grandad was only a block away but too slow to get there first, beaten by a thinner man who got all the headlines. The governor was a burly six foot two and Grandad was even bigger. If second place goes to the ponderous at least they are strong enough to carry a dying man into his home. It was a grisly job while the mangled body, though still talking, was held together with a blanket.

Frank had never been anti-union and in fact was a member of the Printer's Union from days when he and his brother, Ancil, operated the *Caldwell News Tribune.* But the Inner Circle still kept an open file on "the monster who called in the troops in 1899."

The Orchard trial was a sensation west of the Missouri and north of the Snake, enough to bring Clarence E. Darrow from Chicago for the defense and soon make a senator of prosecutor William E. Borah. Harry escaped lynching only through the protective intervention of Ancil and the other Steunenberg brothers. By following our headlines the rest of the country recoiled to learn that Idaho and Iowa were different states but, of course, this soon passed. In many respects the Orchard trial never ended.

Sixty years later I bought a revolver that I really needed: a pearl-handled Colt Commemorative. On its six inch barrel was engraved *Idaho Centennial 1963.*

Many people find history boring but if you have trouble with dates, buy guns.

The date, 1963, may be wrong but Colt needed the business. The centennial year was also an excuse for "The Steunenberg Trial," an opera presented on the stage at the College of Idaho. No native wanted to play Orchard and they brought in somebody who needed the work.

Attendance was light because, competing across the campus was an evening of co-educational mud wrestling. The soprano sang about how Harry got religion in the pen while the tenor strained in counterpoint about the miscreant who was converted by Evaline Belle Steunenberg, the forgiving widow. Occasionally, the choir choked up and trembling cellos hinted of eternal damnation. The villain, a baritone from San Jose, sang as if he had a rope around his neck. In the last act, Harry becomes a helluva gardener, powerfully conveyed by the French horns. This seems factual enough because you can still see his roses today. It was all in English. When the curtain fell to thunderous applause (mud wrestling had ended so the crowd was larger) the assassin's religious conversion had eclipsed the memory of the fragmented victim. After two hours of operatic transfiguration, Harry ascended from opprobrium to haloed folk hero. If the diminutive serial killer hadn't been locked up for rigging that last bomb, he might be your neighbor today. We all have one of these who hides sealed boxes in the garage and tends to borrow things, like a hundred feet of wire and a few fuses. Later on these folks always get religion.

Harry Orchard died April 13, 1954, at age eighty-eight, outliving Darrow by sixteen years, Borah by fourteen—and the governor by a lifetime. In 1991, after a century of hospitality, the grand Saratoga Hotel went down in flames. Natives always thought that with all that bronze and marble there was nothing to burn. But there was.

Back in high school when only teachers owned cars, four of us would often hitchhike to Boise and spend the day staring through the burglar-proof window of Singer's Pawn Shop until we were asked to leave. In those days before marijuana, we sat on the capitol lawn and smoked sagebrush beneath the shade of a gigantic water oak, planted by President Benjamin Harrison on May 8, 1891. This tree was one year late to officially commemorate

Steunenberg home, Caldwell (Idaho Historical Society). A bomb on this gate led to a trial which brought Clarence Darrow from Chicago and made Wm. Borah a senator.

Idaho's 1890 centennial, probably because some press agent sent the president to Iowa by mistake. From this vantage point we admired Steunenberg's statue as he and the pigeons patiently guarded our capitol. We studied the fifty pound plaque at the governor's feet and checked it for typographical errors of which bronze is so unforgiving:

WHEN IN 1899 ORGANIZED LAWLESSNESS CHALLENGED THE POWER OF IDAHO, HE UPHELD THE DIGNITY OF THE STATE, ENFORCED ITS AUTHORITY AND RESTORED LAW AND ORDER WITHIN ITS BOUNDARIES FOR WHICH HE WAS

Saratoga Hotel, Caldwell (Idaho Historical Society). The commercial center of the world if you lived in Idaho. Why else would the street car stop there?

ASSASSINATED IN 1905. RUGGED IN BODY, RES-OLUTE OF MIND, MASSIVE IN THE STRENGTH OF HIS CONVICTIONS, HE WAS OF THE GRANITE HEWN IN GRATEFUL MEMORY OF HIS COURAGE AND DEVOTION TO PUBLIC DUTY. THE PEOPLE OF IDAHO HAVE ERECTED THIS MONUMENT .

The plaque was signed mcmxxvii. (Or maybe it was *sincerely*, mcmxxvii.)

The Caldwell hitch-hikers memorized those noble words and Sam marveled aloud: "Boy, I wish I could talk like that."

My granddad might have been famous too if only he had gotten to 1602 Dearborn first. Second place counts for so little. They don't even get to testify. There is no reason to mention who first reached the dying governor.

He wasn't even a relative.

Our fathers were great fishing friends but Sam and I were even closer because we were too young to argue politics. If Dad was catching more fish, Ray could end any trip by glorifying F.D.R. Once when Ray was ahead, Dad mentioned Alf Landon and the lake suddenly turned sterile.

Since Sam and I lived only a block apart, we were inclined to forget which house was whose. Of course, Sam slept in his own house, but his misplaced jacket could usually be found hanging in my closet. Once a week our mothers would swap clothing, baseball mitts, roller skates or frogs. One item was never exchanged because Sam's dog didn't like me.

We played Kick the Can at his place because that section of Dearborn was better paved, but he emulated Tarzan in my back yard since we had a taller tree. Johnny Weissmuller, the Hollywood Tarzan, could use a stunt man for dangerous scenes but Caldwell's loin-clothed hero swung high over our concrete driveway with my father's admonition: "Don't fall on my car." It was soon obvious that Sam's performance drew bigger crowds, so I volunteered for a less spectacular (some say cowardly) position with the ground crew. Part of this job was passing peanut butter sandwiches as Tarzan zoomed by overhead. Without me, Sam was nothing. The ground crew also supplied bandages to conceal lacerations and abrasions from his mother. When blood oozed through, these incriminating stains were awkwardly disguised with an Eddy's ("Builds sound bodies eight ways") bread wrapper. The real Tarzan did not always tell Jane when he fell out of a tree. Once he stayed overnight—we listened to *Jack Armstrong, The all-American Boy* and baked brownies—while waiting for facial swelling to subside. This ruse worked OK for ecchymoses but a broken wrist is a hard secret to keep indefinitely. During his three weeks in a cast, we played Kick the Can until the flying target broke the plaster. I said I was sorry.

While grounded, he passed the time watching a foul-mouthed bum re-shingle his dad's roof. This usually meant someone owed Ray money. The carpenter held a hammer in one hand and nails in his mouth while carefully guarding a pint of something in a paper sack. It was apparently something about the hammer and his left thumb that evoked a stream of profanity. The shingles were scattered but the pint was intact. Sam's mother hustled her innocent son inside, safely sequestered from sub-human swearing no Methodist should hear. Sam could play with his Lincoln Logs for an hour. It might soothe his ears. Soon after his release, my arboreal partner knocked at the door, wide-eyed and breathless: "There's a bad man on our roof. He eats nails and says God Damn." His protective mother was given to health fads which fortunately changed monthly. The family was turning yellow from carrot juice until mysteriously, the blender, jammed.

Shamelessly, she moved on to massive doses of cod liver oil which no guest escaped. I learned to swallow without protest because the reward was a Toll House cookie and hers were the finest. Fads come and go and some are actually worse than carrot juice or cod liver oil. It was just a question of time until Sam fortified our friendship by warning me to avoid his house for the next thirty days: "This month it's enemas."

GET YOUR OWN DAMNED ARK.

~ Noah

W hen the town's most venerable family donated some of their sizable estate, a golf course was born though it was a tough breech delivery requiring forceps. During the early years, there were periods of apnea when the town links was threatened by real estate developers.

The Sebrees had once owned the Saratoga Hotel which ranked with the Waldorf-Astoria, a fancy building somewhere in New York. Nobody had ever been to the Big Apple but after the locals compared hotel photographs the Little Apple won easily.

Howard Sebree operated many farms and several forests and finally bought a newspaper to explain how come he owned so much stuff. All that remained of their nineteenth century grandeur was the rambling mansion whose six crumbling chimneys glowered from behind a wrought iron fence, much of it over-wrought. Family fortunes had somehow vanished as evidenced by a vast, uneven verandah with peeling pillars which hinted at the elegance within. One entire floor was devoted to a chandeliered ballroom with an elevated bandstand where abandoned music stands suggested that some Idahoans could read music. The Italian stained glass windows had caused several BB guns to be impounded. Mine was later returned when a hapless pigeon took the rap. No white stakes were necessary along the newly graded fairway because the PGA had declared that any haunted mansion was officially out of bounds. Beweeded and dilapidated, this was the residence of the widow Sebree. It was she who once had flashed that beguiling western smile—white teeth and a tight dress worked in 1883 just as today— which may have influenced lonely easterners like Robert Strahorn who was otherwise occupied surveying the

Oregon Short line across the Snake River. She served tea and charm while her husband and Robert were joined by Col. Dewey where the plotting trio huddled in the parlor of her grand new house. After the Civil War, the enterprising Colonel had built the toll road to Silver City. He had even more money than Howard, and both would soon have a lot more. While sketching the proposed train route, they surreptitiously purchased worthless—but not for long—trackside property. Thirty miles to the east, Boise posed as the capital of the world: the Gem state's Mecca of culture, the cosmopolitan home of a museum with a gift shop, and the mother of Arrowrock Dam. Even Indians wore three piece suits, with a feather tastefully peeking from the lapel.

Boise had everything—*except a railroad.* The lucrative track advanced only as far as Nampa and ended right where the Colonel commanded—just a block away from the doorsteps of his Dewey Palace. Only the Taj Mahal was more magnificent.

One imprudent Boise businessman had foolishly crossed the Colonel with one of those sweet business deals that went sour. The culprit tried to recover with a few railroad jokes, but the Colonel never smiled. Dewey swore revenge, not only on the Boisean but his entire town.

"Weeds will obliterate your depot before you get a railroad." Other details have been lost, probably because Dewey had the perpetrator's name deleted from every textbook of Idaho history. Vengeance was swift. Strahorn's tracks stranded the capital. Boise folks with good ears might hear a distant whistle, but to see a train up close they had to come to Canyon county. The ignominy only increased. It was years before the Oregon Shortline finally arrived, and Boiseans celebrated with a pretentious display of flags, bells and whistles and the mayor would roll into town riding on the cow catcher. Gentlemen in high hats and ladies with parasols circled the dignitaries whose cummerbunds were even more colorful than the bunting of

Dewey Palace, Nampa (Idaho Historical Society) Colonel Dewey's answer to the Taj Mahal. The Oregon Shortline Railroad ended right here because the Colonel said so.

the speaker's platform. Democrats stood at the rear as Sen. Borah addressed the throng. The roar of the "Lion of Idaho" traveled down the tracks of the Union Pacific until he could be heard in Omaha. Boise's Chinatown joined the pageantry with pride, since they laid the track. While the band played Sousa, brotherhood prevailed and every Oriental from Boise to Beijing was a Republican. What could go wrong?

Nampa, home of the Taj Mahal, insisted that the cogs in the their roundhouse suddenly jammed. Since workmen could not turn the locomotive to the East, and Boise dignitaries were waiting, they thought it best to stoke up the boilers anyway and ignore the consequences. Twenty minutes later, the engine steamed into Boise BACKWARDS!

Who would not like a state where you can park anywhere?

Ignominious? Yes. Humiliating? Damn right. Unintentional? Not likely. Nothing in this world is harder to cancel than a parade. These tales are relegated to obscurity down at the Carnegie Library where, even on microfilm, Col. Dewey remains forever rich. Not so for Howard. From a rickety back porch, his destitute widow struggled to operate the Oaklawn Dairy, but business was so bad that there was no hint of life on the premises. Four of us had always wanted to see inside, and Sam assured the other three that Mrs. Sebree had died sometime during the Revolutionary War and—just to test your courage—her mansion was haunted. Since Sam was seven months older, he was already an established authority on sex, as evidence of which, he confided that the Queen of England was dismayed that common people also enjoyed bedroom pursuits. The Queen concluded: "It's much too good for them."

Any kid who knew this much about sex was probably also right about the old house being empty. Four adventurers, brave beyond belief, pried off a shutter and squeezed into Caldwell's only haunted mansion. Should they be caught, the plan was to pose as government agents sent to investigate apparitions.

The spooky room was right out of a Boris Karloff movie, and even young eyes accommodated slowly to the formidable darkness. Then suddenly beyond the cobwebs they beheld terror surpassing Karloff—a living, breathing Mrs. Sebree, seated in a faded brocade rocker, sipping unsold milk from a tarnished silver cup. Perhaps she was not a genuine ghost, but close enough to induce a prepubertal cardiac arrest.

Sam escaped first but later pretended this was only to enlarge an opening for the others. Sleep was fitful for a month and none of the intruders ever drank milk again. This traumatic experience taught valuable lessons which served me to this very day: A) Accomplices dare not reveal your cowardice without revealing their own. B) It is better to knock at the door and buy a pint of milk than be guilty of a forced entry. C) The widow Sebree was not killed in the Revolutionary War. She was captured by the British. D) Sam lied about sex.

HELP ME BE THE MAN MY DOG THINKS I AM.
~ Guide Posts

A good hymn should state its business and move on to the offertory. Hold the hymnal high. Move your lips with the choir. Maintain a contemplative forehead. When you miss a note frown at somebody . . . anybody. Beware of any theme with political overtones. One

congregation was once held captive by a possessed preacher whose sermon "He Walks With Me" became an excuse to
deify Franklin D. Roosevelt. Within an hour he had converted the Holy Trinity into a quartet.

We borrow other people's music from European clas-
sics to Negro spirituals but the hierarchy decided that
black songs lacked dignity. No longer can we escape harmonic boredom with the spontaneous majesty of "Swing
Low Sweet Chariot" as it soars anonymously, simply,
unforgettably. But if "Swing Low" is segregated there is a
symphonic poem from Finland that isn't. Jan Sibeleus
wrote it and no words can ruin it. "Finlandia" can bring
out the Finn in a Comanche. Sometimes in Helsinki it
sounds like a lachrymose lament but living near Russia
could account for this. When words and music are inspired
a century apart on different continents there is bound to
be a certain imbalance. No ecclesiastical tampering could
dim the glory of Sibeleus. On the other hand, Dvorak suffered quite a bit. Beethoven and Brahms did good work
but should have added their own lyrics to avoid predictable plagiarism. Eventually some unimaginative
zealot will be driven to add his own tepid words. This
should be a capital offense. Even God would not commute
the sentence.

Latter day lyricists had to hyphenate syllables which
were then shoehorned until the clefs squealed. Note values were stretched, bent or ignored in a frenetic attempt
to come out even. Will called these the Catch-Up Hymns
and they could not be better named.

He could not read music but he did not hesitate to
advise his son who was similarly ignorant. Despite all
those lines, circles and dots there are just four parts. The
tenor sings up here near the top and usually gets more
notes than the rest of us. Never stand too close to tenors.
Most of them are not worth knowing and will try to lead
you off key. However, a prudent doctor should be cordial to

these people who tend to strain on high notes and many develop hernias.

"Next is the lead, the part you already knew before they began singing. Temperamental sopranos guard these notes jealously. If you intrude in their domain they glare, cinch up their choir robes and pretend to be angels, though most angels don't talk like that. Everyone wants to be a bass because it's so manly. The bass rumbles down here so he can ignore all those higher horizontal lines where the girls belong. Some careless composers may slip a bass note above middle C but I frankly doubt it. Anyway some tenor can handle it while he's resting. The bass gets three, maybe four notes and if he misses one nobody cares as long as it's low. Good ones can make windows tremble and a bona fide *basso profundo* can fracture stained glass." Only one part remained: "The baritone takes what's left over."

Civilized folks make music harder than it needs to be. On distant islands, pagans wearing grass ensembles stomp bare feet to the beat of a bleached human femur against a coconut. Their incomprehensible chants intrigued Will until one weekend when there was snow on the golf course he decided to translate their entire language. Without conjugating a bunch of South Sea verbs, it was his conclusion that sacrificing a virgin to a volcano was a Hollywood fabrication, and while this may be a big break for a teenage starlet it was a needless waste of a perfectly good virgin. Caucasians have never comprehended Polynesian culture whose history is largely verbal.

What little they do write is with a stick in the sand so Will had to work fast: "The original ritual does not mention virginity. Only that this was her first *volcano*."

If there was anything worth seeing in the outside world, Idaho kids were too isolated to care much about it. They already had all the excitement they could handle. During roping and branding, local ranchers humored town kids by pretending they needed extra hands. A harmless old horse was provided, they ate with real cowboys and earned a silver dollar just to show up. Training began by watching a Gene Autry movie after which they were herded to Memorial Park and competed by roping statues: Grover Cleveland 10 points, Teddy Roosevelt 20 points. Senator Borah was worth 100 since this was Idaho. One mother smeared Unguentine to a rope burn after Sam's lasso snagged Teddy's wrist which left a bronze hand trying frantically to beckon from the grass. Worse yet the score counted. I could never beat Sam. The foreman didn't pay by the cow and deducted a dime for roping the front legs of your own horse. Sam and his surly mount barely spoke anyway and by now he was so attached to the calves that his branding was limited to fence posts. There were enormous cattle drives in Jordan Valley which were hard to miss since they ran right through the town. Hooved hordes roamed for a hundred miles to the south and enveloped northern Nevada in choking dust where a bandana over the face was more than a fashion statement.

They never made a movie here because Hollywood was afraid of that many cows. Cattle have been romanticized because branding and castration are such macho things. A less publicized aspect of western Americana was the Turkey Round Up. Around Emmett, feathered droves covered the low hills leading to Squaw Butte where they roamed like sheep and were even guarded by—get this— turkey dogs. These were actually sheep dogs who never made the big time. A litter of fifteen pups was worth about a dollar. After years of random in-breeding they are often mistaken for coyotes. Though usually maligned, turkeys could survive on grasshoppers and achieved their avian

apogee during the Depression when these birds and bootleg booze were the only cash crops. With a roasted drum-
stick and a shot of moonshine the Depression could be
downright euphoric. The turkey's first natural enemy was
Thanksgiving but almost anything could kill them.
Fledglings succumbed even to magpies. They even overdid
sociability and would crowd together until they smoth-
ered. Homicide and suicide were about 50:50. Heaven
itself conspired to wipe them out. Their necks were never
designed for looking up and when hail dropped so did they.
If water dishes were not shallow they would drown.

Stewart Cruickshank, an Emmett turkey veteran,
became a reluctant authority on mortality and confided:
They died just to be dyin." If turkeys encountered a
snake—never hard to do—they would form a feathery circle, not to make trouble but just marvel at the wonder of
it all. The birds would stare until dark when the snake
finally turned in. They achieved bizarre dignity on Turkey
Day when the town band had to march gingerly as they
straddled the interurban tracks up Cleveland Boulevard.
Right behind, came the city council leading turkeys on a
leash. Embarrassment was rampant. The mayor—he wore
a dashing feather suit—pushed a perambulator with a big
Tom in a derby and a heavily sedated hen in a bonnet. The
Turkey Day Parade glorified birds but degraded humans.
Kids watched from the curb where they all vowed never to
go into politics.

Hitchhiking was high art back when the thirty mile
trip to Boise came in ten mile segments and
entailed several transfers. To evoke sympathy and
guarantee a ride, the most pathetic kid walked ahead. I
hated this part. License plates for Idaho's forty-four coun-

ties are identified by a unique alpha-numeric system, understood only by third generation natives, and occasional Californians who instinctively appreciate the occult. Those plates beginning with 2-C proudly proclaim Canyon County. (1-C means Camas and 3-C signifies Caribou, if that helps you any.) It was important for these hitchhikers to avoid 2-C plates followed by numbers higher than 10,000 because this meant NAMPA. The Nampa Bulldogs had just crushed the Caldwell Cougars in football, basketball, and track so, with adolescent discrimination, we screened the plates to avoid any driver whose Bulldog conversation was predictable. We never rode with the enemy.

It never occurred to us that by waiting for a winning year we could walk forever. On today's Interstate, Boise is only a forty minute trip and the main diversion is watching the wrecker haul away vestiges of some collision which you escaped by only seconds. Some accidents are uniquely western, like a steer through the radiator, but most are mundane stuff that you can see in New Jersey.

Boiseans have always been inclined to brag, but once upon a time it was indeed forgivable when a unique monument to the modern culinary age opened in 1932. With the dollar saved by hitch-hiking, we could dine like royalty at the Mechanafe, a food palace which emphasized volume, speed and machinery, the embodiment of every kid's dream. You did not have to be high school graduates, which we would not be for another year, to marvel at the wonder of it all. Not everybody in Caldwell had seen it. This landmark was touted as "100% waiterless" and bore a superficial and misleading resemblance to Horn and Hardart's cafe which New Yorkers called the Auto-Mat.

Years later, and against my will, I found myself in New York where I verified the existence of the Statue of Liberty which looked a lot like its picture. The Empire State Building was around somewhere, but I was there to find Governor's Island where they let the lucky ones out of the army. Next on my list was the Auto-Mat which was no more than overpriced sandwiches hiding behind a smeared glass door. I tried one which had every reason to hide and remembered those halcyon days when we gorged at our beloved Mechanafe:

"It's electrical. It's fascinating. It's sanitary." Our clean shirts proved we were out of town as we lined up on a long counter facing two elaborate conveyors going in opposite directions. The top belt brought your waiterless order while the bottom carried the dishes back to the kitchen which probably was not entirely electrical, fascinating and sanitary but who cared? There were dozens of uneaten rolls on the out-bound plates and after you wiped off the gravy these kept you going until your hamburger traveled by. Every hobo along the Boise River had already discovered this, and many of those dishes fairly glistened before they made it down to the sink.

One day after the war this one-of-a-kind cafe closed its doors forever, and Eighth Street would never be the same. Who caused this lamentable loss? Riparian vagrants or kids like us? During the Great Shame of 1938 we avoided Nampa by hiking the long route through Middleton, a town whose minuscule enrollment allowed them to field only a six-man football squad. This was five more than their track team, one farm boy who, without warning, swept past Caldwell in the 100 yard dash. Now we were ridiculed in two towns. A hitchhiker cannot avoid both Middleton and Nampa without detouring through Montana.

CHAPTER SIX

Idaho is well diversified with silver mines up north, green farms down south and timber in the middle. Because of such bounty, folks in the Gem State probably suffered less than others during the Great Depression. California staggered under the assault of the destitute dust bowl but very few found their way to Idaho. They didn't know where it was. Most of us saw our first bread line, not on local streets, but on a movie screen right after the rooster crowed for the Pathe Movie-Tone News. As if this were not enough misery, the Huree Theater in the 1930s invariably featured F.D.R. with that jutting presidential jaw holding his theatrical cigarette holder. Good fathers taught their sons to look away, often rendering them immune to the Roosevelt charisma. Those attending the Saturday matinee agreed that Buck Rogers would make a better president anyway with Flash Gordon as his secretary of state.

Apparently the Depression had spread even to Europe because the news reels also disclosed the pathetic state of French bicycles whose Tour de France racing tyres resembled a loop of atrophic garden hose or a dead snake. Those poor devils had to ride standing up to avoid that narrow seat which made them pump all the harder by threatening castration. This contraption was further compounded by complex gears, twisted cables and other unreliable Gaulic gadgets including—of all things—*front wheel brakes*. Soup kitchens and bread lines were bad enough, but the French

155

seemed to be really suffering. We left the movie, squinted gratefully in the sunlight, and returned to our bikes which were always left unlocked like everything else in town. We embraced the wheels and vowed to ride on the rims rather than forsake balloon tires.

The gearless American Schwinn worked fine with two pedals, one chain and a New Departure brake on the rear axle. When the back wheel stopped so did the whole bike. The French still don't know about this. The stylish veloci-pede of Canyon County trend-setters was tastefully cus-tomized with an enormous saddle seat, steerhorn handle-bars (double-chromed) with red (never black) rubber grips from which dangled outlandish two-foot streamers. At paper route speeds they often entangled the chain which could stop the bike before you planned. Knee lacerations were a small price to pay for class, but chain grease on the streamer was bad for business and implied that your cus-tomers had a careless paper boy.

One fad without lasting merit crept in from Middleton and soon swept the valley: the clatter card. This device was anchored to a fender strut with a clothes pin so that the card roared realistically against the spokes. The clat-ter simulated a motor, so exhilarating to kids, so annoying to adults, hence a double joy. Any stiff material would do but something from a poker deck was acoustically superi-or and distinctly more durable. As luck would have it, my father played poker. I selected the Queen of Hearts from what looked like an old discarded deck. Dad would never miss it, or so I thought. Next Friday, Will's Republican cronies huddled around the kitchen table, each with a green visor and a stack of dimes. (A few years later when dimes were stamped with Roosevelt's profile they aban-doned the game completely.) After dealing the first hand my perfidy was discovered and I was called to the table. But not to play. Buying a new deck put quite a dent in my allowance. I got to keep the old cards, enough to supply the entire neighborhood but I didn't have fifty-one friends. My luck requisitioning clothes pins wasn't much better. Mother's fresh laundry—neighbors always said hers was the whitest—fell in the dirt. The shirts belonged to the same man who only last Friday had bet on a Queen high flush . . . and LOST. A boy's outlook grows dim when he can't appeal to either parent. Was it all worth it just to hear the pseudo-motorization of the chattering Queen of Hearts? There was a downside, for the clatter was only an illusion, but the dogs were real. On my first paper delivery, I was chased by a solitary cur who made off with a chunk of Levis torn from where most people sit. As word got around an entire pack howled in pursuit and, since my pants were already shredded, they decided instead to chew up *The Idaho Daily Statesman*. With a superhuman effort, I salvaged the sports section for one of my best customers. There is a lot of heroism in the paper business. Things got worse in the spring when the pack mustered several new litters which passed from cute to ugly in record time. Here's an idea: Why not use the clatter card for puttering around and remove it during the paper route? Never crossed my mind. Eventually the Queen of Clatter de-chromed a two and a half inch section of the spokes but, fortunately, this defect covered nicely with rust.

This idiotic vogue was superseded by the glorious diagonal handlebar braces. These stylish struts, more costly than a dozen poker decks, extended from the red hand grips (never black) down to the nut holding the front axle thus providing outlandish support to handlebars that never required any in the first place. At this unfortunate convergence, various other structures competed for space: fender struts, reflectors, and a basket heavy laden with the *Caldwell News Tribune* (*The Idaho Daily Statesman* had fired me). This combination of relentless torque conspired to eventually strip the threads until the wheel fell off. In 1938 these chrome rods came in a variety of diameters which were tailored to express a man's individualism as well as school loyalty. Highly polished but understated three-eighths inch struts set Caldwell apart from the ostentatious quarter-inch size which identified Parma . . . and certainly Nampa, that tasteless Half-Inch Crowd.

W hy, you may ask, would some kid pump his Schwinn through crushed gravel past haunted houses and wild animals? Because just beyond the sod house a drain ditch curved to the right and ended abruptly at my grandparents' house. Its rooms were a curious series of lean-tos and featured the original sunken living room which later became so fashionable and presumably intentional.

In the kitchen, also sunken, Grandma Mary introduced me to culinary delights which magically materialized from imported Nebraska recipes which she hid in the barn because Europe's greatest chefs had tried to steal them. She conducted a kitchen symphony with melodious pans, the rumbling bass of a wood fire and the harmonious chant of a cast iron kettle, all directed by a magic baton which resembled a spatula. When the Sisters of the Grange pestered her for trade secrets she may have omitted a few key ingredients. After all, when Rembrandt painted he never wrote things down either. Her gooseberry pie (one cup of sugar per berry) won a blue ribbon at the Idaho State Fair, where trophies eluded Grandad Bill who took his best hog the same year but it died in the holding pen. He brought it home still warm, and Mary awarded him a *Superior Sausage Award.*

But I wasn't at the farm just to eat. I had important work to do which no one else could handle, grubbing out a gigantic gooseberry bush which was larger than a national forest and sustained a complete eco-system with at least two endangered species, three counting me. Despite hoe, shovel, and machete its relentless growth outpaced all attempts at extermination which, in fact, amounted to cultivation. In the leafy darkness one could still make out the frightening forms of garden spiders, yellow and black and about a pound a piece, but these only prompted Grandma's lecture about their usefulness. In the evening I could expect the same fiction about bats. We were too far inland to discuss sharks and too far north for Gila monsters. But it was not spiders, nor cobras—yes, there were cobras in there—but the skin-shredding gooseberry branches that drew just enough blood for a little sympathy and an honorable escape. Now I could help Grandad who was extremely busy sharpening my grubbing tools. Near the chicken coop was his grindstone where for hours he straddled a green seat, factory-contoured in Davenport, Iowa, for a rump smaller than his but undeniable proof that once upon a time he had owned a John Deere tractor. He was perpetually honing mowing machine blades or Mary's kitchen knives but only the latter saw much action. Grinding was slow but very important. Slow because the broken wheel struggled on a bent axle. Important because he said so. He studiously scrutinized rusty blades and, with a professional demeanor, he thumbed them for sharpness or, most likely, dullness. He then returned to the wheel which, stone deaf to the message from the pedals, finally rotated with granite reluctance. Grandad never gave up. This was all he did.

Just a toss away rose a mountain of tobacco tins, mostly Prince Albert and Velvet but several collectibles from Scotland, a gift from some cousin with enough money to get out of Nebraska—and who wouldn't? Each tin held only an ounce and a half which was gone by noon. Through budgetary constraints and unique logic, he bought by the ounce but smoked by the pound. He did save money by making his own corn cob pipes and was shocked to learn that Gen. Douglas Mac Arthur paid good money for his. Surrounded by singed chicken feathers, manure, and pipe smoke, Grandad was easy to find. From this inexhaustible supply of tobacco cans, my father borrowed some for fishing. They fit snugly in a shirt pocket and even the most determined grasshopper never escaped. You could pay more but you couldn't do better.

These cans and a few gooseberries proved to be the chief products of the farm. God put this interesting old man right here solely for his grandson's enjoyment. One Thanksgiving the candles caught his beard on fire and I was probably wrong to applaud. Momentarily incapacitated, Bill deferred the blessing to Mary who also asked God to heal his swollen eyelids. (And he did get better.) Next week, I pedaled out with Sam who liked to play Tarzan in the big maple tree. And Sam had never seen a sunken living room.

Every one in grade school had heard about the flaming beard and we hoped for an encore. He rarely denied his grandson any favor but the man who owned the beard was no fool: "You can't always count on a controlled burn." We concealed our disappointment by collecting tobacco cans and eating gooseberries, once we found the sugar. It was years before I realized that Bill was a dreadful farmer but by then no one cared because he had been such a great Grandad. He had been much too busy grinding and smoking to mention the day he dashed to the side of an assassinated governor twenty years before I was born. Was he modest or just forgetful?

Questions were always welcome but his answers were invariably obscure barnyard metaphors. His jealous mules thought he was talking to them and nuzzled up to intrude on the conversation. I learned to resent them, and they knew it.

Irrigation in Idaho was like tampering with God's plan. After generations of dry farming in Nebraska, where the water came straight from heaven, the transition was more than Grandad could handle. He was always one gopher behind in maintaining his ditches and when a major rupture flooded his neighbor, Grandad was busy elsewhere, sharpening his shovel.

One dry year, the entire Grange over-implored the Deity until a deluge flooded the Snake River. This was despite Bill's admonition: "Don't all pray at once." Plowing was slow because of lengthy conversations with his pampered white mules, and when they looked tired, all plowing stopped. In an attempt to modernize the farm, my father provided a tractor from which Bill siphoned all the gas to kill weeds. Pheasants migrated from South Dakota just to hide in high weeds and dine on low corn. They were on their last kernel before Bill remembered the crop was even out there. Most harvests were disappointing because he often forgot to plant.

While transforming bounty to famine he resisted advice from successful neighbors, but in 1934 all I could see was a wonderful old man who seemed to enjoy the company of a little kid.

Every farmer was a presumed mechanic, capable of servicing his own equipment. With more pride than ability, he serviced his tractor unto extinction, salvaging only that green seat, and this only because it had no moving parts. With a few twists of baling wire this was crudely attached to the grinding wheel as a tribute to his ingenuity and a memorial to John Deere. It is possible to become a surgeon and never understand a car engine—or even how to lift the hood.

Most of my knack for mechanics I learned from my Grandad.

Trees evoke poetry because they live longer than most people and are generally more reliable. Longfellow glorified a chestnut to save the village blacksmith from oblivion. An oak on the letterhead makes banks seem more trustworthy.

Conversely, that fig leaf in the Garden of Eden achieved dubious status, since in the long run, covering Eve didn't help much. Similarly, just because a walnut gavel calls Congress to order, it's not fair to blame the entire tree. During the Crusades, the Gisor Elm shaded Christian knights where kings, at least those who could write, signed treaties and paid ransom for a kidnapped princess if she was cute enough. Eventually, this historic tree was hacked down by disgruntled French when some battle with England went sour.

Rivaling the Gisor were the grand elms which lined Dearborn Street in my home town. I thought they were unique but later learned that almost every road in Idaho was similarly adorned with discounted elms supplied by the benevolent County Agricultural Agent who also sold weeds.

For a kid on a bike these trees whizzed by because Dearborn was almost paved. Then after a jolting shortcut through the barren College of Idaho campus, the route turned south on Indiana Ave. The depth of the dust helped differentiate avenues from streets. Caldwell's row of elms ended where isolated farms of decreasing prosperity were separated by trees that were less decorative and more functional, usually Lombardi windbreaks and locust groves which were later harvested for fence posts of which none were more durable. In time, Dutch Elm disease devastated Caldwell, but on the outlying farms poplar, locust, and willow proved immune to any blight, a toughness shared by the homesteaders who planted them. One fine spruce declared that this proud farmer had once left his crops long enough to travel north, perhaps as far as

Cascade, to introduce evergreens to the world of sagebrush.

After the seedling was transplanted, a farm wife (who probably had absolutely nothing else to do) took charge of watering and the nearby bucket proved she took her job seriously. Eventually the spruce towered over the house and its roots enveloped the staves of an abandoned bucket in an embrace of perpetual thanks.

Very few along this five mile stretch were native Idahoans. Even Grandad Bill's white mules were born in Nebraska where stubbornness was equated with aristocracy. Every ranch revealed its own nostalgia; a fancy picket fence or a uniquely louvered hen house, anything to remind them of home so there were no castles. It was a curious mix: a Kansas fence around a Missouri garden tended by a farm wife in an Iowa bonnet. They could easily pass for Amish except these women swore more. While the bulk of the exodus came from the Midwest, one exception was a homesick Pennsylvanian who replicated an oaken barn reminiscent of his Brandywine valley. The cupola alone was bigger than most stables and the weather vane weighed twenty pounds. Deserving of his Clydesdales, he designed a special tandem wagon to haul massive ponderosa from Idaho City which he squared and smoothed with an archaic adze. Soon the gambrel roof was supported by meticulously fitted timbers and secured by hand-hewn dowels. There were no visible nails. It was a Herculean task, but he had plenty of help from curious neighbors who had never before seen a real carpenter or a gambrel roof, or for that matter, any roof that didn't leak. Tapping the last dowel, he thanked his neighbors who finally got the idea only when a recognizable verb emerged at the end of the sentence. The magnificent barn was not complete until he painted a mural of a Swiss brown cow surrounded by alpine flowers. In authentic Pennsylvania Dutch, he transformed his special spot to be shared by the world. Idahoans who would never venture farther east than Wyoming, now could travel the road from Lancaster to Gettysburg.

This devout Lutheran hesitated to milk his cows because it was such a personal thing. Livestock in that barn lived better than their owner. Master German cabinet makers do not allow splinters even in a cattle stall. On our first encounter, the German rushed out to unwrap a bike chain from my ankle. A pathetic limp earned an invitation to his kitchen and an appointment to tour his barn.

During a provincial childhood I had never heard any kind of foreign accent but after generous servings of bratwurst, the farmer's English seemed to improve.

Next to the plate heaped with cheese was a Dutch Bible about the size of a footlocker and when this food was blessed, by God, it stayed blessed. This stalwart gentleman personified Old World hospitality and introduced the guest to whole hog sausage, a delicacy denied the American-born unless one is on good terms with an *essenmeister* who owns a whole hog. After several servings of *liebkuchen* and *liederkranz*, I confessed that I had exaggerated the pain in my ankle. The host responded with more food which always cured lying back in the old country. Several years later, I needed recommendations for medical school. The grades were up to the applicant but character references could be tough. Then I remembered the old Dutchman who had enough character for both of us. Since he could not write in English he insisted on telephoning Portland. He drove his tractor to a pay phone where my character was never mentioned as he visited, dime after dime, with the Dean of Admission as they exchanged recipes for whole hog sausage.

The Dutch barn with its unforgettable mural was my favorite and the first to burn down. When the ashes cooled, I collected a bucket of hand forged nails but never knew what to do with the brass weathervane. After such a grievous loss even weather wasn't what it used to be. The barn was survived by another memorable but less combustible structure. Tucked between sunflowers and sagebrush, one farm displayed a midwest anachronism: a sod hut dutifully duplicated in memory of the plains states.

I would always remember that special spring when wildflowers sprouted profusely from its dirt roof, nostalgic blossoms from seeds carried two thousand miles and lovingly protected in the apron of a homesick Midwest housewife. Only an apron can do this.

THERE'S SOMETHING ABOUT RADIO
THEY'RE NOT TELLING US.
                              ~ Robert Benchley

A cursory glance of Mary's kitchen sadly revealed the absence of running water and electricity which evoked unsolicited pity from city folks. Mary saw this only as a blessing. Pipes can freeze and she never feared electrocution. The well was nearby and its therapeutic waters were not dissipated by coursing through those lead pipes later so decried by band wagon environmentalists. Here dwelt the perpetual hostess. I wrongly assumed that family cooking should be limited to blood relatives but hers included my entire grade school class, many of whom preferred to drop in when I wasn't there. She fed ravenous threshers by the score and on light days she collared strangers who had only stopped to admire the old sod house just down the road. The table was always set because the whole world looked hungry.

The parting of the Red Sea is a spectacular story but the gustatory miracles are more personal. Leading this category would be Christ's blessing of five barley loaves and two small fishes to feed the multitude on the shores of Galilee. This involved the most people and was better publicized but Mary came in a close second. Surely it was not a wood stove fuming on an uneven floor. It had to be the *magic Houdini table* . . . the only one in Idaho.

After releasing secret levers, two hungry recruits tugged at each end until the massive center pedestal widened triumphantly. Finally, twenty pound leaves were dropped into the chasm to augment the area but, alas, eager to flatten the unwary finger.

The table kept score with bloody thumbprints, and thus began the concept of recording casualties. Our air force picked up on this idea when, for every enemy zero shot down, American Mustangs painted a rising sun on the fuselage. The sturdy infrastructure was requisite to support the weight of the impending banquet and when heavy elbows flanked every plate, the added strain could be enormous. The oak surface was badly pocked by forks which had missed their mark but every blemish was covered with a magnificent table cloth from Mary's mother. Once, far away—and in a far grander home —this gracious linen and lace had spread hospitably across the longest table in Nebraska and yea, even unto Iowa.

This Sunday, the Houdini table stood as an oaken witness to an afternoon of unrepentant gluttony: fried chicken, double fried fritters and pies usually served whole; verily, a cornucopia of coronary cloggers. In silent salivation, we waited as Grandad slowly took his chair at the head of the table where he surveyed the bounteous spread and invariably proclaimed:

"This meal looks Larrupin' Good" . . . a judgment so predictable that all lips synched in grateful silence. Grandma had done her job and this was his. He wasted valuable gorging time but we knew the prayer would be short. The patriarch ceremoniously tied his stained canvas bib which was adjusted to catch what his beard might miss. He blessed the food and none deserved it more. The countdown had begun.

Too much chicken isn't good for you, so platters of beef and pork were stacked on a table that still refused to sag. Variety was important but grease was king. As if ashamed, vegetables hid beneath the gravy with a viscosity of S.A.E. 60. Whenever it was too thick to flow, Grandma thinned it with a cup of cream. Many of her finest creations are regrettably extinct, but plastic replicas may be seen in the Great Lipid Hall at the Smithsonian which commemorates America's capitulation to the calorie.

Here is recalled her whole hog sausage which in real life had to be eaten fast before your arteries snapped shut.

The wizard could simultaneously monitor the table in front and the stove behind and still wipe my mouth which was often. (Remember, I was just a kid.) Food levitated from all directions until a dozen platters materialized. One hand passed mashed potatoes while another stacked corn on the cob neater than logs at a Boise Cascade mill. Her third hand—quite bizarre when I think about it years later—caressed a cauldron of soup behind her back, nudged a drum stick or fearlessly plunged a fork into an angry kettle from which, like an Indian fishing Shoshone Falls, she always came up with something. Cook and stove observed a secret alliance and without a glance at the belching Monarch she would baptize a fritter and casually toss some wood dangerously deep into the heart of the flame. At such a sight we sucked in our collective breath. Grandma then acknowledged our inspiratory approbation by holding high a triumphant arm that once again had escaped incineration.

Through years of culinary legerdemain she never sustained a blister as she stirred, as she spooned, as she stoked. Important! She never handled black coal during meals. This was bad etiquette.

Harry Houdini, the table's namesake, was a famous escape artist who in 1926 captivated the nation with his most death-defying stunt. He was chained and handcuffed inside a weighted trunk which was heaved (by friends, I suppose) into the frigid Detroit river.

Harry wasn't worried. Mary was his backup.

LET THERE BE LIGHT WAS THE LORD'S IDEA; IT TOOK EDISON TO ADD A SWITCH.

Rural electrification almost forgot Grandad's farm. While progressive neighbors along Karcher Road strung wires to propitiate the kilowatt, one stubborn old man still poured kerosene and trimmed wicks, waiting for the fad to pass. Bill had too many lanterns to throw away. By 1932 the proliferation of power poles marched across his property right up to the drafty walls where, barricaded in his kitchen, he held the 20th century at bay. In his own private corner a cluster of lanterns flickered and smoked to bestow a luminous yellow glow to his magnificent Morris chair; a three hundred pound expanse of walnut and tufted horsehide. Regal as a Romanoff throne, personal as a Kennedy rocker, not even the madam's bed at the Mustang ranch could equal its seductive embrace. By merely dropping a heavy knobbed bar—especially heavy when you're only ten—into different slots, its variable positions bestowed sinful comfort. William Morris (1834-1896) invented lots of swell Victorian things but surely he built this enormous chair with my Grandad in mind. I sat in it twice, once with permission, and settled in to marvel at Bill's stereopticon, the embryonic pioneer of 3-D photography. Four by six cards with separate images for each eye, were dropped into the slot and the world was yours: castles on the Rhine, the Isle of Capri, or the wonders of Egypt viewed safely from America without the risk of diarrhea. To bring strained eyes back on track I thumbed through the illustrated Edgar Rice Burroughs with that cryptic "Me Tarzan, You Jane" dialogue which was tailored to my age. Most of Bill's library featured more pictures than print, whereas his wife had gone to school longer—actually twice as long—and appreciated varied authors including some with funny French names. Puberty was closing in and the titles alone suggested that this language had a lot to offer a curious kid.

Mary always read standing up so she could do three things at once. At dawn she raced the light and invariably won. At top speed this lady could correct mistakes before they even happened. On the open back porch, she cranked a stubborn De Laval cream separator into submission though it was hard to keep it level on a floor that wasn't. It got cool out there when the snow drifted in, but then she suggested other chores for her grandson, such as tending the stove in the kitchen where it just happened to be warm. Her quick hand could intercept an egg before it hit the straw. On the blackest of nights, Mary would strike off for the barn without a lantern, gallop back with an apron-full of unbroken eggs and kill a weasel on the way. Her practiced eye surveyed the hen house and low producers were admonished only once. Once was enough, because even the dumbest fowl knew how Bill loved fried chicken. Today's gracious egg-gatherer (bonnet, apron, that sort of thing) might be tomorrow's executioner. Mary didn't fool around. Catching a chicken demands lightning reflexes and learning to think like a chicken.

A recent study by the U.S. Dept., of Agriculture has established the odds at 3 to 1 in favor of the hen, depending on the enclosure and speed of the pursuer. In this particular barnyard most gaps in the fence were larger than the chicken, analogous to a bullfight where the arena is vaguely confined to downtown Madrid. Complacent white leghorns clucked derisively at Mary's woeful weapon, formerly an axe. Its pathetic state was typical of all equipment on this farm, a few twists of rusted wire straining to secure the head to a shattered handle whose ash splinters were more dangerous than the business end. Gripping the ex-axe in her right hand, she needed only her left to snare the quarry's neck.

Mary never swung twice. Maybe not even once, since it was a common belief that under her transfixing glare some victims died of fright. Most headless chickens run about aimlessly, whereas Mary's flopped obligingly toward the kitchen as if nothing worse could happen. Awaiting the bird (except for the head) was a cast iron skillet sputtering bacon grease over an archaic Monarch wood range. Its electrical counterpart had once been seriously considered until an over-eager salesman belittled wood in order to extol a 220 volt stove. Terms like volts, amps and watts were mysterious enough but 220 of anything was not in Grandma's budget.

For several years she and her wood stove continued to live in the Snake River Valley which, forsaking reality for image, was later renamed Treasure Valley, though this country always had more snakes than treasure. With this felicitous proximity, there were many memorable meals in Mary's kitchen, and since she was my personal Grandmother, I got to eat there too. In a few years the government insisted that I compare her food with that of an army mess hall where every recruit seemed to remember a grandmother just like mine.

WHO ELSE COULD WEAR A HAT LIKE THIS
AND GET AWAY WITH IT?
                              ~ Abraham Lincoln

Mary's father had been a Union doctor in the Civil war. Major David King became my favorite ancestor as I paraded around the barnyard with a hero's sword. It glittered victoriously through many charges beyond the hen house and across the stubble field. One October, while slashing across corn stalks, the blade seemed unusually dull.

With such a blunt weapon I might even lose the next skirmish so naturally I took it to Grandad's grinding wheel where—and just in time—the warrior was intercepted by Mary who patiently explained that this was not a fighting saber but purely ceremonial. Which is why ceremonies are so dull. A smarter kid would have figured this out from all that ornate engraving. Her father had worn it once in a parade but waged most of the war with a scalpel, or more often a saw. One unlikely medical tool was the shovel he shared with the burial squad. When the chaplain was busy elsewhere—and why wouldn't he be?—Dr. King offered grave-side prayers which were all the harder when he knew full well that the mound covered amputated arms and legs.

Mary's only other souvenir was a Confederate leather pouch given the doctor by an Alabama soldier when this Northern surgeon saved a Southern leg. I carried the pouch through many imaginary battle including my longest day when I stormed the heights of Vicksburg. Single-handed I took the city but also managed to lose Mary's irreplaceable souvenir. My grief was so genuine that Grandma baked some sugar cookies. This saccharine solace was the ultimate sign of forgiveness.

After dark I borrowed her kerosene lantern—I was always borrowing something—to resume what would be a futile search but became entangled in barbed wire which could happen to anybody. Somehow I wound up on the wrong side of the fence and dropped the lantern. At least that's where the fire started. Volunteers finally put it out and that was the night I got to meet all the neighbors. Around midnight, I staggered though Mary's door without pouch, lantern or shoes. Grandma baked another dozen cookies, this time with raisins.

Dr. King's other daughter, Martha, remained in Nebraska. Every girl in those days was named either Martha or Mary, prosaic perhaps but better than Moonbeam or Cher. On my tenth birthday Martha sent a letter instead of a present. After sulking for a week about no gift I finally realized from the unsteady hand that I would not hear from Mary's sister again. I can share her letter with you now because I still have it.

She described the Depression in the Midwest, further worsened by a drought and after a page or so she began remembering her father: ". . . a good doctor who drove a good team . . . loved to hunt and brought home many wild turkeys and prairie chickens . . . I have a sample ballot of when he was running on the same ticket with Abraham Lincoln . . . my sister has his sword and a confederate bullet pouch . . . for poor patients he canceled their bill and often bought them groceries . . . one of his lodges erected a monument to him and held a touching ceremony on the occasion of the unveiling . . . ." How fortunate that Martha, rather than Mary, kept that ballot which surely would have been inside the C.S.A. pouch the day I lost it.

Stonewall Jackson once led a famous raid to capture a shipment of chloroform for the South, and I could picture my great grandfather guarding the Federal train. Most Northerners recognized Jackson since his picture had been in all the papers:

"General Jackson, you can't have it."

Once Stonewall got a glimpse of Dr. King's saber he wheeled his cavalry and rode away empty handed, but without profanity, for Jackson was a Presbyterian. I don't know what they teach today, but we had to prepare a term paper on the Civil War. The entire class felt that mine deserved an A, but I got a D for lying.

Another D awaited when I envisioned my ancestor at Chancellorsville where exploding shells started a forest fire which encircled hundreds of wounded. My own imagination magnified Major King's participation. The great doctor ministered to Union and Confederates alike (Mary's actual recollection) and saved every one (my version). Placing my great-grandfather central to every battle was simply adolescent exaggeration, but eventually all my schoolmates would grow up to see other wars where no hyperbole was necessary.

Just holding an ancestor's sword evoked fabrications of the Civil War and were at least as accurate as professorial convolutions of history where the South wins the war. Deep in the Nebraska heartland there is a memorial to Major David King which honors a Civil war veteran, but Mary's son-in-law could think of another reason. Will knew plenty about the doctor business since that's what he did:

"David King's monument was all the more imposing because half the town owed him money." I inherited the Major's sword and later gave it to my son who has always taken better care of heirlooms than his father ever did.

To this day it has never been sharpened.

North of the sod house one surviving waterwheel struggled against the current of the Methodist Ditch, named by the congregation which dug it.

The same God who provided the water in the first place must have tossed in a few extra shovels because Baptists and Presbyterians also had their own ditch. Many canals and significant laterals were named this way until they ran out of churches. Trouble began when one deacon decided to christen a conduit after his daughter whose name turned out to be the same as the preacher's mistress only with different spelling. Jean vs. Jeanne was enough for a splinter group to organize a new church. This entire mess could have been avoided if they had only waited a few years when they could name a church after Lana, Hedy, or Bambi. One was called the Government Ditch because it was so crooked.

Had there been a Mormon Ditch, this water would surely flow faster than anywhere else—and even uphill if the bishop so commanded.

Many years later when I pedaled by, it was as if the old water-wheel could not stop turning. Leaking wooden lifters no longer carried anything to anywhere but spilled just enough to create a roadside oasis. Just like a witching wand, some mysterious force pulled the handlebars toward the cool grass and my bike refused to move beyond the shade.

Another mile, and just proximal to Grandad's farm, was a haunted Victorian mansion, three stories precariously stacked with sagging shutters, garish gables and more broken stained glass than a cathedral with an unpaid mortgage. A few scalloped shingles still pretended to be a roof but most were scattered over the brown yard where invading briars hoped to conceal the shame. Here was a monument to a long departed prosperity, built with wealth brought from Missouri to be dissipated in the sagebrush after land promoters promised unlimited Boise River water. To beat the greedy crowd the Missourians arrived prematurely, even before Arrowrock Dam became a reality.

Within the decaying mansion dwelt the standard ghost and I often glimpsed the ethereal face of a shrouded lady gazing from the tower window, not someone you would take to the prom but for a kid with acne those were desperate days.

A shredded flag on the turret waved frantically to warn of two frothing mongrels, the kind that never get the color right—one blue eye, one brown eye and fangs in a ghastly shade of yellow. Old age and no sheep can make dispositions ugly, causing locals to speculate that they were part of a litter produced after the Hound of The Baskervilles bred with a Tasmanian Devil.

These beasts ascended straight from hell to sulk and stalk from the carriage house where the mansion's last vestige of grandeur suffered the ultimate deprecation.

From here they launched unprovoked assaults until one day enormous jaws grazed my leg, overshot the frightened target, and punctured a tire. With old dogs the teeth are the last to go.

It was assumed that these beasts had no owner, or had already devoured him. They had taken over the abandoned house—didn't even pay taxes—and except for the ghost upstairs, neighbors thought it was unoccupied.

While the snarling dog struggled to pull his fangs from my tire, a voice proclaimed: "I seen you when you done it. Your damn tire could have broken my dog's teeth." A frothing hulk was baring teeth of canine yellow and proved that people DO look like their pets and bathe about as often.

My father never resorted to crude language but this very day I experienced a crash course in profanity which spewed the nebulous logic of an animal owner defending his pet no matter what. I escaped with my life only by riding the rims into dad's office where he responded to my plight: "I have encountered the same thing when driving a car. After swerving into a ditch to avoid contact, what driv-

er among us has not accidentally struck an animal? Only
when fur blends with asphalt does a worthless mongrel
become man's best friend and valued at about two thousand dollars. Yesterday's ignored cur is suddenly a cherished member of the family who dines at their feet and
shares their food stamps. Even a pedigree is fabricated,
certainly the only one in this family. Sobbing children,
probably borrowed, appear from nowhere. You would think
they had never seen a flat dog before. Precocious actors
are programmed to cradle the fur in a lacrimose embrace
but can't remember the dog's name. No impact is welcome
but each is different. Coyotes and raccoons are indistin-
guishable when the chrome meets the fur, whereas a horse
makes a fairly strong statement. The same scenario
applies to cats though this usually draws a smaller
crowd."

With a knowing nod, the doctor reached into his medical bag and retrieved what was soon to be THE ANSWER.
But surely this syringe could not have much effect on mad
dogs unless you caught them first.

We shall see. To his wife's shame, Will lugged the tools
of his trade in a laundry sac until she replaced it with a
medical grip like doctors carry in the movies. Nothing
symbolizes this proud profession like brass and cowhide
and only when he promised to carry it at all times did she
refer to him as Doctor.

When Will came to town in 1919, drugs were found
only at the Drug Store. Morphia was man's salvation from
agony. Cocaine was a mucosal anesthetic and marijuana
grew where it belonged, across the fence with the other
weeds. Then some Californian discovered that you didn't
have to break a leg to enjoy narcotics which were a helluva lot more fun without the pain. These addicts invaded
Idaho in stolen cars and more than once broke into Will's
office in search of a fix. The jimmied lock on his beloved
bag had not worked for years and the forlorn strap had

been slashed, sutured and slashed yet again. An ugly laceration along one side testified to a hasty entry and one impatient junkie had even violated the bottom. (Today's judgmental world is quick to blame some hop head for desecrating a medical grip just because there is an ampule of morphine inside, but omniscient psychologists tell us that the perpetrator was probably a hard-working, churchgoing tax payer with a healthy curiosity and a harmless fetish for cutting leather.) My father loved that grip but this doctor was not looking for sympathy.

He wanted revenge. The punishment must fit the crime, *exactly* fit the crime. Will's retribution would be appropriate, instructive, and innovative.

He replaced the contents of a MORPHINE bottle with dilute STRYCHNINE. With diabolical whimsy, this dilution was carefully calculated to be sublethal and educational. Just like a light dose of gonorrhea. No need to disturb the Skull & Crossbones since this label seemed to fit both drugs equally well. Nobody died but beneath bridges from the Snake to the Columbia there were several convulsions and two conversions. Junkies spread the word: One Idaho doctor had some really bad morphine. Will prophesied:

"Dilute strychnine in this very syringe has already saved some human souls and can now do the same for two unrepentant dogs. Son, we are not a vindictive family. What may seem cruel is actually the road to canine salvation. Dilute ammonia, just like strychnine, will teach good manners . . . and FAST! Operation Ammonia will repress anger in any beast, whether he be inherently evil or just the product of an unhappy childhood." He handed me a 20cc positive control Luer Lock syringe featuring a metal thumb ring over the plunger and two rings on the barrel for the index and middle fingers: "It's glass. It's expensive. And I want it back."

Attached to the business end was an 18 gauge needle, carefully blunted to render it harmless to a juvenile cyclist who was born awkward. Furthermore, friends had noticed an embarrassing tremor whenever dogs barked. All the chickens were not in Grandad's barnyard. I pretended to have forgotten the way to the farm, to which my father gave me a powerful shove.

The carriage house was still there and the snarling malcontents rushed on cue. This would be their last day of terror as they embarked on a crash course in instant domestication. Two squirts surpassed all expectation. The howl was heard in Nampa. Tails slumped. Ears dragged the ground. Sagging jaws revealed the yellow fangs and the enamel was wrinkling before my eyes. Two quivering lumps of fur collapsed in docile supplication. No doubt about it. They wanted to be friends! And all of this through the miracle of chemistry.

How lasting was the benign transformation?

One even eloped with a cat.

Weenie (don't ask how he got that name) was Grandad's venerable neighbor who had helped raise me. Whenever Grandpa was busy I could always cross the fence and pretend I was helping Weenie. But his greetings had been chilly ever since the Great Sturgeon Debacle. Weenie had caught sturgeon up to sixteen feet but recently surpassed this with a state record that made the *Idaho Daily Statesman*. He took special pride that an out-of-town paper had even spelled "Weenie" right, as if you could possibly spell it wrong. Casting a ham on a hay hook can be hard work until he and Bill had devised a giant sling shot from a tractor inner tube to catapult the bait effortlessly out to the middle of the Snake

River. Eventually, they landed an ancient monster who was probably swimming during the Revolutionary War. Weenie dashed to borrow a camera which verified an enormous chondrostei that outlasted the dinosaurs just by being a bottom feeder. Its primitive head extended beyond the seat down to the wagon tongue and the other end— and this was far, far away—dragged in the dirt beyond the tail gate. I begged to take this irreplaceable photograph to show my friends and it never came back. Weenie took it mighty hard, but Bill shrugged it off because he had been sulking ever since William Jennings Bryan failed in his bid for the presidency long before I was born. My father could relate to this as he fumed over the incessant re-election of Franklin Delano Roosevelt but there was still a flicker of hope. Grandad, on the other hand, swore never to vote again and he reinforced this vow by dying two years before the 1944 election. Bill was as stubborn as those two white mules that treated his grandson with aristocratic contempt even when he dropped by after the war to see if they would warm up to a uniform but they mistook him for a Nazi.

Bill and Mary celebrated their golden wedding anniversary on September 13, 1941, where I crashed the party, pretending to be just another farmer. I had learned to operate the grinding wheel in lieu of work, and could visit for hours if there was a fence to lean on. As an ersatz farmer, about all I knew was that corn stood high, and beans grew low. Wheat was somewhere in between. Pheasants could hide in sugar beets though no one knew how they did it.

I could never tell oats from barley, but the green stuff that smelled just like chewing gum was probably mint. Hail was bad. The government was worse. Every barn roof leaked unless it was built by a German. He tried to explain roofing but nobody could understand him.

One anniversary guest arrived late after a long search for a tie—he thought it was only for funerals—and joined well-wishers around the Kool Aid bowl. Every guest was proud to know Bill and Mary and nothing proved this like a tie, even if it did not match their overalls.

Complaining is the *sine qua non* of farming but there is risk of addiction. Agriculturists Anonymous became the support group for these pathetic victims who struggled for rehabilitation and mainstream acceptance. Meetings began with a generic prayer which the Supreme Court declared unconstitutional until the group's composition was 10% Muslim. They borrowed the Twelve Steps from another anonymous group (which could not be all that anonymous or nobody would even know where to borrow the steps). They swore never to borrow equipment, give up the straw hat and stop complaining about the weather. So the first three steps were almost insurmountable.

Neighbors helped by locking up their tools, most of which were already borrowed. The straw hat was a habit especially tough to kick. Some fought valiantly, even gave it up for almost a year, but kept a spare hidden in the closet despite countless warnings from a veteran sponsor. This, of course, set them up for their insidious moral collapse which began by wearing the thing secretly only in the out-house. Within a month the poor devils were right back where they started and in no time had disgraced themselves in public.

Even harder than renouncing the straw hat was to stop bitching about the weather. Weenie Moyer went through the Twelve Steps several times but always relapsed. The lost sturgeon picture didn't help his disposition, though he seemed glad to see my dad since the doctor had co-signed his notes at the bank for the last ten years.

Weenie was already Canyon County's most eloquent moaner, having earlier mastered this art while dry-farming back in Nebraska. But this year Weenie was blessed when he alone had guessed exactly what to plant and wound up with a bumper crop and record high prices. This happy news almost eclipsed Bill and Mary's anniversary. Here was a chance to redeem myself, so I horned in to join farmers who toasted Weenie with Kool Aid and surrounded him with effusive congratulations. An unsmiling Weenie delayed his response until he could look me straight in the eye: "It took a lot out of the soil."

IF YOUR RETRIEVER GOES AFTER A DUCK BUT BRINGS BACK A FRISBEE, YOU PAID TOO MUCH FOR THAT DOG.

After years of faithful service on Grandad's farm, I moved on to a job with a dairy. It was Grandad's idea. To drive a dairy truck, one must first learn to drive. Few of life's triumphs can equal that of graduating from handlebars to steering wheel. Important high school athletes speak to a boy in car. Girls beckon. Acne fades. Every state enforces age requirements, and to drive in Idaho you should be at least twelve, unless you are really big for your age. Since the L.D.S. church emphasized achievement, precocious little Mormons learned to double clutch while still in diapers, made Eagle Scout by ten and bishop before eighteen.

Methodists had to wait until they could stretch up to the windshield and in later life can be identified by their long necks. Presbyterians were usually chauffeured. Idaho had a few driving regulations but the Republican legislature was too tight-fisted to print them. They reasoned that kids learned to hot wire an ignition by word of mouth and a fancy manual would only dignify auto theft.

Accompanied by a perspiring father, juvenile driving trainees crashed across the Owyhee desert, cutting a swath through acres of sagebrush where lacerating lava lurked beneath every tumbleweed. Where other cars stored a spare tire, these carried an extra oil pan. Quick learners such as myself immediately mastered right, left and forward. Reverse would not be necessary unless I parked in Boise, and that could be years away. After an hour of negotiating sagebrush, I was ready to drive a milk route for the Home Dairy before they hired some Mormon. This job paid better than a paper route plus all the milk you could drink and with a day that began at 3:45 a.m. this could be quite a bit.

Since I had delivered the *Idaho Daily Statesman* to some of the dairy customers only I could answer a question that has long troubled mankind: "Which upsets people most: No milk or no paper?" I was supposed to keep track of each customer's preference, raw milk or pasteurized. This was hard to remember since they were both the same color, and I was already worrying about identifying those houses with the meanest dogs. Better my client contract brucellosis than a nice kid like me die from rabies.

In those days, disposable containers were a distant dream, so after the route I washed bottles by the score: pints, half pints and those weird quarts with an hour glass constriction near the top to sequestrate the cream. This, of course, brought up the question: "Why does cream rise to the top?" It was the owner of the Home Dairy who provided the erudite answer: "So people can get it." By now the dairy business was in my blood, and I was still learning. One would think that such thick glass would be almost impossible to break but it wasn't. Only the boss handled the heavy case of fancy bottles, designed specifically for Bulgarian buttermilk. He lucked on to these at a Montana auction when someone, presumably a Bulgarian, went bankrupt. Ornately etched with hydrofluoric acid, they resembled museum decanters and would today be highly collectable, that is if someone had not dropped the entire case. But remember, I had been up since 3:45 a.m.

The next morning seemed darker than usual when suddenly two drivers met at the same intersection. One may have forgotten to turn on his headlights, or so said a witness. Bad things happen when you slam the brakes with a full load. Milk, butter and cheese shifted forward and jammed the hapless driver's chest against the steering wheel. I'd still be trapped but someone got tired of hearing the horn. Extrication took a while after which I heard that my savior had switched to another dairy. But with dawn still far away, there was plenty of time for real trouble so I pushed on to deliver the unbroken bottles.

Next on my route was Glen Evans, whose fish fly business was doing so well that he had recently splurged on a valuable AKC German short-haired pointer.

The dog may be man's best friend in the daylight but after dark they picture themselves as heroic guardians, the consequences of watching too many Lassie movies. On our first encounter, I was no more than a suspicious stranger who forgot to bring dog food. You would think his pedigree alone might have guaranteed good manners but the beast lunged out of nowhere. White teeth on a black night present a frightening contrast and sudden panic evoked the same reflex that slammed on the brakes just twenty minutes before.

I took a sudden swing with the only weapon handy, a heavy quart of milk. The hound dropped like a stone. GOOD because he couldn't bite. BAD because he was probably dead. A man of honor would knock on the door and admit his cowardly crime. On the other hand, who wants to be awakened this time of day? So I wiped the blood off the bottle and left it on the doorstep.

Maybe raw. Maybe pasteurized. Oh Lord, the world was quiet as I walked back to the truck. Young pups must

be hard to kill and have softer skulls than most folks realize. This dog roused from his coma and grew up to be a fine
hunter. I even had the gall to borrow the hound since Glen
was known for his generosity. We hit it off quite well
because the dog did not recognize me—or anybody else for
that matter. He could hold a stance just like a real pointer but lost his composure when some cat chased him from
the field. Despite that costly pedigree, this handsome animal never entered any dog shows because of a disqualify-
ing deformity. Behind his left ear was a deep concavity
which conformed perfectly to a quart of milk. Everybody
wondered about this, but as far as I was concerned, the
less said the better.

CHAPTER
SEVEN

My White Loggers had just been anointed with a copious layer of Hubbard's Shoe Grease when the letter arrived from the University of Oregon Medical School. They had the gall to mention that my transcript from the College of Idaho was short on credits. It looked just fine to me but the UOMS demanded another course in physics and— get this—an 'A' would really help. Who do these people think they are? I already had plans for the summer. Four of us had organized a momentous adventure in the Sawtooths, but suddenly I hoped the remaining three would get lost without me. My crash course in physics was hosted by Buck Steunenberg back in the days when no student called him Buck. Ancil Steunenberg was the scion of an illustrious Idaho family which included an assassinated governor but, since I didn't do it, we got along quite well.

We met at 7:00 a.m. in the gloomy caverns of Sterry Hall while the sun was shining on Sawtooth Lake where unworthy comrades were catching their limit before noon. In this scholarly dungeon one bare bulb struggled to glow against a blackboard which became even blacker as the filament faltered. The student was reluctant to mention this because Buck was blind with corneal tuberculosis, a disability quickly dismissed since he taught from a big black book which had been published with his name on the cover. Some blind folks are hard to fool. The bulb flickered from white to yellow to out which I emphasized with exaggerated stumbling and other pathetic histrionics. It was all so simple: *The College of Idaho needed a new light bulb.*

In well-endowed colleges this would probably be replaced, but the C of I was a penurious institution and the professor's response illuminated the essence of a school which had barely survived the Great Depression.

I lived only six blocks down Dearborn Street and was not too surprised to hear: "Tomorrow, why don't you bring a new bulb from home?" The College of Idaho would spoon feed pre-med students if they brought their own spoon.

The professor of German at the College of Idaho was born in Bergen, Norway, and turned out students with a unique Scandinavian accent. Knute's course culminated with a dreaded book report for which all were warned the first day but still pretended surprise. Trusting poor penmanship to conceal a perilous translation, I cranked out the mandatory ten pages which friends critiqued. After prolonged derisive laughter, they referred me to Adriana, the resident campus ghost writer and linguistic savior of many desperate freshmen. I bought her a Coke with extra ice. Adriana was expecting me. Her version was flawless. It was almost like another language. Perfection invites suspicion, so for authenticity she suggested sprinkling the report with a few intentional errors. I could handle that. I was only one of many that this dear girl smuggled though the labyrinth of German verbs and on to medical school. She was declared a campus treasure and in case of an air raid, Adriana was to be saved first. After investing two years in this language, I grew overconfident and subscribed to a German scientific journal to provide some light reading in medical school. Somehow the publisher in Munich learned about that ghostwritten book report because they refused to mail it.

Just as well. By then, Adriana was married to a man who refused to loan her for the weekend.

After a lifetime of preparation, many now in medical school felt more guilt than triumph since no Germans were shooting at anybody in Portland and med students sequestered on Marquam Hill were safer than they deserved to be. Most of my old friends were not this lucky.

Dale had entered the war even before his country did by joining the Royal Canadian Air Force. He became the town's first war hero and the *Caldwell News Tribune* followed every sortie until he was shot down over Holland. The story of his death filled page one, including pictures of a curly-haired kid sharing smiles with his winning teams in football, basketball and track. Dale excelled in any sport played on grass, maple or cinders. His day began with farm chores at 4:00 a.m., after which this remarkable lad managed to letter in three sports and still captain teams in debate and chess. Budgetary constraints of small town newspapers limited the number of photo reproductions, but Dale could be featured by omitting shots of FDR with his theatrical cigarette holder. Relegating Roosevelt to page two actually increased subscriptions.

During all those years since the world lost a brave young pilot, physics and medicine have made monumental contributions and great books have been written. Whenever someone receives a Nobel prize, I find myself thinking, "That could have been Dale." Sam was with the infantry in France where a 2nd Lt. has a better chance of being killed than promoted. He had already survived an adventurous childhood and enjoyed risky games. He played Tarzan with alarming realism and most kids would have used up all their luck swinging high above a concrete driveway on frayed ropes.

Al's eyesight washed him out of the Air Force but he was deemed suitable for a suicide glider squadron. A man without a parachute or engine is almost better off if he can't see too well. The University of Oregon Medical

School had accepted sixty-five freshmen, most of whom were summarily indoctrinated at Ft. Lewis, Washington.

If patriotism was not a sufficient motivator, the United States Army promised that those who flunked out would be sent far, far away. A handful were in the navy program because, after all, the ocean was only ninety miles away. Oregon boasted a medical school many years before it occurred to Washington. When my father graduated during the first World War, Will's school was a gray cluster of expropriated buildings down on Lovejoy Street and the abandoned warehouse may have been used to store cadavers.

To improve the view, the school was eventually moved to Marquam Hill, probably so I couldn't find it. The great eastern centers like Johns Hopkins were located closer to indigent patients until slum overgrowth obscured the hallowed halls of Halsted, Welch and Osler. From the commanding heights of Multnomah County Hospital, fortunate Oregon students walked to class through towering evergreens, dense ferns and, if you were not in a hurry, even a waterfall. Marquam Hill was a microcosm of the northwest's grandest greenery and an idyllic home if it were not for demanding professors determined to spoil it all. Oregon accepted a small quota of Idaho boys and some from other states wore Phi Beta Kappa keys. No one back home had ever heard of this organization but Idahoans have never been joiners. But what the hell! The key did not fit any lock anyway. To my left in biochemistry stood the son of a Nobel prize winning physicist. I had heard of Nobel since some of the kids back home liked to play with his dynamite. To my right was the math wizard from Oregon State who had been embraced and feted by the Dean and three trustees. On opening day they tripped over their gowns in the rush to welcome the wizard and stepped on my foot as if to punctuate my insignificance. Across the lab table another freshman who already had a doctorate in chemistry frowned when I took two matches to light my Bunsen Burner.

When I first boarded the Portland Rose with a one way ticket, my father's last words had been: "Son, you're as smart as any of them." Hoping for paternal reinforcement, my first letter from home confided: "Maybe you're not as smart as I thought."

After six weeks depression only deepened. Two classmates—one actually a Phi Beta Kappa—had flunked out and were ushered unceremoniously into the U.S infantry. These poor devils had never learned to fake their lab results. The survivors remained in alphabetical order from aardvark to zebra, inhaling the pungent world of biochemistry. Even urine takes on a lot of class when boiled in an Erlenmeyer flask.

Pathologists on television lead interesting lives, wear nice suits and solve murders after which the surviving widow turns out to be a rich nymphomaniac who can't thank the doctor enough. But pathologists in the real world wear cheap suits, try to pay off the mortgage and at the end of a boring day drive home in an old car to a wife who is by no means a nymphomaniac, at least as far as he can tell. He spends most of his life fretting about cancer cells which are devious mimics and never to be trusted. Under the microscope many pitfalls lurk to waylay the unwary pathologist where even a perfectly normal placenta is a terrifying sight and easily mistaken for malignancy. To meet the diagnostic criteria for cancer, not only must the individual cells be abnormal but they must be re-located in some strange place where they do not belong. Even though placental cells look wild they are situated exactly where God intended—inside somebody's uterus, taking care of a baby.

Even without medical school you know what crazy things the female pelvis can do. Medical terms often share the same Greek root. It is no accident that both hysterectomy and hysteria are derived from *hyster*. Think about it.

Hunching over a microscope is not for everybody but a few men like George Papanicolaou apparently enjoyed it. Before his monumental discovery, a diagnostic biopsy required a chunk of tissue if you could get at it and were not easily discouraged by bleeding so George searched tirelessly for a simple but reliable shortcut. He began with cancer of the cervix by smearing cells on a slide and looking at them for ten years during which period his golf handicap skyrocketed.

Just like skin peeling after a sunburn, the cervix sheds cells continuously and is accessible to anyone who can find the vagina. Reliable identification took practice, but once perfected, George's technique would save lives all over the world—including people we don't even like.

Walter Chrysler and Willis Dodge made sure they were remembered, but scientists can't stick their names on a hood ornament. George Papanicolaou should be a household word just like Conrad Roentgen and Marie Curie. Milk drinkers everywhere toast Louis Pasteur who saved them from brucellosis. Extract of Lord Lister is gargled every morning as Listerine. Edison became a light bulb. Poor George was not so lucky. He took a lifetime to describe those ugly cells which today are scanned impersonally by a computer until his forgotten name has become the PAP SMEAR.

PAP is ignominious enough, even for a Greek, but smear seems downright insulting.

Bacteriology can be quite tedious because the subjects are so small. Parasitology was downright creepy because when you looked through the microscope something at the other end seemed to be looking back. Hunching over such disagreeable organisms is all the harder when outside the sun is shining, though in Portland this only happened twice. Then one afternoon Stan and Bill got lucky when it was discovered that their inoculated rabbit was blessed with a very high titre for Tularemia—sufficient to extract a useful serum. The professor would excuse them to the animal surgery suite but only if they knew how to bleed the rabbit. As it turned out there was nothing these lads did not know and they already enjoyed a few special advantages. Bill was the governor's son and Stan's status was even more enviable. He was a Canadian citizen who, should he flunk out, would escape the U.S. army draft which strongly motivated the rest of the class. Only last week the crafty Canadian had a mighty close call when the bacteriology instructor borrowed his microscope to check a slide of E Coli. Instead of bacilli he focused on a pornographic picture purchased in the lobby of the Burnside Burlesque. The lens was still on low power and Stan insisted that with higher magnification he was looking for gonorrhea. Many of the faculty recognized the erotic creature, and even the dean had long suspected that she might be a carrier.

Stan always landed on his feet by sucking up to the profs. With wartime rationing he was a good man to know because that man could really siphon gas. Professor Sears entrusted Bill and Stan with the keys which unlocked a spotless white room filled with expensive equipment. Cradling the tularemic rodent, two aspirant surgeons swaggered to the operating table. This assignment should take about twenty minutes after which the East Moreland golf course beckoned just across the Ross Island bridge . . . and the sun was still shining. The governor's son would take charge of ether anesthesia while a confident Canadian shaved the groin, preparatory to cannulating the femoral artery. But it was not to be. The furtive femoral eluded them even with the anatomy text opened as an unerring guide. Finally they changed books but, these too, only confirmed that the boys were lost. Surgeons are inclined to sweat more than other people. Failure in the groin directed them to the neck, home of the carotid artery. Through a cervical incision, much longer than it needed to be, Stan dissected while the anesthesiologist also served as the page turner but Bill was hovering too close to the ether vapors and kept dropping off. Occasionally he roused long enough to hear Stan's disquieting words: "We should have stayed in the groin. There's too much important stuff in the neck." Time passed. The rabbit slept on.

In desperation, they located an anatomy atlas which for some reason was kept under a glass dome, a limited edition, leather bound, gold trimmed, and autographed by the personal physician of Queen Elizabeth. The only other copy was in the royal museum in Edinburgh. Books are hard to handle with slippery hands and this one was abandoned, badly smeared with rodent fur and human sweat. Everything in it was wrong. You can't trust those foreigners. British book binders must do sloppy work because several pages fell out when it hit the floor. Back under the glass dome it even smelled different. The sun was sinking when they accidentally stumbled across the maligned carotid, for which a conduit was prepared to siphon off the tularemic blood. In those days, plastic was yet to be invented so cannulas had to be hand-fashioned from glass tubing which was scored and snapped. It was then fire polished over a Bunsen Burner to smooth the rough edge which otherwise can accidentally saw through the blood vessel at the worst possible moment. A spectacular column of blood spurted to the ceiling to announce that these surgeons had forgotten *step three*.

Excitement turned to panic when the patient suddenly woke up and did what rabbits do best . . . pretend it's being chased by a coyote. This immaculate operating suite would never be white again. With sanguinary leaps he covered every centimeter of the recently endowed floor. Then, without a care in the world—at least as far as you could tell—he circled the gleaming wall like a motorcycle in a hippodrome.

Centrifugal force is a wonderful thing. Nothing escaped. Bill and Stan were sent down to get blood and, by God, they got blood.

It was mighty dark outside when the curious boss arrived to check on his scholarly research team. A sense of humor was not prevalent among academics in this medical school and the Chief of Bacteriolgy had none.Dr. Sears entered the surgery suite to witness a most unprofessional scene.

Ingloriously every vestige of scientific discipline had collapsed, and in desperation . . . and in the name of science . . . they had beheaded the rabbit.

One man was straining to wring the furry corpse and the other knelt below, holding a stainless steel bucket which was filling fast.

Those cherished hopes for a Nobel prize seemed to have vanished. Later that year there was a major epidemic of tularemia.

Stan was spared deportation when Alberta didn't want him either. Sensitive Canadians abhorred any cruelty to animals beyond mushing dogs over thin ice, or clubbing an occasional seal.

The governor commuted his son's execution, probably because Bill always carried a lucky rabbit's foot.

One student became an orthopedist; the other a neurosurgeon.

Where do you think doctors come from anyway?

BEETHOVEN WAS SO DEAF THAT HE THOUGHT
HE WAS A PAINTER.
~ George Carlin

Professors are paid to keep students worried so they
were dumbfounded by the inscrutable Krasnopolsky who
remained casual through the entire ordeal. He studied
when he felt like it which might be any day now. He captivated the entire class with noon piano concerts which
distracted lesser students who could ill afford to be late for
the next class.

Eric had been a child prodigy who performed in
Warsaw and Vladinir Horowitz was his godfather. Despite
classical training his musical tastes were catholic and he
played jazz with a Polish accent. When Kraz learned that
I had once met Duke Ellington (or so I said) there was
instant bonding between a Krakow Jew and an Idaho gen-
tile. With state of the art cactus needles we played 78
RPMs of Brahms and Bach mingled with Basie or
Lunceford. Kraz professed to know Beethoven's final
thoughts on his chorale symphony: "How do I end this
thing?" He also confided personal details on the finale of
The Shostokovich Ninth Symphony which was so frenetic
that the piccolo player had to take a shower before his curtain call. Friends with varied musical talents wanted to
join in and one trumpeter blew out his lip on the tuning
note.

Eric was a renaissance man. Before medical school,
with nothing better to do, he graduated *cum laude* from
MIT. After leaving Boston, he became a varsity swimmer
at the University of Oregon. For reasons never understood, such gifted people seem to thrive only on the immediate challenge and what should be a lasting triumph was
for him ephemeral. During his junior year, the Polish
prodigy suddenly quit school, probably compelled to dig a
ditch in someplace like Nepal. His piano gathered dust.

Professors were perplexed. Remaining classmates became so depressed that several were shamed into psychiatry.

As long as pneumonia starts with a p some words will be hard to spell. This is why doctors cheat with memory devices such as Limericks, Mnemonics (Hell, there's another one) and acronyms. Catchy rhymes were especially useful to organize the chaos of anatomy and, whether homely or handsome, most of us are composed of these essentials: A) The basic skeleton with 206 bones (more or less). This may have changed. B) Muscles attaching to this and that. C) Vessels nourishing structures here and there. D) Assorted nerves wandering aimlessly in and out of A, B and C and ending in confusion.

Check your doctor's diploma. Make sure he knows all this stuff. One guy never got beyond the bones. He suspected that the vertebrae were in the back somewhere and became a chiropractor. This saved him years of school and in six months he earned more money than any real doctor.

Others were tempted to abandon medicine when one cynical instructor stood up in front of impressionable freshmen and proclaimed (get this) the female breast was actually no more than a modified sweat gland. Verily, a cruel disclosure to altruistic students, some of whom were so young that they still believed in the tooth fairy.

The professor never knew who slashed his tires.

To spare you four years in medical school let us now share this time honored crutch for the twelve cranial nerves: "On Old Olympus Tiny Top, A Fat-Assed German Viewed A Hop." For the gifted student this quickly translates to: 1) Olfactory, 2) Optic, 3) Occulomotor, 4) Trochlear, 5) Trigeminal, etc. We could go on but this is heavy stuff. Eight wrist bones are entirely too many, considering the size of the wrist. Our Creator made a lot of mistakes like this, but it's too late now. Next time wrist anatomy is discussed at a formal dinner, just remember: "Never Lower Tillie's Pants. Mother Might Come Home." That's eight, or should be. This equates to: Navicular, Lunate, Triangularis, Pisiforme, etc. The rest were forgotten right after the quiz. Most of these are lewd because med students always forgot the clean ones. There are German counterparts for students in Heidelberg but (and who's surprised) the filthiest ones are in French. Some deserve to be remembered if only for their sheer loveliness

The Lingual Nerve
Took a hell of a swerve
Around the Hyoglossus
Well I'll be fucked
Said Wharton's duct
I think it's going to cross us

Since this is mouth anatomy, the version from Paris was even more disgusting.

After graduation, there were three verses left over, two rhapsodic poems and one Limerick. What did they mean? Some of the fellows could fit theirs in by remembering a particular exam where they did poorly. But I did poorly in so many that I could never really be sure. I loaned one to a urologist since their life is pure poetry:

A THOUSAND PLAGUES CAN STRIKE A MAN
BUT V.D. IS THE MEANUS
THIS RASH ON ME
LORD, LET IT BE
JUST MEASLES OF THE PENIS

I WOULD NEVER JOIN ANY CLUB THAT WOULD
HAVE ME AS A MEMBER.

~ Groucho Marx

Meet Your Professor Night was a boring event for which attendance was mandatory. Perspiring people with nothing in common were herded into a small room for an evening of exhausting amiability. Since it was dreaded by teachers and students alike, it clearly met the first criterion of a tradition that would never die. The sham was worsened by forbidding alcohol so the chief of surgery took a few belts before he left home. So did his wife.

This spectacle was held on Sam Jackson Road in a white colonial building that passed as a fraternity and housed more booze than members. This was confirmed when one of them became an Admiral in the navy. The brethren were forewarned so all whiskey had to be smuggled to a place of presumed security across the street. That would be in my dank basement room which was barely habitable but ideal for hiding contraband. I was paid a dollar to protect the cache of Jim Beam and Old Crow, but most of it was cheap Southern Comfort, that ineluctable interloper of war time rationing. But this duplicity was short lived.

That same afternoon some anonymous abstainer gained entry to desecrate the stash which was momentarily unguarded while I had to attend a class. Or so I said. The crusader poured every bottle, jug and decanter down the toilet. The distinctive Haig & Haig pinch bottle became a damned expensive candle holder and still reminds me of that day when I lost most of my friends. The fraternity's *ad hoc* Committee on Booze had listed—notarized, as I remember—every bottle and easily confirmed that sixteen quarts had gurgled into oblivion, enough to clean every sewer pipe from Portland to Salem. Most bourbon had disappeared with a single flush, but a fifth of Jack Daniels took forever.

Tennessee's famous Sipping Whiskey can't be rushed, and it was slowly savored by an appreciative porcelain bowl. I was never invited to join the fraternity.

AROUSAL WILL ALWAYS PASS BUT SOMETIMES IT TAKES A YEAR.

During the sleepless grind of medical school, chemistry is an innocuous pursuit, but anatomy can screw up a man's concentration with recurrent images of the female form. She begins as a noble abstraction of muscle, nerves and vessels but after a few hours is transformed into an erotic phantasy.

One of the married Pfc's taunted celibate classmates by arriving with a knowing grin and his web belt unbuckled. He went home a private and returned a general. These students were composed of three groups A) Doctor's kids who had not yet heard about sex. B) Minister's sons who were against it. C) Farm boys who thought artificial insemination was the only way to go. It was their shared hope that medical school would resolve these sexual conflicts but anatomy teaches only the name of everything, not necessarily where it goes. What little they knew about overcoming female resistance had to be learned from B movies where the beautiful starlet is pursued by a dapper leading man with a pencil mustache. His success is assured by a French accent, a cigarette in one hand, a Scotch and soda in the other and around his neck . . . an ascot. Seized with passion and bent—often seriously bent—on seduction, one amorous freshman borrowed a

cigarette and intoned an unforgettable line from a forget-
table movie:

He: "I'll be gentle."

She: "Don't you dare."

He fled in a panic.

Out-dazzling every female in Portland were identical
twins tagged the "Dolly Sisters" after a current movie featuring June Haver and Betty Grable. This film (yes, it was
in living color) won no Academy Awards which only proves
that the awards are fixed. Actually, Hollywood had nothing to compare with these twins who differed only in their
sex drives and came to be known as Prudence and
Prurient . . . names which identified their sexual inclina-
tions and clearly defined the goal. But fate threw a curve
and many batters struck out. They were truly identical
only above the navel. Prurient was beautiful and it took
just a little wine to take the chill off her ovaries. Prudence
was equally gorgeous but came with a factory sealed
vulva. When hope runs even higher than testosterone it
was vital that a suitor know one girl from the other. This
could be frustrating and expensive. Ordinary people ate.
They dined. You could sell tickets on the beach when they
wore bathing suits. The Queen of England drew obedient
stares, but never dislocated her subject's eyeballs. The
Queen can bestow knighthood. These twins could do a helluva lot better than that. The Dolly Sisters were gorgeous
high-maintenance creatures who did not date poor medical students. Until one day it happened. Crouched over
my five dollar roll top desk, I was memorizing the
sphenopalatine ganglion when I heard the unctuous voice
of my roommate, hoping to negotiate one of his painfully
frequent short term loans. I had developed a high titre
immunity to his whining appeals, but this time the dividends could be enormous. Don had spent a month locating
a car with three gallons of gas (the owner didn't know
about it yet) after which he finagled a date with the Dolly

Sisters by the same devious means. His partner in conquest was another freshman, who had already mastered
the sphenopalatine ganglion, and had bought (or
siphoned) enough gas for a madcap evening of reckless
seduction. Wayne swore he could tell Prudence from
Prurient and had foolishly announced this in public. As
things turned out he was mistaken.

Don wondered which twin he would get, but Wayne
could be cruel: "You wouldn't know the difference."
Thoughts of getting the wrong twin was making them
testy but my own lot was sorrier as I stared once again at
the sphenopalatine ganglion, learning absolutely nothing.

Don and Wayne burned gas they couldn't replace and
spent money they didn't have, and all Portland drooled
while two Pfc's paraded these coveted creatures. Should
The Oregonian cover such an event in the society section
or the sports page? They actually ate twice that evening
just to see men drop their forks when the girls entered the
dining room of the Benson Hotel. So far, this resembled a
movie which was seriously over budget. As bankruptcy
loomed, even the script was about to fail them. "I'll be gentle" never achieved critical acclaim because it was never
uttered. They searched for some place—*any place*—to
park but you can't stop on a bridge and in Multnomah
county that's about all there is. They crossed the
Willamette a dozen times until they ran out of gas. Just as
well. By then even the engine was in heat. Each lad was
stranded with the same unwrapped condom he had carried since high school (when they were called rubbers) but
the world must never know. Wayne bluffed shamelessly as
he swaggered across the campus with that unmistakable
smirk of sexual conquest. On the other hand, Don was a
lousy actor and next Monday morning the word was out.

"Poor devil. He got the wrong twin." Instead of derision the class went into mourning. So doctors DO understand. None of us did well on the anatomy quiz which

included the foramina at the base of the skull and, just for the hell of it, the brachial plexus.

The sphenopalatine ganglion was not even mentioned.

There was no level ground on Marquam Hill where two freshmen shared a basement room in a three story house built just well enough to hang on to a steep incline. From the street level you stepped up to the first floor (actually the third) or down to the second (always the second) and the only entrance to their basement cell was from the downside backside outside. Here you entered a dank dungeon not unlike a cave or—you deserve the truth—*exactly* like a cave. Spelunkers rented it on weekends.

My top bunk was supported by sturdy stalactites adjacent to which was a mysterious door that led nowhere. It was lined with rotted plywood to prove that Oregon was rain country as if any verification was necessary. It was here that one never-to-be-promoted Pfc stored his gas mask which was issued so the army could keep track of me. There it decayed in moldy silence for a year until suddenly the commandant ordered a gas drill. Even the Nazis would have given more warning. I stuck a reluctant hand into the forbidding cul de sac but retrieved only a pair of goggles and a coil of rusted wire to which hung a few pathetic shreds of rubber. During the initial panic, I considered going AWOL but would be too easy to track with that powerful aroma of formaldehyde which lingers for months after anatomy dissection. This unpardonable loss was promptly confessed to the colonel, a superannuated doctor who still believed in leeches. It was rumored that long ago he had attended Ford's theater where he was hastily summoned to treat a man in a stove pipe hat with some kind of a head wound. Apparently it had turned out badly. A court martial was mentioned but I adroitly diverted the commandant's attention by admiring his many ribbons. My powerful defense emphasized that the gas mask had never done a thing for me, bad fit and a dreadful color. Could they issue another one, perhaps something in a pastel?

Overwhelmed by such contrition (and because he had a quota of doctors to crank out) the colonel granted a reprieve but ordered me to extra drill time on the parking lot. Here I paid for my transgression where a million seagulls with full cloacas circled overhead, never caring who might be marching below. I left the colonel with my best salute—not too military but quite good for a doctor—and as I passed the sergeant he whispered:

"Destroying government property isn't nearly as serious as picking the wrong twin."

The class of '46 scattered after graduation and some were urged to go far, far away. Thereafter, I rarely saw my old group again unless I owed them money and then chance encounters were uncanny.

Graduation declares that you are now an honest-to-God doctor and while your signature may still be a scrawl, that M.D. suffix will be quite legible . . . at least for the first year.

Every recipient gripped his diploma as if someone might steal it, but my special bonus was delayed until I could finally vacate my med school cave. It still took both hands to force open the mossy door while salamanders scurried. I packed what I could lift and left what I couldn't, which meant a reluctant abandonment of an enormous roll top desk which could comfortably sleep two. My predecessor had sold this monster for five dollars, part of an unholy ritual as successive students passed it from class to class.

It could have been mine for only a dollar, but during the transaction the seller was a graduating senior so I was negotiating from a position of awe.

Massive oaken drawers contained not only my files, but forgotten material from every previous owner. Some cubby holes might be stuffed with Marie Curie's notes on radium or a few Lincoln letters which Abe forgot to mail. I surreptitiously burned one sheet which was an embarrassing memory of once dealing with the student underground. Sol, a barber in his former life, stole exams and sold copies at four bits each to previously honest students. But in neuro-physiology who couldn't use that extra edge? That was my sole contact to the Medical Mafia. The money was non-refundable, the exam was counterfeit and I was lucky to get a D. In addition to selling stolen exams, Sol rented his sister on weekends and still found time to organize a lucrative Portland Barber's Union. He was one of the early pioneers of tax evasion. His sister was not too risky because penicillin had just been discovered.

Sol was kicked out of school during his junior year while he was writing a best seller on medical ethics. With the royalties he started a trailer rental company and made millions. I last saw Sol on the cover of *TIME*.

His sister never writes.

Our five year reunion was canceled because most of the class would be in Korea. The United Nations hawked this conflict as a Police Action but, quite frankly, it looked just like a real war.

By the time we finally got together, nobody remembered medical school but bored each other with exaggerated war stories. The class of 1946 would never get any larger . . . or more boring. Wayne still tried to defend the Great

Twin Treachery, and we were not too surprised to learn
that Prurient now owned the hotel which hosted the
reunion. Looking around the room, it was easy to spot
those who had once dated Prurient. They were still smiling. Those who dated her frigid sister never regained their
self-esteem and went into research. During subsequent
reunions, the smarter doctors learned to guard conversations with any spouse who seemed younger than they
remembered her. This was a different wife.

CHAPTER EIGHT

DADDY, WHAT DID YOU DO IN THE WAR?

Constantinople is a fickle town, sometimes Christian, sometimes Muslim and, compounding the confusion, even changed its name to Istanbul. But time has forgiven her inconstancy and decreed that she will remain forever a Eurasian beauty. Within its city walls, Greek and Arabic literature was guarded and revered at a time when European monarchs could not even sign their names. When St. Paul sent his epistles to Ephesus or Thessalonika, these were the folks who wrote back. Ancient writings liberated from Byzantine libraries (and to this day never returned) led Europe out of the dark ages.

Rome was founded on seven hills by Romulus and Remus and soon the folks down at the forum were singing "It's Gotta Be That Wolf's Milk." Since this worked out so well they tried the same thing in Constantinople where there just happened to be seven hills at the other end of the Mediterranean.

Since the city of Constantine could out-spend Rome and out-sin Sodom, it sent an unmistakable invitation to conquest. The clash of broad swords and scimitars echoed where two continents met at the most besieged city in the world. Much to our Christian shame, this jewel of the Bosporus was pillaged by the Knights of the Fourth Crusade, and had barely recovered when, two centuries later, she suffered mightily when Ottoman hordes sacked the citadel in 1453. The crusader's noble intent had been to save Jerusalem from the Saracens but, somewhere along the way, European troops were mesmerized by Constantinople and especially the Aya Sophia, the apotheosis of Byzantine wealth. Already envenomed by theological schisms, they forgot all about Jerusalem as they stole Sophia's treasure and concentrated on a well-stocked harem. Priceless jeweled reliquaries found their way back to every castle in Europe with enough left over to sponsor another crusade. Hot Damn!

After Constantine embraced the cross in a vision, he built his eponymous city with the rallying cry: *in hoc signe vinces* (by this sign thou shalt conquer). But alas, latter-day crusaders were carried away by the emperor's exhortations (which lived much longer than he did) and, soon enough, Constantinople was pillaged by bad people who had started out so good.

When the army shipped me to Turkey there was still a lot to see in this town and rivalling even India's Taj Mahal was the majestic Aya Sophia, who, even at 1400 years, did not look her age.

When it was completed in 563, Justinian (all these emperors had peculiar Latin names) modestly declared: "Solomon, I have surpassed thee!" People talked this way in 563. Boastful perhaps, but a claim hardly exaggerated because his new cathedral embraced an acre of gold leading to a substantial altar weighing in at 40,000 pounds of silver. To replace stolen jewels, thousands more were stashed in the Topkapi, right next to the harem, so everybody knew where it was. In the center of the nave floor was the *omphalos,* the navel of the world. These Byzantines were inclined to grandiosity which seems even more elegant in Greek. Crafted with ceramics and sapphires, the *omphalos* struggled to endure the endless parade of the devoutly curious. Apparently even shoeless feet are abrasive and with two per pilgrim this can add up.

Blood stains of Crusader knights and Saracen jannisaries had been washed away long before I got there, though I did step in some dog stuff.

Unlike European cathedrals, this one has a roof you can really see. The huge central cupola, like some gigantic Plummer's Helper, seems to levitate the lesser ones. This is not your average roof, intended just to keep the rain out and the people in.

To prove this was an honest-to-Allah mosque, four sentinel minarets were added, one of which has been modernized with loud speakers. The Mullah's amplified call to prayer reminded me of the off-key tenor in our Methodist choir back home. Nostalgia overwhelmed me. Sophia eventually had five minarets, even though the Koran decreed that no mosque in the Muslim world could have more of these than the mother church in Mecca. I forget how they worked this out. Methodists would appoint a committee. Sophia's greater magic is inside but only with your shoes outside. Mine were held hostage until I bought my quota of postcards. Perhaps you received one since I mailed dozens.

A Frankish diarist of the Fourth Crusade described what he beheld in 1204, before Sophia's golden walls were stripped and sagging crusader wagons, bristling with booty, struggled toward Macedonia: "The eye cannot distinguish the limits of this edifice . . . the dome is not a reflection of the sun but a radiance within . . . one hundred chandeliers hung from silver chains as thick as a man's arm and each held twenty and five gold lamps . . . three massive doors, the highest for the emperor (who probably wasn't all that tall) swung on silver hinges . . . ." Today we know that steel hinges swing better, but these early folks just didn't care; and quite honestly, we have never really given silver a chance.

Emperor Justinian selected spectacular columns of every hue: porphyry from Thebes, yellow from Thessaly, red from Cyprus, black from Ba'albak. Ephesus alone contributed eight green ones leaving her temple a little short on columns.

Already a thousand years old, each column was moved assiduously in three sections from the farthest reaches of his empire. How vast the real estate! How cheap the labor! They were rejoined with seams of molten lead and, because the columns varied in height, ingenious craftsmen concealed the discrepancy with massive bases and ornate capitals of carved acanthus, hoping no one would notice. When the church became a mosque (1453 was a bad year for Christians) Islam proscribed the human image and all Christian portraits and mosaics were destroyed and replaced with Arabic tapestries and huge green Koranic discs with pious maxims. On the other hand, it's their country.

Only the angel Gabriel survived the iconoclasts because he served both faiths: the Christian's Angel of Annunciation and Islam's Angel of Truth who revealed the Koran to the Prophet. Arms beckoning and wings folded, Gabriel gazes benevolently from every wall.

This architectural wonder was approached from the Galata Bridge, crossing which, so it is said, one may hear every language in the world. However, only an astute observer who already understands every language in the world would be qualified to make this judgment. Quite frankly, I doubt it and so did everybody else whom I questioned (in English).

Because of the proximity to the west, driving on the bridge is not too risky, but the rules of the road deteriorate in proportion to the distance from Istanbul where each village uses its own interpretation of the Koran to explain the mysteries of internal combustion.

Americans grew up with the automobile and evolved with gears but the middle east was denied this gradual mechanical transition. With a few pistons and a heavy foot, Turks overnight became a nation which gripped a steering wheel with the one hand while still patting their oxen with the other.

Between the whip and the accelerator were many Arabic anomalies: a) Turn off the ignition at all stop signs. This saves gas. b) Whenever possible, drive in reverse. Gas is burned only when going forward. c) Turn off headlights at night. This saves the battery. d) Instead, use the dome light which has a smaller bulb and imparts a festive glow. Now with illumination inside the car, the driver can't see a thing but it shows others you are in the neighborhood. Sitting in a dark taxi, it takes awhile to realize that you are sharing the back seat with a side of beef.

Turks were confident mechanics, ready to undertake major repairs anywhere, anytime. Without hesitation, they would dismantle the entire drive train, dump it in four inches of dust, and work off a prayer rug. Allah would re-start the car and any parts left by the roadside only proved that they used too many gears in Detroit. The Anatolian plateau was strewn with courageous automobiles that almost made it.

MASH hospitals were so popular in Korea that everybody wanted one. After years of camping in Idaho, I knew a lot about tents and the army found out about it. It might have been something I said. Setting up a MASH unit was my chance to stand out without gluing braid on my hat or wearing British riding pants, and soon I was shipped out for Tent Detail in eastern Turkey. Muslims resent being called Muhammadan (KORAN 27:78) so already you know more than the army told me. Keeping the money straight was tricky. NATO decreed the official rate at 2.8 Turkish lire per American dollar. In practice it reached 20:1, clearly an invitation to the black market. I had a few close calls at 40:1, but only our colonel got caught. We still correspond at Christmas. The Turks needed no indoctrination to hate the enemy. From their mother's Muslim womb they had despised the Russians and knew how to express it. No brainwashing was necessary because Turkish inductees (askirs) were born invincible. Despite the language barrier, "Turk kork mas" when spoken through grinding teeth just sounded like "A Turk fears nothing." It could mean nothing else. Turkish *askirs* introduced their own special brand of fighting by infiltrating enemy foxholes to slit North Korean throats. No artery squirts as far as the carotid and these *askirs* were looking for a record. With sadistic discrimination, they killed only one of the occupants, selectively sparing his trench-mate who, with an intact larynx, could spread the word. For sheer panic, nothing could match the bloody Turkish Signature. Bullets are frightening enough, but a slashed jugular conveys a special terror. So silent. So sneaky. So personal. The survivor awoke in a blood spattered foxhole, shared with a frightfully pale comrade who seemed to have been sleeping all the time. Next night nobody slept. You can see how this would work. Both Turkey and Greece were members of the same alliance, but after a thousand ugly years they could only despise each other. NATO urged them to get along and, strictly in the spirit of brotherhood, offered liberal bribes to both. It was in this same spirit that I never mentioned my brief landing in Athens (home of the infidel) on my way to Ankara (home of the faithful). When my DC-3 touched down, I marched across the tarmac at Etimisgut and saluted the Red Crescent like a soldier coming home. Mendacious, to be sure, but if I hoped for promotion this trait would need to be cultivated.

For those of you who served in the army and remained a private, now you know why. Turks had driven the Greeks out in 1920 and, flushed with victory, had since believed that the Russian Air Force was terrified by the Turkish cavalry.

There was no need to change their attitude but I had to work on my own. Those Anatolian recruits not shipped to Korea served along the Russian border which was really not worth seeing except for Mt. Ararat. This peak smiled down on Diyarbakir, a town that frowned back. At 16,800 feet, Ararat sounded even higher when called *Agri Dagi* where the adjective rhymes with the noun, no matter what. During Ottoman conquests they stole just enough of the Persian language to create a poetic hybrid which, by defying grammatical logic, could make common words sound downright Shakespearean. Such speech blends musical Arabic with guttural Slavic so don't stand too close. French is also a beautiful language (so say the French) but less so when a translator explains what they are saying about you. When confronted by natives who didn't understand English, most of us just shouted louder. For the hard of hearing, we offered money.

Astronomy, mathematics and literature had flourished elsewhere in the Arab world but the Turks were endowed with quite another gift: There was nothing they could not destroy. Pillage became a source of national pride. Creating a priceless rug takes many months, sometimes years. Is it not then logical to kidnap the Persian who wove it?

Once upon a time they even stole an alphabet but didn't know what to do with it. Paradoxically, the perpetual snows of Ararat are reached across arid plains of which none are hotter. It is here where tectonic plates from three continents converge to create the mother of earthquakes. Erzurum, Diyarbakir's neighbor, was famous for nothing else.

In terms of hardship, the Turko-Russian border was the virtual equivalent of Korea and this included getting killed, where, not far away, enemy soldiers wore helmets with red stars and carried rifles with telescopic sights. Off-duty American soldiers could pass the time searching Mt. Ararat for Noah's ark but unless you are really into boating this eventually gets boring.

Our headquarters were at Diyarbakir, a city as ancient as Jericho but the walls of the former had been spared the destructive vibration caused by Joshua's trumpets. Here we kept a bunch of expensive airplanes, forgetting that they couldn't take off in heat which surpassed the Sahara and once tied Death valley at 134 degrees. Flight crews sweated under improvised canopies and near each mechanic was a bucket of water for wrenches too hot to handle. Work was slow, but no matter, the plane wasn't going anywhere. Since this wasn't working as an airfield, and NATO was floundering in money, they turned in desperation to the United States Army Medical Corps. Could we help? We could. The solution: Diyarbakir needed a MASH unit but it could cost as much as $200,000. NATO declined. So we settled on $500,000. The camouflage was so effective that we couldn't find the hospital so we suggested a colorful stripe or a perky pastel. All my life I have craved recognition and if only we had squandered an even million a military medal could have been mine. And for two million, maybe an oak leaf cluster.

It was a memorable inauguration. Our first patients were Turks from the nearby border, dangerously hoarse from yelling insults at the Russians. We flew in extra doctors, looked at every throat and saved them all. Now every soldier was ready for the parade. Since it was too hot for the band to touch their horns, we substituted a tape but it melted just before the piccolo bridge on Stars and Stripes Forever. Anyone caught looking at a thermometer was put on report.

Thirst is a problem in a country where even the natives won't drink the water, so they substituted their national drink from which no bacteria and few stomachs survived.

Schnapps, Vodka, Metaxa or Bourbon may identify other people but in Turkey they drank *Raki*: anise in flavor, clear as water, smooth as sandpaper with an alcoholic content known only to Allah and the N.C.O. club.

Good Muslims never drink but for some reason they pass out just like infidels. *Raki* is so perfidious that even before the first swig it betrays the drinker. When mixed with water it turns milky so, when someone is watching, they drink it straight. Milky or clear, Allah will know right away and the next table soon enough. Devoted rakophiles had been known to lose their wagon or even the town they came from.

Some even misplaced Diyarbakir though it had stood reliably in the same spot for about 3000 years. Even at normal temperatures *raki* can be lethal but at 117 degrees a few vultures were seen circling at the periphery of the drill field. These birds marked the boundary beyond which MASH did not make house calls.

Instead we resumed the inspection of our new but untried hospital wherein a Turkish colonel with a yellowing diploma from some phantom medical school was eager to prove his mastery of the scalpel. With the language barrier, and hopelessly outranked, the situation was soon out of control.

The colonel opened the tent flap, pointed at a hapless private and bellowed: "YOU!!"

This monosyllabic exclamation is quite specific in English but mesmerizing in Turkish; all the more so when this officer wore a sword that was not entirely ceremonial. The obedient *askir* hopped on the table and the doctor took out his appendix. Instead of a congressional investigation, the patient returned (jogging as I recall) to his barracks to display his battle scar. Now everybody wanted one.

Somewhere near Diyarbakir there is a jar of formaldehyde packed with normal appendices.

Turks were conscripted without formal notification
since draftees knew better than the government how old
they were. On their eighteenth birthday the army will give
each recruit two pair of boots but he must be present to
pick them up. With a little luck one might kill a Russian.
Failing that, they could practice on Kurds just like their
daddy did. As long as six weeks before their birthday, boys
would be seen trudging from some remote village to an
appointment where none were late. Each wore an
astrakan, an undyed lamb's pelt where one lamb fits all.
When carrying groceries, Americans expect a choice: paper
or plastic. Since Turks had neither, every man, woman
and child carried his own square of netting with a purse
string of rawhide. This took less pocket space than a handkerchief—which nobody carried—and sufficed for the purchase of the day where oranges and eggs were bought by
the pair, not by the dozen. About a hundred Km from
Eskishehir we crossed a stone bridge, deeply rutted by
Roman chariots, and stopped for a draftee with a club foot
who proudly declined a ride. No mere limp would deter
him and the army could get used to it just as he had. He
probably didn't even have a note from his mother. When
he insisted on sharing a small remnant of black bread, we
took an obligatory bite which brought a smile I still
remember.

The Turkish army got a good one there. These recruits
funneled into various induction stations, including
Erzurum in the east, Trabzon on the Black Sea or Antalya
on the Mediterranean where Hadrian's gate has guarded
that scenic harbor since 130 AD. Its good condition today
suggests that Hadrian may still be around.

The road to Antalya had once been traveled by St.
Paul, but these sons of Islam considered Paul no more
than another infidel who did not live long enough to meet

Mohammed. Most of these stripling recruits had never even heard of such distant cities, but had no doubt that they would get there.

During parched treks they shuffled beneath Roman aqueducts, some of which arched for eighty Km, but now those stone ditches carried no water for them. From the turquoised dome of the Whirling Dervish Mosque at Konya, many followed the rusting tracks of the Istanbul-Baghdad railroad, romantically recalled since 1896 as the Orient Express. Like the Cedars of Lebanon, all the trees were only memories so fences were improvised by stacking Greek and Roman statuary, antiquities with nothing better to do. These were casually admixed with quarried granite from a Byzantine coliseum. One section was topped with engraved stone seats, most likely reserved in 130 AD by a wealthy malpractice lawyer who sued the royal soothsayer who scrutinized a goat's gall bladder and prophesied long life for the emperor who, alas, died the next day.

Protruding indifferently, as if to break the monotony, was the head of a marble goddess whose torso and ample stone breasts may be found in California where today they are worshipped by some head-shaven cult wearing designer togas. Even so, this was more respect than any Greek relics ever got in Turkey. Only the goats within these ornate enclosures were more indifferent to antiquities than their Turkish herdsmen to whom one acre of Corinthian columns looks like all the rest. A hundred Greek statues were no more than something for children to hide behind when playing Cowboys and Indians, locally known as Saracens and Infidels.

Far from our MASH tents and deep in a Diyarbakir bazaar was a magnificent tray, regally displayed on a silk Persian rug where the flickering yellow cast of a dozen candles enhanced its exotic beauty, much as a strategic light can show a cheap diamond to great advantage. Some old world craftsman had scrolled intricate designs into a heavy copper disc and tucked yards of gold and silver wire into cuprous canals, tapping the former into the latter with microscopic precision. This would add class to my office if I ever got out of the army. To take possession of this treasure entailed haggling with *Ahmet The Sinister*, a battle I was losing until Sgt. Joe McGlasson appeared, fresh from a recent bargaining triumph in Istanbul. Joe quickly summarized the finer points of doing business in the Middle East. The realistic monetary exchange in descending order was:

POUND - DOLLAR - FRANK - LIRE - DRACHMA - CAMEL - GOAT - SISTER

"A confident manner is essential. Stride disdainfully into the bazaar and belittle the merchandise. Wear a pith helmet. Swat a beggar with your swagger stick. They'll think you're British. Look constantly at your watch but don't sell it. This drives them crazy." Joe got the tray for ten lire, five diddly squats, and a pair of re-soled GI boots without laces. Ahmet, now a broken man, bolted the tent screaming Arabic invectives that required no translation. We later heard that he had gone over to the Russians. McGlasson, like any good sergeant, was a Greek scholar and in the dark catacombs beneath the marble gymnasium was chiseled a warning which he interpreted:

GLADIATORS! DO NOT SPIT ON THE GYM FLOOR.

Hellenic scholars from Bosporus to Boise have questioned this interpretation. But it seems so right.

When the call to serve their country was heard in central Anatolia, boys in Kayseri said goodbye to homes cut from ancient Cappadocian cones and caves which once sheltered Elijah while ravens catered his meals for forty days and forty nights. These Old Testament dwellings now displayed house numbers since Muslims don't rely on some fickle bird to deliver the mail.

Since inductees walked all the way, it took three weeks just to reach the enormous amphitheater at Aspendos, never knowing nor caring that it was built by an army returning from Troy where the siege had gone very well. Reflecting on these lonely, trudging youngsters, I had to re-think my derisive attitude about the intelligence of people who drive in reverse to save gas. This is child-like and has a certain logic for children to whom everything is new. Given the chance, children learn very fast. Every evening along the way, recruits were feted by generous strangers they would never see again, villagers who spoiled them with that unique hospitality which poverty begets. Proud huts flew the red crescent in celebration of a hero who was passing through.

Patriotism was never so eloquent nor so touching. My most enduring memory of these people was their devotion to those dusty draftees as they trudged on to duty that none questioned. We smiled at some of their curious customs, but the Turks taught me a lot and I learned to love them. But maybe because I'm not Greek.

McGlasson traded favors with another sergeant who needed penicillin for his concubine who suffered some undisclosed "condition." We had earlier mastered such benevolent reciprocity when dealing with the black market. They smuggled my tray out of Diyarbakir, securely packed with a valuable Persian rug, abandoned when *Ahmet the Sinister* fled his tent. After it arrived at my A.P.O. in New York, the post office carefully followed the usual sequence and shipped the tray to any state with a short name that begins and ends with a vowel—first to Ohio, then to Iowa, and finally to Idaho. No tray has ever traveled more. I planned a parade the day it arrived but Dad thought that this might conflict with the Caldwell Night Rodeo.

It has hung in the main hall, the reception room, even the laboratory, but it wound up in the bathroom where such art could be most appreciated. Or so I was told. With the studied humility of world class art collector, I awaited the inevitable compliments. My first patient had a better one which he bought at Sears.

CHAPTER NINE

The grand new office was indeed commodious when first occupied but seemed to shrink thereafter. Will's original solo practice was now a group of ten doctors plus a proliferation of ancillary forces—nurses in white uniforms, file clerks in green smocks, insurance specialists in blue skirts, and an interpreter in camouflage. The office manager kept order with a long black whip and got a raise any time he wanted one.

While the rest of his group sought more space, Will unselfishly relinquished part of his own to create an area for EKG's or post-venipuncture patients threatening syncope. This new recovery room was separated from Will's office by a thin wall and a stethoscope made it even thinner. It was here that I conducted vital research on Western Americana though others might misconstrue an ear to the wall as crass eavesdropping.

Today's subject was the unwashed Haywoods. This was not their real name. They had no real name. This grubby assemblage included three generations of a stone age family which were a sickening testimony to the brevity of gestation. After jump-starting a borrowed pickup, the Haywoods smoked into Caldwell, and before the manager could bolt the doors, they stormed into Albertson's and escaped with a truckload of groceries. They had food stamps but this was a training session. The little Haywoods were shoplifting neophytes and still required parental supervision.

After pillaging Albertson's, they laid rubber to the liquor store. Nobody had ever heard of liquor stamps but these welfare warriors counterfeited their own. These were green and red with a profile of Benedict Arnold and today prized by philatelists everywhere.

The grimy horde laid siege to 222 East Logan, where they de-trucked in descending intelligence except the smallest kids who were, of course, trampled by their elders.

Each had received his medical welfare card in utero along with a federal license to spawn forever. Any of the kids could have made the cover of *MAD* magazine. *Take This Job And Shove It* was a song written for them but they were perplexed over the word JOB. Siphoning the treasury without actually going to work is best accomplished by having more kids. The welfare mother's greatest fear is the menopause.

Extra chairs, pulled from under paying patients, were dragged down the hall taking special care to scratch new mahogany panels. Two of the stronger cretins commandeered a davenport which refused to bend around a corner until they removed the stuffing.

Only the office magazines were untouched since none could read. They demanded comics, complained to their congressman and the office got a nasty letter from Washington. The Army of Invincible Ignorance marched under the banner of multigenerational welfare with the battle cry: "We dare you to get us well." Ever sick yet never sick, they succumbed readily to television's disease of the month. Working folks play golf when they can afford it. The chief diversion for welfare recipients is going to the doctor. It's always free.

Television ads, once tailored to the twelve-year-old mind, were dropped to eight just for them. Today they all had a headache. Only the uterus enjoys, and, by God, deserves, more attention than your head. Once during his coffee break, Satan devised the nomenclature for headaches. Our singed copy smelled of brimstone but was still readable: *Exploding, migraine, frontal, occipital, nauseous, etc, etc. . . .* and continuing several pages later . . *.throbbing, splitting, sick, really sick, sinus, cluster, caffeine, closet (for gays), theatrical (hard to cure),or terminal (impossible to cure).* Recently our Surgeon General decreed three additions: *orgasmic (his), ovulative (hers), and overanxious (threesomes).*

The Haywoods suffered from the Chronic Remunerative Headache: "You didn't help us a damned bit. It took a chiropractor to get us well." What a relief to know that he could share such patients with the disciples of quackery!

"We're here about Gramma. Somethin's gotta be done." The doctor pulled out a four by six card and glanced at his Haywood record:

"Delivered seven kids at home . . . one in the swamp . . . don't believe in hospitals or paying bills . . . a touch of gonorrhea here and there but never enough to sterilize anyone . . . several house calls at their pathetic farm; dying sagebrush, flourishing cannabis, a few rustled cattle and poorly tended rocks." This lack of visible means of support did not reconcile with their standard of living because, every year since Ransom E. Olds first created his eponymous conveyance, these parasites somehow managed to drive a new Oldsmobile. The doctor who hoped eventually to own such a car suspected their income was significantly supplemented by operating a still, probably with copper tubing stolen from his office. This would be hidden somewhere up Succor Creek Canyon where they shot fawns every spring.

A second truckload of Haywoods arrived, so ten minutes was devoted to vulgar salutations and much goosing as the seldom-washed embraced the never-washed. Excitement peaked at the arrival of one niece from across the Oregon border. She had missed the last family reunion though her cage had been reserved for a month: "Muriel, it's been ages. You've put on weight. Is that tattoo new?"

So far they had ignored the doctor. He was counting his blessings. Eventually—no one knows why—someone remembered why they came:

"Gramma's doing lousy and she's only ninety-three. Your crummy heart pills make her worse just like she said they would. Your water pills are the wrong color so she just spits them out. She's got that there diabetes and thinks she caught it right here in your office. Everybody knows insulin is a bunch of crap. You know how stubborn she is." He knew.

For every diabetic it was his custom on the first visit to explain their intolerance to sugar and included the debt owed Banting and Best, Toronto researchers who discovered insulin in 1922. This was intended to evoke gratitude among thinking patients who reflected on a monumental discovery that saved a million lives.

But Gramma was a Haywood:

"Any medicine from a couple of Goddam Canadians can't be any good. I won't take it." And the doctor knew that too. After years of diabetic retinopathy and gangrene of a few toes, she made a further declaration:

"Sugar? Hell, I'll eat what I Goddam please." Will penned some quick notes: "The caprice of neglected disease has messed up her eyes and kidneys but spared her vocal cords." No wonder her physician thought she had died ten years ago. She was never weighed in the office because the scales stopped at three hundred pounds. For the very curious, there were always the grain scales at Crookham's warehouse. They never refused anyone but might stencil something on your back.

I was now joined by another sheepish doctor who was equally ashamed to eavesdrop but had no will power and a better stethoscope. There was a recurrent sonorous undertone but through the wall, one could barely differentiate between a belch and a fart until Charlie observed: "I believe the fart draws greater applause."

Two more chairs were dragged in from the waiting room, now unaccountably vacant, but one cowboy whose butt had conformed to bar stools decided to sit up higher than the rest. Soon there was the sickening sound of Levi rivets gouging their track across the polished surface of Will's pampered desk. Diaphragms on both stethoscopes shuddered. That roll top had been a gift from a grateful Basque sheepherder who always self-medicated his annual rattlesnake bite until one struck him in the neck. He surrendered to medical attention only after Will sent a nurse out to tend the flock. The teak and rosewood desk had come from northern Spain and was one of a kind (or had been).

Charles was distraught about that copper gouge because Will had promised him the desk when he was through with it. The way things were going, that could be tomorrow.

At frequent intervals, sticky kids ducked out and dashed to the bathroom because they got a real kick out of hearing the toilet flush, probably more fun than shoplifting. We could hear those happy sounds of childhood: stuffing towels in the ventilator, pissing on the floor or the frantic echo as two kids forced their brother's head deep into the toilet bowl before that final gleeful flush. Water seeping under the door meant they had a tight fit.

Meanwhile the adults, so to speak, got back to Gramma:

"When she ain't coughing blood, she bleeds from the bowels and then passes out. We think she does it for attention. My own crap is brown. My kid's are different shades of green. That's how I tell them apart. Can't really tell the color of Gramma's, what with the outhouse and all. It's dark as hell down there. Some welfare jerk brought us that there indoor plumbing we'd heard so much about, but it kept freezing. Goddam government! I'm gonna sue them. I won last time when the liquor store sold me bad booze and gave me a hangover."

I thought I heard my father loosen his collar.

"You said Gramma was too fat and had the guts to ask her to lose weight when you damn well knew that would hurt her feelings. You know how sensitive she is."

This was news to Will.

"She got her picture in the paper when she had her twelfth baby at 50. Then you warned her not to have any more. It hurt her feelings again. What kind of crap is that?" The captive doctor wasn't sure. Brown? Green? He shuffled cards back a year: Massive edema, frequent diabetic comas, black stools, hemoglobin 8 grams. <u>Not Pregnant</u>! Suspect colon cancer. Urge X-Rays with Barium enema. "Hell NO! Enemas aren't mentioned in the Bible (which she never read) and X-Rays kill people."

They knew all about X and used it to sign their names.

Charlie summarized the situation: "It is customary to trace genealogy through a family tree or, in this case, a weed. Gramma may never reproduce again though, God knows, the appeal is still there. This moribund matriarch is now used to checkmate a hapless physician being held captive in his own office. No buzzer can save him. Tomorrow there will be only memories; a deep gouge on his desk, a plumber's bill to fix the toilet, the charred circle in the parking lot where we gathered together to burn anything they sat on; all those little things that say so much.

"Just beyond this wall I detect some deeper motive. Why all this concern for the first time in thirty years? Let me guess. Gramma had a stroke. That's OK. Gramma can't eat. That's OK. Gramma can't shit. That's OK. Gramma can't talk. That's BAD. Why? Gramma always kept the keys to the still. Now they are hidden behind the uncertain curtain of aphasia. Without the still they might never drive a new Olds again.

(Charlie made medicine very exciting; part Mayo and part Agatha Christie. They had heard every voice except Will's. Could he have slipped out the window? They dared not hope.)

"With a myocardium thoroughly infiltrated by fat, her exhausted heart struggles to pump bacon-blood through choked arteries and quite frankly, IT LOOKS BAD. They have ignored morbid obesity, diabetes, heart failure and amusing strokes. Bloody stools are designated as 'strange shit.' It's what makes Gramma different. Since all medication was forever free it could not be any good. So it was vilified, discarded or, better yet, sold."

Charlie was not through. "After three generations of increasing dependence on the government, these recipients exemplify the Law of Unintended Consequences. As a result, the Haywoods are afflicted by the incurable CUD triad: Critical, Ungrateful. and Demanding. Finally, and just for variety, Gramma has a touch of hemoptysis where a neglected colon cancer has metastasized to her lungs. Easily the funniest thing yet."

Charlie's monologue was interrupted from beyond the wall:

"Dammit doc. I'll say it one more time. We want YOU to do something."

"What do you think?" Then from every quarter the office echoed:

"Yea doc, what do you *really* think?"

REALLY is a harmless enough word, but with the right inflection somehow implies that without it you would certainly lie. The doctor addressed the multitude for the first time and said what he *really* thought: "She *could* die."

THE BEAUTY WAS IN THE SIMPLICITY.

Some patients phoned for an appointment while others tapped impatiently on the doctor's window. Traditionalists still registered at the front desk while favored cronies were smuggled through the side door. This included some golfer ready to pay an over-due bet or the local priest prepared to confess a social disease. *Golfing Digest* was scanned by the former while the latter read *Playboy*. The office Bible was kept in the lab so the technician could refer to it and explain aberrant results.

Eventually patients in the main lobby became aware of side-door favoritism and demanded reform from which evolved an expeditious routing of humanity that became the envy of the western world.

Hal and Myrtle had been doctor and nurse for thirty years and, to avoid bottle necks, they devised a speedy communication system combining the best features of semaphore, sign language and mind reading. Myrtle was an Idaho farm girl who was never hampered by delicate Latin terminology:

"Snap into it, doctor. The babe in room three wants her vagina re-bored before her husband gets home from the army." The doctor dashed down the hall, but the patient was missing. So it was through necessity that medical pantomime replaced the spoken word. "Put the next lady in stirrups" took little work.

Hand signals soon became reliable, almost infallible, until one day at top speed, the fingers became a confusing blur. It was time for a pelvic exam and, just like a hundred other times, Hal beckoned Myrtle by raising his right arm and extending his index and middle fingers straight toward heaven. The signal was unmistakable. From Caldwell to Chicago, from Lourdes to London, from the Mayo Clinic to Allegemankrankerhaus auf Main—all of the medical world recognized this as the universal sign for a pelvic exam. What else could two fingers mean? Let me tell you. From the far end of the corridor another patient was leaving, to whom Myrtle smiled and said:

"That will be two dollars."

Names often appear in curious clusters. Some may be associated by ending with double consonants such as Derr, Batt, Foxx, Gott or Carr. Such coincidence erupted in the local hospital when, within a few hours, they admitted The Four Kings of Trauma:

1) Herman King suffered an acute hemorrhagic pancreatitis when his horse stopped before he did and jammed his belly against the saddle horn. Herman was barely out of shock when a stretcher brought in another King:

2) Davie King was a local paper boy who raced a Ford to a tie. His papers went undelivered while the lad was whisked to the Emergency Room with a ruptured spleen. It was during Dave's splenectomy that a notorious ladies' man joined the parade of identical names.

3) Stud King was shot by his wife, not once but twice, because she was really mad. Weeping nymphomaniacs from Payette to Mountain Home packed the waiting room, though most of them had alleviated their sorrow by picking up men in heat before the surgery even began. Does this sound like your waiting room?

Stud was hospitalized the longest due to .22 caliber perforations of the colon, duodenum and liver (and, as I learned with chagrin at his second operation, also the right kidney). Since Roy Rogers always packed a macho forty-five, all lesser calibers have been maligned as unmanly toys, yet when fired by a spouse who means business but hates noise, the .22 can be downright meaningful.

Investigators prefer this little gun when the victims are together in bed because Exhibit ONE stays in the mattress.

4) To complete this quaint quartet, the police escorted the King of Thieves, grand theft auto, whose bloody forehead bore the three pronged imprint of a Mercedes steering wheel. Starting in Florida, he sped and swore and swerved for three thousand miles—a long trip, to be sure, but he really liked this car. He picked up some bad marijuana in Nevada—my guess would be Las Vegas since Reno's was always high quality—causing him to miss a curve between Marsing and Caldwell. German cars usually stop just like ours, but the crash victim insisted that the same dealer who sold him bad grass had also stolen the brake pedal. Removing his handcuffs delayed the surgery while the cops ransacked the kitchen for donuts, pretending to hunt for the key.

All of the Kings got well but Stud King lost his regal ways with women and was forced to abdicate. My father was now retired but remained curious about anything unusual at the hospital.

"Dad, what would you say if I had four Kings?"

"I would say that is a very good hand."

❧

For the duration of any hospitalization, it will be an uphill fight to get your name back. Once those heavy glass doors close behind you, your name becomes a number which, while your back is turned, is transformed into some revolting pathological entity.

The receptionist wears a name tag because she is afraid the same thing will happen to her. Forget your birth certificate. You are now an inflamed gall bladder, a protruded disc, a thyroid adenoma or (who has not known one of these?) an anal fistula.

The patient's name will appear, of course, at the base of his bed where only the doctor can see it, so he can pretend to remember you. Caldwell's operating room supervisor always called for the next case in a voice that did not require amplification. When admonished she only grew louder: "Roll in the HYSTERECTOMY. GALLBLADDER to Room 3. HERNIA in 4." She finally decided to tone it down when one patient, anxiously awaiting a hemorrhoidectomy, turned and whispered:

"My surgery is very personal. Forget the alias. My name is Herb."

Because The Reverend W. A. Spooner taught at Oxford, he presumably knew lots of words but became famous by mixing them up. Other professors tried to ignored his slips from the lectern but no one could cover for him when "Our dear old queen" came out as "Our queer old dean." His speaking engagements declined but his name endured as the epitome of transposition. I heard my first major spoonerism over an archaic Atwater Kent radio when a commanding baritone voice introduced: "The President of the United States—Hoobert Heever." The memorable slips need not be funny but they must be mortifying.

I didn't deliver babies—the noise grated my delicate nerves—and whenever some pregnant lady found her way into my office, I sent her staggering to some one who did that kind of work.

One expectant mother hesitated to bother her obstetrician after midnight so, instead, she would call me to ask how come this was taking so long. I conjured a few classy

Latin platitudes but they seemed hollow. It was too late for *Caveat Emptor* to prevent a pregnancy and *Tempis Fugit* only made her mad. The months dragged on with two false labors and culminated with an IV drip of pitocin to induce delivery. Soon thereafter, I spied her, trim as ever, as she crossed the packed hospital lobby. I rejoiced at her post partum state and formulated a most original salutation: "I see you finally had that baby." Surrounded by strangers she waved and shouted. What she *intended* to say was "The doctor gave me a SHOT OF PIT."

Norman was a landmark. When Caldwell needed a new hospital, the city council town moved Norman first and then built around him. This old man was history wearing a tool belt. A massive moustache partially concealed a hare lip but never that perpetual smile. Norman knew who he was: "I'm a janitor, not a custodian. Custodians work in jails."

He was born at Givens Hot Springs in a long-gone two story hotel which had once been a most welcome stop for stage passengers travelling from Winnemucca to Idaho. Trail dust was washed away in the Givens Pool until it left the water muddy. Passengers were then sufficiently refreshed to roll on to Boise which was laughingly called a destination since there were few others.

Norman was home-schooled on an isolated homestead and learned to read and write just like his parents, which was very little. His only brother was killed in a runaway, which left Norman to tend the sagebrush alone. Aside from a commanding view of the Snake River, the family farm had little to offer. The Great Depression peaked right here where alkali blew under every door and rabbits got to the alfalfa before the cattle had a chance. On the bright side, gopher tails brought two bits a dozen. His mother's butter-and-egg money had gone to Boise surgeons for multiple attempts to repair his cleft palate but eventually speech therapists in Spokane had abandoned him to a lifetime of hypernasality.

Norman was hard to understand but a wonder to watch. Frozen cogs, stubborn levers and dead switches magically succumbed to his wizardry. No squeak escaped his oil can. Every sound was muffled because noise was anathema to convalescence. Every patient was HIS. He sought to emulate the quiet atmosphere of a library, a cathedral or perhaps the total silence of the local high school gym when Caldwell had a losing basketball team. His domain included the parking lot, where a single wave of a callused palm silenced hot rods and even the hospital administrator's motor cycle.

Though he had never seen an elevator before, he soon commanded this one to go up and down (sideways if you preferred). I was stranded once between floors but was not completely alone because the thoughtful Norman had just rolled the hot food cart aboard. He never left the hospital because, in his absence, something might break.

Norman ate lunch with a knife, a fork and a wrench.

But mechanical triumphs were not enough and he hankered for something more intellectually stimulating. Medical centers in far-off California were using a new-fangled embosser to print identification tags, so our hospital bought one even though we already knew everybody's name. The device arrived with a dozen blanks upon which Norman was to print: Radiotherapist, Inhalation therapist, Physiotherapist. There were others but you get the idea.

Beyond the forgivable misspelling, the spacing was tricky and the wastebasket soon overflowed with rejected tags. They ordered more blanks (twice) and soon the Caldwell Memorial Hospital was over budget. It would have been sensible to abandon the entire misadventure but young trainees had already stolen white coats from the physician's lounge and threatened to quit if they couldn't wear name tags just like doctors on TV. They craved recognition more than graduation and the diabolical embosser now took on a life of its own. Finally, in tactful desperation it was suggested that Norman should stamp only THERAPIST which would cover all variants and at least avert a student insurrection. The spelling was perfect but the spacer betrayed Norman when the last thirty tags proclaimed: THE   RAPIST

BUY RUB-O
RUB IT ON BRISKLY
SEE HOW IT RELIEVES
THE IRRITATION
CAUSED BY THE RUBBING
                                    ~ Henry Morgan

Galileo was branded a heretic for observing that the earth orbited around the sun. Propelled by job security, the pope insisted that the earth was the center of the universe so people must, perforce, revolve around the church. An orderly universe begets an obedient congregation. With the weight of superstition on its back, scientists crawled slowly through the resistant mud of the middle ages. They corrected their mistakes but the rejected falsehoods were collected and legitimized by GAG, the Grand Army of the Gullible. They mustered in Europe, crossed the Atlantic, stopped in Salem to hang a few witches, bought a printing press and later a TV station. The IQ of a cult leader is usually lower than that of his flock but GAG also recruited many college graduates.

(Which has nothing to do with IQ.) Education should convey immunity, but the susceptible elite seem eager to embrace any mystic cult that blends alchemy, pyramids, magnets, astrology and pin ball machines. The master con man can predict the end of the world and administer a high colonic irrigation while you are waiting.

Reputable physicians are at a disadvantage. They are trained to be accountable while predators can promise anything without personal consequences. If a fraudulent nostrum kills somebody, Congress responds with a new law to impose harsher restrictions on orthodox medicine. Responding to lobbyists, their laws exempt the quack who has a constitutional right to earn a living—or a killing. Veterinarians go to school for many years to take care of your dog, but humans will turn their lives over to a high school dropout with a nice smile. These pretentious opportunists don't even know what they don't know, but they do know the way to the bank.

Foreign origin and an exotic label seem to possess unique therapeutic powers. Just across the border, is a perpetual array of novel cancer nostrums where Mexican Laetrile is still in vogue. Most Mexicans are too smart to use this junk, but gringos think it smells like almonds. Even more expensive was Krebiozan, the rage of the 1960's, which came from Yugoslavia and any drug smuggled that far had to be good.

Why do we allow unscrupulous opportunists to milk the wealth of desperation from the cancer cow? Because their victims fall into predictable categories: 1) Patients actually cured by orthodox treatment but simply refuse to believe it. 2) Those who never had a malignancy in the first place. The devoted neurotic can magnify dandruff into cancer. 3) The incurable: "We could have cured him. Why did you wait so long?" This masterful alibi shifts the blame north of the border where some uncaring doctor intentionally delayed alternative treatment.

The jet replaced the propeller. This is called Progress. Penicillin replaced the poultice. This is called Profit. Voodoo and electromagnetism have been revived by any quack who can afford a forged diploma and an hour on television.

With an odious mix of arrogance and ignorance, pitchmen who flunked high school chemistry lecture on vitamins and belittle the profession that discovered them in the first place.

THE KING'S BEEN SHOT!
SOMEBODY CALL A CHIROPRACTOR.

The doctor had rendered his usual quality care but the patient refused to leave while customers piled up in the waiting room. Every physician dreads this costly impasse but she was determined to tell all about her sister's miracle. She probably thought Will was a priest. The object of this particular marvel had failed to conceive after five years of marriage, and cruel neighbors whispered about Barren Barbara.

Infertility clinics had failed. "All they ever did was take her money." Finally her childless sister consulted a highly recommended chiropractor who palpated her spine professionally and frowned theatrically. With facile grace he finally homed in on her *Baby Vertebra*. Behold! It was seriously misaligned and obviously responsible for her infertility. Incompetent M.D.s had so long ignored this vital bone of fecundity that multiple manipulations would be necessary. Weekly visits would be good. Daily would be better. Money was no object. Sure enough! In just four months she was pregnant. "Doctor, what do you have to say about that?"

"I would say that the chiropractor was not sterile."

Joe flew his B-17 over Berlin until there was nothing left to bomb. Winning the war was important, but by then he was addicted to flying.

After the war, his planes kept getting smaller until there was room only for Joe and a few canisters of insect spray. Crop dusting was less satisfying than bombing Nazis, but at least he was killing something. Surrounded by pressurized poisons, he exterminated various pests throughout Southwestern Idaho where every emergency room knew him on sight. Lord knows, he flew well enough. It was that crazy cargo. Most medical cabinets kept an ampule of prostigmine with his name on it.

Sophisticated antidotes struggled to keep pace as sprays became more chemically complex. Joe tried them all. Toxicologists were just a phone call away at Idaho State University and, without Joe, the Pocatello Poison Center would be nothing. One lowly pharmacology instructor was promoted to full professor just because he exchanged Christmas cards with the famous but oft-poisoned pilot. Insurance was a problem, and the only agent who would cover him was another pilot who worked out a sliding scale whereby the lower Joe flew the higher his premiums.

Through his enormous respect for power poles, he had already outlived most of his contemporaries. Memorizing the terrain paid off when he was temporarily blinded after a defective valve filled the cabin with noxious fumes. He suddenly remembered a nearby canal and, with uncanny timing, he ditched the plane and jumped upstream while the current sluiced the toxins downstream toward Wilder (where nobody much cared). He straightened the prop and anchored the wings with a little baling wire, and his Stinson was ready to fly again.

Despite federal admonitions, the Geological Survey hired him for some aerial photography but, instead of mapping the designated area, he shot ten rolls of the Jarbidge River as it coursed from the Humboldts to its confluence with the Bruneau. This would give him an inside track to the biggest native trout in Idaho. He should have hired a photographer, but hesitated to share this piscatorial cornucopia with any other man. Flying about three feet above the water, Joe spotted a pool teeming with trout but had to drop even lower to see what flies they were eating.

Yes, he did clip the wing but only because he released the controls to hold the camera. It could have happened to anybody . He would have straightened the prop again but couldn't find it. Pilots do well in the air but have trouble on the ground. Range bulls occasionally leave the plateau and wander down into box canyons where Jarbidge water and knee high grass sustains them, but they grow surly in isolation without any attractive heifers.

There are also rattlesnakes down there but these are innocuous when compared to a snorting bull at close quarters. The quick-witted pilot remembered that nothing distracts man or beast like a camera. The range bull, now known as a canyon bull, had never been photographed before and is probably still posing. Joe finally climbed to the rim where he was relieved to see a rescue squad, but it turned out to be the Geological Survey who had come to cancel his contract.

Most of his aerial pictures were blurred but one revealed a group of happy-go-lucky rustlers, huddling over a sagebrush fire, branding cattle that were not theirs. The governor's brother in law was sharply defined and the negative alone was worth two hundred dollars.

Between crashes, Joe continued to give flying lessons while wearing a body cast which is more restrictive than a seat belt: "Learn to fly. All it takes is me and money." It took me two years, maybe three, to solo, which entitled me to read flying magazines. *The Crash and Burn Gazette* had recently featured Joe on the cover.

By then, I was hanging around the airport, wearing a leather helmet and a long white scarf. Nobody noticed.

One August most of Joe's fractures had healed when he touched down and hurriedly took on gas. The breathless pilot explained that he had hit the jackpot.

Crop dusting or blackmailing the governor paid well, but controlling the current grasshopper infestations was a pilot's dream since it meant federal money and the usual obscene budget. Was he headed to pick up more spray?

"HELL NO. I work for the government. I'm going for more grasshoppers."

Herman was the master of auscultation, a craft he perfected in North Dakota. During one midnight blizzard, the weary doctor was summoned to the home of some cardiac cripple but it was all a ruse. Grandpa was fine but the pipes were frozen. The family needed the stethoscope and medically trained ears to follow the water's turbulence until it suddenly stopped. The family supplied the blowtorch. The doctor can't bring everything. The icy embolus melted. Water flowed. The family rejoiced. Grandpa leaped out of bed, completely cured. A blowtorch triumphed where digitalis had failed.

Such duplicity would seem unworthy of this ethical German community but Herman could overlook it since he was as German as the rest of them. He had not acquired that Lawrence Welk accent at some eastern medical school. His last name was so ludicrously polysyllabic that his signature required an elongated prescription pad. He preferred to be called Herm, but that was not even the part that needed shortening.

During the long drive home, he was hailed by a forlorn figure and the doctor stopped more out of curiosity than compassion. No sane man would dare venture out in such forbidding weather. He was lightly clad but proved to have even less sense than clothing. He hadn't seen Grand Forks in a while and tonight was the night. God said so. God had probably just paid his bar tab. By relying on prayer instead of preparation, he routinely implored the Lord for his transportation. If no car stopped, a voice told him it was even OK to lie down in the center lane.

Suddenly the doctor had a vision of his own: "The Lord has his hands full. I don't bother him unless it's important, but I do try to keep communication routes open. Now I know why my prayers are rarely answered. Nobody else can get through because people like you keep the lines tied up." By now the car smelled pretty bad, and the hitch-hiker declared derisively that he had no particular destination. The driver nudged him out at a spot precisely fitting that description.

Herman's fame as the master of auscultation spread as far as the Mayo Clinic where Rochester had frozen pipes of their own, hundreds of stethoscopes, and probably a blow torch. The uglier the winter the more his phone rang. Maybe someone was sick, but more likely it was just too damned cold to call a plumber. Reason enough to take a job in Idaho.

My father and I escorted Herman through the local medical museum but he had already seen most of the artifacts: "Back home, I worked with tools just like those." Herman was an inveterate hunter and only low flying geese could make him late for the office. His first patient recoiled, thinking the goose blood was human. Always stuffed in his trunk was a pair of Ted Williams white thermal coveralls. Crawling on his belly, he could pass for a Finnish ski trooper sneaking up on an unwary Russian, until one sub-zero morning, he thought he recognized some ganders he had known on the Missouri flyway. He ground sluiced another man's decoys and it was too late to blend in with the snow. After profuse apologies, he shared his thermos of coffee and was so contrite that he picked up a new patient.

From goose hunters alone, Herman built up a huge practice. Geese tolerate the cold better than pheasants. Herman had been spoiled in North Dakota where China roosters froze in the field and could be harvested without firing a shot. Idaho pheasants never froze and had the gall to fly or, worse yet, run forever. A year's supply of shells could be gone by noon. With such expensive hunting, Herman worked nights and weekends just to support his habit.

When studying abdominal X-Rays, it is not unusual to visualize a cluster of radio-opaque pellets in the right lower quadrant. Idaho radiologists recognize these as buckshot. Depending on how fast you chew, some shot is inadvertently ingested and wanders downstream to eventually lodge in the appendix.

In Canyon county this is one way to tell patients apart.

Herman's pellets were number 5's. Mine were 7-1/2.

CHAPTER
TEN

To day's backpackers owe a profound debt to those early woodsmen who, pungent and hirsute, blazed Idaho trails in the days before dehydrated food and designer boots. They did not really eat rocks or wrestle grizzlies, but by discarding hyperbole and distilling the useful, our generation can benefit mightily from their pioneer experiences. These woodsy tips could spare you an expensive helicopter rescue:

Bears are black. Cougars are tan. Hunters are orange. Porcupines are not as edible as they say.

Be sure that the warranty on your back has not expired.

Some World War II packs have a hole in the bottom.

Never adopt a bear cub, even the cute ones.

Bring a coat even if it's out of style.

A loose lid on the syrup can sweeten your entire pack.

Matches dropped in the toilet should be replaced, not dried.

Two left gloves do not a pair make.

After two weeks, sugar and coffee are the same color.

Avoid camping with a doctor.

When you run out of food, try an old Indian trick; retrace your steps and find a cafe.

After the age of fifty, bring either cheese or toilet paper. You won't need both.

Don't rent a llama because folks will think you are a Buddhist, and there's a lot of bigotry in the woods. In any event, some myopic hunter will mistake it for a mountain goat, so you should never stand too close.

The Idaho elk season is not official until some hunter shoots his own pack animal. At checking stations, game wardens try not to be surprised at the variety of trophies draped across the hood of some Mercedes. One common Idaho aberration is a dressed-out mule with an elk tag in its ear. This would embarrass the average man, but a Californian can even explain those horseshoes.

With the passing years, there are additional risks which are unique to the primitive area. Not every bearded recluse is a picturesque mountain man. That side arm suggests that he may be growing marijuana. And an Uzzi means he has a bumper crop.

SOME GELDINGS DESERVE IT.

After the war, four Idaho boys had some ammunition left which was just the right caliber for a trophy elk. One hunter's belt sagged with a Nazi dagger, recently liberated, but adding a German Luger caused his pants to fall off.

We slept in goosedown sleeping bags, dined on T-bone steaks and read Biddle's Journal of Lewis and Clark by the camp fire. In 1805 *The Corps of Discovery* often relied on dogs—roasted, boiled or even shish ka-pup—but these latter-day *voyageurs* renounced authentic pioneer cuisine and opted for bovine over canine. We snacked on Hershey bars which soften in hot weather but can be reconstituted by brief immersion in a cool stream, an old Indian trick. Through some misguided mistrust of chocolate, this crowd preferred Pay Days which don't melt. This candy bar is covered with peanuts which can also be used to trap squirrels which are quite tasty with forest mushrooms, of which the most beautiful species are poisonous. Four bottles of Chardonnay were broken en route by an abstemious pack horse which frowned on drinking and already disliked these over-dressed hunters. After the first mile on the trail, a brand new Stetson blew away and a mule stopped to pee on it. This never happened to John Wayne. After the Nazi surrender it had been Sam's onerous duty to destroy any arms confiscated from German homes. For several agonizing days, scores of priceless old guns succumbed to an electric hacksaw, but this sergeant salvaged one pristine rifle which just happened to be the length of a GI duffel bag. Quite mysteriously, it wound up in Idaho. This beautifully engraved Austrian Drilling featured a side-by-side 16 gauge shotgun mounted over a single 9.3 x 74 mm rifle barrel which fired a 270 grain cartridge.

Where the Selway joins the Lochsa, a huge bull with a splendid rack had never seen such a gun and moved up to admire it. Curious elk are an easy shot. When dressed and quartered with a Nazi dagger, the meat was contested by a snarling blur of fur, claws and fangs.

Wolverines are fearless carnivores, forever eager to re-affirm their legendary ferocity. They are usually associated with Michigan where they are seldom seen but nevertheless claimed by a football team to enhance their reputation in the Big Ten. With such an intimidating name, it's hard to explain how the Wolverines could ever lose to the Golden Gophers of Minnesota whose mascot is a subterranean rodent, more pungent than golden. The foul disposition of these Lochsa wolverines emptied the camp faster than an accordionist playing *Lady of Spain.* This ugly pair were begging to be shot, but instead Sam pulleyed the coveted prize up to a high limb. It remained beyond their reach, but the tree took a terrible beating. It would have been better to surrender the elk since the meat was tougher than the antlers, and we could not stick a fork in the gravy.

To compound the insult, the packer threatened to sue the group because his horses refused ever to work again. Beyond the fire, beady eyes surveyed this mutiny with approval. Wolverines not only growl. They can snicker. The entire Lewis and Clark budget was far less than the cost of a 20th century elk hunt. However, the hide made great gloves which averaged out to $475 a pair. This is a bargain compared to bagging a half ton grizzly and hiring a taxidermist.

No one goes thirsty in the Sawtooths. By just standing still almost anywhere, parched hikers can hear the sound of water. Not so in the Crags. Here the adaptable limber pine declares that these are Idaho's driest mountains, their trails, the dustiest.

There is an unmarked spring near Cathedral Rock and four miles later an equally obscure trickle near the base of Mt. Aggipah. For the backpacker accustomed to the Sawtooths, there is a tendency to hike right past these because he is not thirsty. *But he soon will be.*

Every trailhead evokes high hopes. Your pack seems light (you're standing still) and it's only three miles (not even close). Trail signs point to assorted lakes and, just for laughs, include the distance to each with the tacit promise: *Trust me. I'm from the government.*

Markers are cut from rustic pine and shaped like an arrow as if the Indians had something to do with it. Actually these Forest Service signs are distributed from Ogden, Utah, because Mormons do such nice work. Most destinations, even when you know better, seem to be three miles but only because the jammed Ogden router was stuck on three. For the five to ten mile range, three is close enough. For serious mileage you might see 13 but a three is always there (unless it's 30 when they leave off the zero). Some signs have been corrected by disgruntled woodsmen who like to whittle. Conflicting advice is nailed to a single post: RIGHT, LEFT and GO BACK. People come from everywhere just to experience the Idaho wilderness, and guessing their origin is part of the sport. Each group is unique. Misspelled words mean New York. Spray paint means Detroit. Arabs write from right to left just like kids from San Francisco. One well-carved spruce proves that sexual deviancy is out of the closet and into the woods. The reaction of bark to trauma varies with the species, and aspen lacerations may turn out as either cameos or intaglios. One unfortunate Douglas fir has been the recipient of complaints about the IRS and other oppressive bureaucracies. It has been carved high, wide and deep with such fervor that the Great Tax Tree seems to be dying. Certain comments border on treason which the tree has sealed with patriotic pitch. Reading between the lines, ax marks on a fallen signpost testify to a really bad trip. 'Tis now time to forget those misleading signs and place your trust in equally unreliable government maps.

Just at cloud level there is a pass of grueling granite between Gentian and Ship Island Lake where a million alpine flowers cling to every cleft as if to prove that you are on the right trail. In the shimmering valley below, bear grass blooms in profusion and in another mile you can hear Waterfall Creek shouting that it could have no other name. With such spectacular scenery the destination hardly matters.

Actually, after dark it *does* matter.

The switchbacks up to Ship Island Lake carve two miles of granite, and at many turns fellow hikers could be out of sight for several minutes. Periodically, like hippies in a harmonic convergence, several climbers might be stacked vertically in puffing proximity.

It was here that a furtive man devised his diabolical plan to move to the head of the pack. Ray, the master of deception, always made the first cast and every year his trail mates almost admired his creative duplicity. On the steep ascent there was more sweat than oxygen, and every time they passed on a switch back, Ray would fabricate some pointless question. The winded victim always answered, to which Ray only said "HUH?" This was repeated at every zigzag—one short question, one long answer and huh—where courteous men, of course, responded until they were cyanotic. Aching lungs were wasting precious oxygen that they had planned to use for other things.

Two men staggered and collapsed under a solicitous spruce while the third sprinted ahead. Once again the cunning Ray would get his line in the water first. Luke wondered aloud, "Why do we let him do this to us?" Will confessed: "On the way up I once even thought of pushing him off the cliff." Luke shrugged: "You would have been forgiven since Ray is a New Dealer and God—of this I am certain—is a Republican. Remember last year? We saw his pole leaning against a tree and concluded that he was out gathering firewood." The crafty Ray had carried two rods and one was only a decoy. When no wood turned up they caught him sneaking to the bank on his hands and knees. Overcome by admiration, his companions murmured, "What a guy!!"

A three pound veteran rainbow scanned the shore of Ship Island Lake for the impending arrival of Idaho's foremost fishing triumvirate. Fish don't get this big without knowing the characteristics of their antagonist: A) Ray caught the most. B) Will managed the biggest. C) Luke's creel was usually empty. Dogs and cats liked Luke, but fish were cruelly indifferent. It was not that he didn't feed them. He just never got his grasshopper back.

Luke took solace in the scriptures and remembered that on the Sea of Galilee even Christ's disciples were not always lucky and learned not to bitch about it. Today, however, after ten years in third place, his patience was about to pay unexpected dividends. With a smug smile and a sagging creel, Ray arrived at camp never dreaming this was to be his day of atonement. As always, Luke would do the cooking because his hands never smelled like fish and the aroma of those frying onions was enough to tease a Sioux out of North Dakota. So far they had not seen another soul when Will thought he glimpsed movement across the lake. Luke agreed: "I can't quite make out that hat but it looks like a ranger to me." It was common knowledge that the Curse of the Crags patrolled this area. He was relentless, incorruptible, and tougher than John Wayne. Even the Forest Service was afraid of him.

A few years before, an over-limit fisherman had tried to bribe this ranger for which he was shot on the spot. This happened only once but you know how those stories can circulate. In one variation the body was staked to a tree as a warning to other game hogs but this is not true, certainly not in a state with a Republican governor. The figure vanished along the north shore though a preoccupied Ray never looked up from his piscine bounty. Suddenly the hiker returned to full view: "I think you're right, Luke. He's Fish and Game and coming this way." Luke had better eyes, having never strained them cleaning fish, and started to say "no" but stopped short with a sardonic grin. An opportunity with unlimited possibilities flashed through his inventive mind. After a decade of settling for the bronze medal, he listened as the wheels of justice began to grind:

"Ray, don't let him catch you over the limit. Grab your creel and disappear. Don't make a sound and we'll get rid

Mother moose has fenced in her calf because it's so ugly.

of this guy." Ray dove headlong into a narrow pup tent accompanied by every mosquito not otherwise occupied. There they remained trapped behind a tightly zipped tent flap ready to feast on a prisoner immobilized in a canvas nightmare. Only at that moment did Will see that this stranger was no ranger but the show had begun. From this very moment, a couple of amateurs would improvise an Academy Award performance with a script handed down from heaven and edited in hell. The newly arrived "Ranger" could be the star. During his escape, Ray had

jammed the odorous creel ahead of him so he was now facing the rear of a stifling tent, inhaling fish caught hours
before and ripening fast. Rigidly confined in sweltering
heat and fearing suffocation, he confessed to God the sins
of a game hog and swore to mend his ways. The answer to
his prayer came from a voice beyond the tent: "Welcome
mister. Pull up a rock and have some coffee." Through the
drone of insects the prisoner could hear the guest slowly
sipping from a mug that only this morning had been his.
Such camp encounters were usually no more than a cordial exchange of fishing tips or maybe sharing half a candy
bar. But this evening, after an effusive welcome, Will and
Luke surprised their guest with unexpected hospitality.
The Challis National Forest had never known such glee
since Lewis and Clark crossed the Lemhi pass.

"How's the coffee? Too hot?"

"Just right."

"Have some more. We've got plenty." After another
gallon or so, the victim in the tent dared to hope that the
guest quaffing from another man's mug might convulse
from a caffeine overdose. There are things a suffocating
game hog hates to hear and here's one: "How about another pot?" That was the voice of his beloved brother-in-law.
The trustworthy Luke had never let him down but now he
would have to drown him—*first thing in the morning*.
Mosquitoes, probably piqued over their confinement,
sucked all the blood they could handle but a few gluttons
persisted—crimson, bloated and belching. Ray had never
seen six inch welts before. Surely it could not get worse . . .
but it did.

Will decided it was time to chime in: "We have a stack
of huckleberry pancakes left over from breakfast. They are
great with peanut butter but maybe you'd prefer Luke's
favorite, bacon grease." The stranger smacked his lips: "I'd
be a fool to say no to that." Doubly betrayed! A second
Brutus had thrust the blade even deeper. Will had been

Swinging bridge, recently desmantled because too many people enjoyed it. There was nothing on the other side anyway.

his fishing partner for years and easily his best friend . . . until today. Now he would have to drown him too. What a lousy fishing trip.

With a sinking sun the fictitious ranger felt compelled to move down the trail but even this was painfully prolonged: "What hospitality! I haven't eaten pancakes since my wife left me." He wanted their names for his Christmas card list and Ray roused from his coma while they searched the woods for a piece of paper. These things take time. Before leaving there was one last question: "Who's the guy in the tent?" And the tent came alive, filling the woods with decaying fish and assorted oaths. Aspen quivered. Spruce dropped their needles. Cougars sprinted for Wyoming. Skunks thought it was something they did.

The trembling dinner guest regretted ever meeting these people and was about to return the pancakes when suddenly the victim smiled through his welts and actually began to applaud. Ray had ignored humiliation by realizing exactly what had happened and how much he deserved it. He appreciated the spontaneity and ingenuity but most of all he marveled at the unlikely perpetrator, a patient man who had been cleaning someone else's fish for ten years.

Never before had Ray so admired his brother-in-law. There are jokes. There are pranks. This was genius.

Later, well beyond the odor of dead fish, three silhouettes hunkered by a campfire which soon flickered low as if to complement a sky full of stars close enough to touch. The same power that wrote the scenario which turned a lowly ranger into a star, had established the firmament eons ago, but it seemed He had tailored it for this very night.

After an hour of silence the Idaho woods heard the last words of the day: "I'll bet you were mad enough to drown us."

I daho rarely made the papers unless an important politician got lost in the woods or if someone shot a trophy elk out of season. To the New Yorker we were still Iowa. This worked both ways because many westerners thought Lake Erie was a state.

But once, for two weeks, Idaho made the big time.

Loon Lake was destined for national wartime fame, later eclipsed by the Normandy invasion, but still lingering locally as cracker-barrel lore. In Idaho's back country, one winter is just like another, and Loon reposed in icy silence until 1943 when, on February 13th, a McCall bush pilot was ferrying supplies to snowbound mining camps at Warren and Yellow Pine: The *Idaho Statesman* quoted Penn Stohr who "noticed the tops of a string of trees had been clipped off on the south shore of the lake. Then I saw the army bomber. It was a two-motored plane and it was lying on its belly at a 45 degree angle to the lake about 50 feet from the shore . . . wings sheared off as the plane landed. The fuselage did not appear to be damaged. They had a flag pole stuck up on a log stage they had built on the ice of the lake with one of the men's shirts flapping in the breeze."

On 29 JAN 43 the bomber had crash-landed at Loon where the fuselage still marks the path and the wings are not far away.

A B-23 from Tonopah to McChord Field had gone down in a blizzard, and Stohr's sighting was not until two weeks later. With the prop still turning, Penn unloaded, practically jettisoned, his supplies and returned to the crash site to pick up five survivors who, so the story goes, were extremely glad to see him. After two weeks of starvation these airmen were not as heavy as they used to be but still more weight than the plane could safely carry in one trip. So twice Stohr landed his ski-equipped Travel-Air on dangerous ice. The Douglas B-23 carried the secret Norden bomb sight and the army was upset about some civilian prowling around just to rescue some freezing crewmen. If Penn had any felonious intent, there was not enough remaining daylight for a third landing to haul away a bombsight; and even if he had stolen it, no one in McCall could afford to buy it.

Just before the crash, through chattering teeth, the pilot, 1st Lt. Robert Orr, discussed the options and a short list it was. In a hurried vote among the seven aboard they vetoed parachuting into blinding snow, realizing that even if they didn't hang up in the trees they would be hopelessly scattered. Out of fuel and with a momentary window in the clouds, they were allowed just one attempt to land on the ice but Loon Lake is not very big and never intended for this sort of thing. They overshot into the trees where they were doubly blessed with limber jackpines to ease the landing and no gas to explode. Attesting to God's intervention, there remains even today a wide path of topless trees, scalped by some heavenly lawnmower.

Crash injuries immobilized four at the site, but two days later as the radio failed, Schermerhorn, Freeborg and Pruitt started down a narrow canyon in waist deep snow and waiting ahead was another forty-two miles of the same or worse. For two sub-zero weeks in increments of fifty yards, the lead man pushed the snow ahead while the two following awaited their turn to be the plow. When the crust was not thick enough to bear their weight, they crawled on all fours.

They had salvaged a shotgun but most game had better sense than to be out in such weather. A few feeble-minded squirrels ventured out to see if it was spring yet, but it takes about a dozen of these to sustain life. If the shotgun pattern is too tight it takes a lot more. There was no time to cook the meat and fur is hard to swallow.

Two airmen struggled into the McCall ranger station on February 18th, and a search party snowshoed back to the CCC camp where Pruitt remained with frozen feet.

Since his toes didn't fall off, he was not discharged **nor did he ask to be**. After 1943 there was still plenty of war left, and hikers who ever since have passed that crumpled fuselage are bound to wonder what happened to the crew. Every man survived and was sent to various theaters of the war—some with snow, some without—and so thoroughly scattered that they never saw each other again. While the crew were thawing out, the characteristic military solution was to render the plane useless even as a refuge for elk hunters for whom getting lost is part of the hunt. Army brass suddenly materialized (this doubled McCall's population) and commandeered a dog sled after screening all dogs to exclude any Nazi sympathizers. One suspicious Dachshund was rejected, but with those short legs he could never pull much anyway. They accepted a German pointer who passed as English. Thus was dispatched a squad to machine gun the fuselage, as if it hadn't been through enough already. Rather than a dog sled, the locals suggested aerial strafing which would be good practice with no risk of returning ground fire. However, GHQ was not too keen on sending another plane over the primitive area. Word gets around. It was only after the army was sure they had won the war that Stohr was commended for his heroism. By that time the old Norden bomb sight had been replaced by the Sperry and the Russians had stolen both.

In 1991, the *McCall Star News* reported that Ed Freeborg, now sixty-eight and living in Portland, returned to fly one more time over Loon Lake. After fifty years, most of McCall's citizens had not heard about Ed or even his war. Sgt. Freeborg was encouraged to amplify on his saga. A touch of exaggeration, or even fabrication, might rejuvenate a tired old story which, frankly, nobody in the following generation wanted to hear again. Perhaps that frigid ordeal of forty-two days in deep snow could be improved with some Hollywood effects. Adding a woman to the story might help. Perhaps one of the sled dogs could be a bitch. But Ed was laconic, more Portland than Hollywood:

"We were young and just began to walk." That was it. No drama. No frills. His succinct summary speaks volumes about the men who fought a war from which so many did not return.

For Penn Stohr this was not his last adventure. Airplane drivers went out of their way to shake this bush pilot's hand, hoping some of his luck would rub off. Neophytes listened and learned from a pilot who could double their life expectancy.

While other intermountain airports were improving, Idaho's seemed only to get shorter. With a plane that was never in a hangar, Penn lived most of his life in the air, and that 1943 bomber wreckage was only one of many he spotted. A small forest fire was a good tip. Many remote strips along the Middle Fork of the Salmon were unforgiving cul de sacs where you got just one chance. There was no level ground but landing uphill slowed the plane down and when you turned around it gave the mandatory boost on take off. Mid-air collisions were rare because "the nearest plane was most likely in Montana."

Once off the ground, bush pilots banked safely down river, never up. But if a careless flyer took a wrong turn those to whom he had just waved goodbye heard the ominous sound of a Lycoming engine straining to escape an enclosing canyon. Then suddenly they heard no more. Penn knew where to find the plane which would not be far from two other wrecks.

The lure of the primitive area was the main reason to fly, and once they had soloed, beginners adjusted their goggles and headed for Indian Creek or dirt strips even smaller.

Stohr held impromptu clinics at places like Johnson Creek and Meyers Cove, dealing with recurring mishaps and the predictable personalities that invite them:

Survivor returns 48 years after 1943 bomber crash at Loon Lake. (Star News, McCall)

A) The important doctor compelled to hurry back to the hospital no matter what. B) The confident lawyer who, after many triumphs in court, could only conclude that he

Miner's cabin, Salmon River. When the gold petered out, prospectors stuck around just for the view.

was equally invincible in the air. C) The veteran who took off overloaded in the heat of the day, though it had not seemed all that hot after a couple of cold beers. D) For hunters, Penn left nothing to chance:

"When there's no room inside the aircraft, don't strap your elk to the tail."

More than once he had walked away from "unanticipated" forest landings which are often fatal to pilots and always hard on planes.

"Pick your spot before it's picked for you. Trees may be bad but big rocks are worse. Look for a grove of aspen (the white ones) or young lodgepoles (the straight ones) which when struck (caressed) near the top might be sufficiently limber to ease you down to the ground. If all you have are large Ponderosa, try to slip the ship between two that are separated at least the width of the fuselage. Wider is even better. It's OK to shear off the wings. This will help slow you down. Just watch the nose. That's where you are. You can fix the plane later."

He survived several unanticipated landings and established a record no one cared to surpass. Penn continued this humdrum routine until June 20, 1957, when he and his 1929 Ford Tri-motor died together near Townsend, Montana, where none of the trees were quite suitable. His admirers were inclined to blame the Montana forest rather than the Idaho pilot. The sister ship continued to serve Idaho back county for many years and today that tri-motor has been beautifully restored by his son.

Penn was somewhere else when I first saw the Loon Lake plane, a hike sustained by five salami sandwiches and a light dinner wine. After half a century, old machine gun holes and new vandalism remain as a tribute to eight indestructible airmen, one valiant pilot and the durability of aluminum. That glorious old wreck would attract more spectators than Mount Rushmore if the trail were better.

The most curious survivor is the leather pilot's chair with faded arms intact. The seat belt and a few twists of wire anchor it to a water-logged fishing raft. Hikers always inquire about Idaho's famous floating anachronism. If you have the time and like to travel, why not tramp into Loon Lake and wait on the shore? Before you run out of salami, some lonely backpacker will rush to embrace you even if he never had one friend back home. This is a lonely place.

The conversation is predictable: 1) "Is this Wyoming?" 2) "Are you going to finish that sandwich?" Answer these two questions anyway you wish because you are only waiting for the third: 3) "How come that fishing raft has such a swell seat?" Now has he unwittingly set the stage so you can do justice to a little known chapter of a European war, partially fought in Idaho snow.

Embellish as you see fit, but stop talking before dark because it's hard to sleep in a plane where wind whistles through a hundred bullet holes.

If he doubts your story, just whisper that his purloined sandwich, delicious as it was, contained elk dung garnished with just-picked mushrooms of questionable origin. The last man who ate one had a convulsion. Then point the way to Cheyenne.

EVERY DAY IS A GIFT.
THAT'S WHY THEY CALL IT THE PRESENT.
~ Paul Harvey

After flunking basic woodsmanship I lost my merit badge for fire building when an alert scoutmaster confiscated my lighter fluid. I got even by showing him tracks leading to a cave. He pushed ahead only to awaken a hibernating bear. Promotion to Eagle Scout was now out of the question. The lesson was clear: Better a Boy Scout travel with someone who smokes than borrow matches from a stranger. All subsequent knowledge of Idaho's mountains evolved from a series of misadventures because success is a less instructive teacher. For pre-war hikers, camping under the stars could mean a merit badge, but the night sky lost its luster during the campaign in northern Italy, which was now deep with snow and thick with Nazis. Facing them were Americans, hurriedly shipped from North Africa and still wearing summer uniforms. Such flimsy attire was ill-suited for the Alps until Sam appeared at dawn wearing his sleeping bag, creatively modified with two holes for the feet. This improvised attire covered the stripes of rank but woe to the imprudent soldier who failed to recognize his own sergeant. They looked like penguins but the enemy learned not to laugh at them.

It was now ten years later when the veteran penguins again succumbed to the siren call of the Sawtooths. Had the European campaign taught them anything? Apparently not.

TOXAWAY LAKE, headwaters of the Salmon River.

5:00 a.m., Mountain Standard Time. Four shivering mountaineers jockey for position around a struggling fire. 5:05 a.m. Some klutz trips over the coffee pot which extinguishes the fire. I am summarily ostracized. Nothing else worth mentioning.

ARDETH LAKE, headwaters of the Payette River.

6:00 a.m. We are a year older and getting up an hour later. Reluctant fire nursed with just enough kerosene (no merit badge for this) to thaw the same frigid quartet. Coincidence, God of the Klutz, repeats last year's coffee pot mishap. Fire drenched. Box of matches also wet. Justice is swift. Culprit banished to the deep woods. Old pals keep his boots. Friendship running thin.

CRAMER LAKES, headwaters of the world. Here is a scene to fill a Thomas Moran canvas, but he died before he could paint it.

Like a queen and her court, four shimmering lakes are joined by waterfalls and create a calendar foreground with multiple reflections of Mt. Cramer, a regal peak with a diamond-shaped crown of white granite. This dominant landmark makes the tacit promise: "Keep your eye on me and you will never get lost."

However an asterisk at the base of the diamond refers to a footnote a thousand feet below where 'tis chiseled: "Don't count on it in the fog."

Cramer Lake, from an oil. Painted by a grateful patient who didn't expect to survive her surgery.

On the shores of middle Cramer Lake, four campers, colder but wiser, stoke two fires: one for cooking and holding bears at bay, and another, six feet away, just for coffee.

This year my boots have been returned without the laces, but I am still on probation and must remain outside a circle drawn in the frost. Its thirty foot diameter seems overly insulting, and I am relegated to scrounging for wood. As a sullen protest most of it is wet. The group is distracted when somebody hollers BEAR! The surly wood gatherer sneaks inside their damned circle, stands too close to the fire and scorches his boots. This evokes hilarity of the crudest sort. I retaliate by kicking the coffee pot, only to learn that I am the only one who hasn't yet had a cup. My Cramer Lake adventure ends with acute caffeine withdrawal.

Moving eastward to another range might change our luck. Despite sketchy maps and imaginary trails, we somehow made camp at the base of Castle Peak where the snow never melts. This year I brought an extra pair of boots, intending just to photograph the scenery and drink coffee. From my sleeping bag I heard quaint forest sounds which, alas, included those of a porcupine chewing unguarded boots. Only hot coffee could assuage my grief but the pot had tipped over. The porcupine? Not likely. While my boots nourished the porcupine, the focal plane shutter froze tight on my Leica, which is now for sale (in case you are interested). The only documentary of this trip was a postcard I picked up in Challis.

Chamberlain Lake lies above timberline. No wood means no fire but nothing boils at this altitude anyway. And I couldn't burn my boots. Here was the only lake where we ever caught California golden trout, perhaps the best thing to come from that state. Though reputedly delicious, this fish is only fair uncooked. Since I had selected this site, the other three conferred without me. I remained a member of the group because the only black ball available was an elk turd.

We moved our camp down into the trees with acres of dry wood, but unfortunately the granite boulders never separated the width of a sleeping bag. This situation was conducive to insomnia until the benevolent camp physician dispensed 1-1/2 grains of Nembutal—White Cloud Rock Softeners. In a single night I was forgiven all those drowned fires and modestly accepted my new role of camp hero, knowing it could not last long since I had forgotten the toilet paper. But they would not know this for several hours and, even then, one at a time. You would not think that spilled coffee, burned boots and toilet paper could evoke fireside insults for another twenty years . . . but they can.

As the years passed, these backpackers with stiffening joints came to envy men on horseback who smiled as they crowded us off the trail and moved on to commandeer the best campsites where they also ate better. Hiking lost its appeal. My boots were about shot anyway. The transition to horses should be simple but my saddle kept falling off. Among our group, Charlie alone understood livestock and bore the permanent stamp of a boy raised on a Kansas farm. On his arrival, horses whinnied in the next county. Mares went into heat. Intractable mules begged for a burden just to admire Charlie's diamond hitch that never slipped. By contrast, I was Idaho-born and had learned absolutely nothing.

I went to rodeos only for the hot dogs. Charles recommended mounting the saddle from the left side, a revolutionary concept, but even when I was aboard, my stirrups dragged the ground. One still aches at the end of the trail only in different places, and the animal selects the campsite, preferring grass over scenery. The experienced rider has a customized saddle but I was too modest to have that part of me measured.

After years of backpacking by the ounce, a horse now hauled provisions by the pound. Men who once had rationed dehydrated food were suddenly transformed into unrepentant trencherman and gluttony ruled the woods. It was pay back time for all those Spartan breakfasts and twenty thousand calories should just about do it. Without shame, we stacked flap jacks you could hide behind. Syrup seeped up our arms but never enough to hamper eating. Each platter was a monument to culinary stratification with a thick slab of ham as a foundation so the load would not shift. Then in ascending order: six eggs, hash browns, sausage, fried onions, biscuits and gravy. Somewhere in this obscene mountain of food was a rasher of bacon, whatever that is, but it must be small since ours got lost. There was one sprig of parsley.

Just within reach of every diner was a gallon of coffee heated by its own private fire. All I could kick over was my own. Which I did. There was one sad note. We were so preoccupied with gluttony that one starving squirrel, hoping for a crumb, ventured too close and we ate him.

One more confession: With stomachs dangerously distended and squirrel fur in their teeth, the mountaineers lapsed into a state of euphoria, and rather than wash the dishes they casually tossed them behind a giant mountain ash with enough berries to hide a truck. In defense of this crass assault on the environment, these doctors dismissed it as high altitude hypoxia. The evidence was later uncovered by a Mormon scout troop and reported to the Sierra Club. This case is pending but we still must explain that missing squirrel since the Challis National Forest is one short.

The size of this group never varied much and distilled down to four. We were not exclusive. No one else wanted to join. Ads in the *Idaho Statesman* drew no response. For thirty years we were drawn to those mountains for the enigmatic ritual of the unshaven and pungent to refuel the myth that last year's disaster had been a triumph.

Somewhere in Idaho dwells the perfect camper. He never burns his boots. His coffee is always hot. He never gets lost. But who wants to travel with him? When nothing goes wrong there can't be much worth remembering.

As the group cartographer rolled up his maps, he proclaimed, "Enos Lake is hiding in the Payette National Forest, somewhere north of the 45th latitude, east of Oregon and west of Montana." With a touch of repressed optimism, he finally concluded: "If we pay attention we shouldn't wander into Canada but I have researched Alberta just in case." Planning these trips cannot be taken lightly. Magellan had gone through the same thing, and though his crew finished the voyage, Ferdinand didn't make it back. The Enos Lake expedition could be in trouble because for orientation, most surgeons are inclined to consult an anatomy text. Since Charlie had moved here from the flat lands of Kansas he revered the mountains more than most. He stopped frequently to admire the peaks which was also a welcome opportunity to take on more oxygen. His group had to be scrupulous in planning their route because if half a dozen doctors got lost the rest of the world might not be too quick to send out a search party. Disgruntled patients seem to be everywhere. The backpacking standards were not too high because this year a Baltimore psychiatrist would join them. Mac was conducting a well-funded study on why Indians seem to be normal and psychiatrists are so crazy. To achieve balance and dilute the doctors, there was one musician who had once auditioned with Artie Shaw but before he could sign a contract he was drafted and sent to Korea with the band that won the war.

When Bill got back to Idaho, the world had forsaken anyone who could read music in favor of 1000 watt guitars which were often short-circuited by "artists" urinating on stage. For three years this bunch had probed all the wrong routes to Enos, attempting the Loon Lake Trail twice just to admire the wrecked B-23 bomber which made Loon Lake famous in 1943. We preferred summer travel because during winter, the plane was often occupied by hibernating bears. A compass was about as useful as holding a cross in front of Dracula, since these innovative doctors had recalibrated theirs by bending the needle . . . but just a little. During one failed attempt, we had started up the Secesh River which shores were once settled by

Confederate secessionists in the 1860s, a sentimental choice because its tributaries drained from the south. Their progeny now look like the rest of us, though they can still effect that obsequious drawl when begging for credit. Following blaze marks ended in disappointment at the base of a Douglas fir which was pathetically hacked by the tomahawk of some lovesick Brave: BEAR-IN-HEAT LOVES MOONEYES. A romantic inscription to be sure, but no help today. Trails in the Payette were poorly maintained because Idaho's budget was siphoned into the Sawtooths, prompted by the proximity of Sun Valley's vulgar wealth. Forest Service toadies even built a bridge over Hell Roaring Creek so snake skin boots would not get wet.

Payette rangers did their best with what they had and nailed up trail markers in the back country. These were always inaccurate, but just seeing them was reassuring. It meant somebody else had been here and, since there were no skeletons around, they probably made it back. After annual abortive attempts, we decided to descend Lick Creek summit and avoid Hum Lake, named after mosquitoes planted by secessionists in a subversive effort to infect abolitionists with malaria. The trail divided and one arm coursed north. Time to flip a coin. Shamefully, I repocketed my quarter when the rich Baltimore psychiatrist produced a Krugerrand and promised we could all take turns flipping it. We followed dust, measured not in inches but feet, only to find the trail divided again: west to Twenty Mile Creek (the name says it all) or east along Loon Creek which was known to be haunted. An Indian hex must be strong medicine because, behold, next morning the sun rose in the west.

The woods grew intimate, but eventually opened onto wind-fallen trees which taxed footwork and abandoned the hiker eight feet above the forest floor with a choice of jumping or, if no one was looking, creeping back on hands and knees. Eventually we escaped this maze to flounder in the shimmering green chaos of chaparral which resisted every step like some unseen linebacker determined to push you out of bounds. The crest was not far away, ready to confirm that the air is thinnest just when you need it most. At 9287 feet we straddled South Loon Mountain with each boot hugging opposite sides of the peak and toes pointing to different states. Suddenly, triumph dispelled dyspnea when directly below was Enos *himself*. The prize was not large, measuring less than a mile east to west, but very deep and obviously with a lot of personality. After eluding us for three years, Enos beckoned at 45 degrees 5' 30" N. and 115 degrees 50' 20" E. Today's panorama was doubtless more welcome than the one seen from that plummeting World War II bomber.

Bill: "I saw a fish jump."

Sam: "That's over a thousand feet down."

Mac: "He was big enough to see from here, and there were two."

Charlie acquiesced. Charlie wanted to believe. But the day was almost gone, and this would be the year just to survey the scene. It was a long way down, longer coming back, even longer after dark. The General Staff devoted the remaining daylight to planning next year's strategy.

These were not the precipitous cliffs of career climbers with cams, crampons and carabiners. However, the descent would deserve cautious respect where shifting shale extended almost to the lake shore, and your arrival could be quite premature. Emerging here and there along the shard slides were clumps of struggling pine and alpine brush. Our group would return with several lengths of rope to serially anchor one island cluster to another; enough to facilitate descent, save your pants and maybe your life. Ropes were precautionary, some might say cowardly, but we would be lugging out heavy creels and with ropes we would look like real mountaineers. It would be

Loon and Enos Lakes are not this close together from the ground.

next August before *THE DAY* when we stood transfixed on the banks of Enos Lake, almost reluctant to cast lest reality kill the dream. Every past disappointment was rewarded with such teeming generosity that we did, in fact, need ropes to haul out the fish. Our campfires were the first. We met trout that had never even seen an Indian. Enos was the lake of which it could be truly said: Two flies. Two fish. Voracious rainbows bent many hooks but we brought extras and soon every man's creel was full.

But not for Sam. Early that spring with ice still on the shore, he had kayaked alone down the South Fork of the Payette River while his usual boating comrades decided to wait for the water to simmer down. Sam had written about class V rapids for several outdoor magazines and his exploits were widely admired by veteran river runners.

The man who had conquered the Middle Fork of the Salmon, even the Fraser in Canada, drowned on a far less famous river within sight of Idaho Highway 21.

Sam's billfold contained the usual family snapshots plus one of Dale, his high school buddy who had died in the war. His sons inherited his fishing gear in which they were surprised to find a dog-eared Forest Service map where one lake was circled and its coordinates noted: 45 degrees 5' 30" N. 115 degrees 50' 20" E. In the margin near Enos Lake he had added a big red exclamation mark.

After Will, Ray, and Luke found the route into Ship Island Lake, the next generation launched mountain conquests of their own. Backpacking for them would be facilitated by recently acquired military training. Their fathers had been forced to rely on the obsolete methods of World War One. The local boys were so confident that I even recruited an old medical school classmate who now practiced psychiatry in Baltimore and was actually proud of it. Johns Hopkins had just published his last paper: *Modern Psychiatry's Answer To Impotence . . . Kill Yourself.*

Psychiatrists have no shame and Mac arrived in a coonskin hat (just like the one I wore in surgery). He completely reorganized the group, appointed himself treasurer and to the rest assigned code names: Jack, Bobby, Teddy and Genghis. We had planned for Ship Island Lake in August, but instead found ourselves trying to start a wet fire in the chill of September. With typical eastern duplicity, Mac blamed his tardiness on the time zones. The difference between Baltimore and Boise was not two hours after all . . . but one month. And we bought it. Natives of the Mountain Time Zone are gullible by nature. Many don't even own a watch.

The mercury cracked the bottom of the thermometer and the group was trapped in the Second Great Ice Age. It may have been this year's stew or last year's dish rag, but the long night ahead would be forever engraved in the annals of bowel pathology. Back in the civilized world, it is mandatory that next to every toilet is an issue of the *Reader's Digest* and it is not *bone fide* diarrhea until you have read this from cover to cover. At Ship Island Lake, only a foolish man would dare violate a contract with his bowel. At midnight a cry arose. Mac had been stricken in the prime of life. Cramps may be a personal matter, but diarrhea involves depletion of the entire camp's toilet paper. This particular dysentery was that western greenish variety so debilitating to the eastern colon.

At first his hasty tent departures were quite civil as he excused himself for stepping in my face when he was still continent.

Barely audible peristalsis advanced to an ominous roar, signifying a bowel in total revolt. His flashlight failed completely. The night before it had seemed dim while reading *The Ultimate Forest Survival: Cannibalism. . . We taste a lot like chicken.* Speed was paramount, but while both hands struggled to bend the frozen tent flap, the toilet paper blew away. Through the endless ordeal, fearful cramps hurled him into the darkness. Into a tree? He didn't care. Over a cliff? He didn't care. Idaho's Big Horn Crags had seen dehydration, even delirium, many times but tonight the cliffs echoed the trembling mantra of a man failing fast. How many nights until morning? His last plaintive cry was largely muffled by a howling gale:

"This time I may not get back. Just tell my wife a bear ate me." But he was not that lucky. Bears are too smart to eat what has already made a human that sick. Without a flashlight he never found the same spot twice, but by the light of day his trail was clear enough. Since no horse would go near him, trusty comrades rigged a litter and carried Mac down the Cathedral Rock trail, stopping occasionally to prop him up for a picture. He was a big man but easy to handle once he lapsed into a coma.

The victim recovered but probably suffered some brain damage because he returned the following year. We agreed to cook nothing, avoided the dish rag and ate only candy bars.

This time, the tent flap did not freeze shut, and the psychiatrist's camp notes culminated in a scientific monogram that shook the western world, following which Mac was inducted into the International Psycho-analytical Society where even normal members wore purple suits.

His monumental work conformed to the customary rigid medical format: a prospective, randomized, placebo-controlled study with a ten page bibliography and a forged endorsement by Sigmund Freud.

For several years, our camping bible had been "Identification of Edible Mushrooms That Can't Quite Kill You." This classic was superseded when every trail mate received a package from Baltimore (with postage due). Mac had sent each of us a leather-bound reprint of his critically acclaimed dissertation which was presented in London in English and later, in Paris, by his French mistress.

The title was tastefully embossed in gold:

HOW I KICKED THE PAYDAY HABIT

CHAPTER ELEVEN

CRAZY HORSE WAS SPUNKY.

~ George Armstrong Custer

Eighteen seventy-eight was a bad year to be a doctor at Silver City. An early snow had clogged the Dewey Toll Road, stranding a dozen freight wagons with a predictable effect in food prices or, God forbid, whiskey.

The town physician was expecting medical supplies, primitive potions which had changed but little since the Napoleonic Wars. Ambrose Pare, Bonaparte's battlefield physician, would have felt quite at home once he grew accustomed to the domestic wines. Everybody in Silver City seemed to be grinding something, from ore through a stamp mill to some pharmaceutical powder from Dr. Purdy's mortar and pestle. A week before the blizzard the victims of a mine explosion had exhausted the morphine supply, and the doctor had to requisition a few vials of opium from a Chinaman who would probably go into withdrawal, trading one emergency for another. It would be another sixty years before penicillin hit the scene so, until then, gonorrhea would be free to run its capricious course, including urethral strictures and—with a little luck—sterility.

Otis Purdy learned patience from listening to his father's sermons where he sat immobile for three hours every Sunday, four if the devil was gaining ground.

Sweating in August or shivering in January, he and nine siblings packed the front row bench built for six. These cramped little Christians pretended to concentrate as Dad intoned exactly what they would all hear for the rest of the week. Reason enough for Otis to come west for his health.

Purdy was a contemporary of the legendary Doc Holiday who coughed all over Tombstone, but coming West did not improve his health either. On the other hand, Holiday was a dentist and in the days before anesthesia a lot of patients might want to kill him.

Nothing was going right in Owyhee County. Ten years earlier the pine and juniper on War Eagle Mountain had been stripped for firewood until the terrain above ground was as inhospitable as the tunnels beneath. Mine shafts collapsed. Miners drank too much. The former only aggravated the latter. Chinese had been easy to rob but were starting to fight back, and those ragged dagger wounds in the neck were hard to suture without ligating the carotid artery and a tourniquet was out of the question.

Back in good old China, their ancestors once discovered gunpowder but relegated its use to harmless firecrackers. But this generation knew all about dynamite and occasionally punctuated grievances by detonating a few sticks. When miners brought grimy shirts to the Chinese laundry, the proprietor handed them a bar of soap with succinct instructions. The demand for Mail Order Brides soared, but delivery took six months and most refused to do windows or laundry. The once affable superintendent at the Blue Bucket grew testy. Ore carts jumped the tracks every day for no special reason. Why can't people get along?

Silver production sagged and Pittsburgh bankers who built this town, turned up the pressure with angry telegrams, followed by Pinkerton detectives. Could things get worse? They could.

Buffalo Horn didn't have to immigrate. He was born in Idaho back when it was called something else. Like his father and grandfather, young B.H. thought he belonged here. Indian tribes were in turmoil and those eastern emollients applied against Mohawks and Seminoles were rejuvenated. Sarah Winnemucca urged her father to pacify his restless Paiutes.

She made the chief realize that it took eighteen years to grow a new Paiute warrior whereas the supply of white soldiers seemed inexhaustible. Even Chief Tendoy moved his Lemhis to Lord knows where. But farther south, Pocatello's peace mission was shouted down by angry Bannock braves who were starving at Ft. Hall. Buffalo Horn shouted the loudest.

A treaty with superfluous signatures had promised the Camas Prairie to the Bannocks but a government clerk, the archetype of those hired today, had typed *Kansas* instead of *Camas* and, naturally, refused to correct the error. Telegraphers tapped the happy news over the *Long Tongue* (verily, Indians are poets) and hundreds of homesteaders steamed west on the *Iron Horse*. The Midwest poured into the Far West. Camas bulbs that had fed the red man for a thousand years were plowed under.

For every million stolen acres, our condescending government graciously named some forlorn town after an important chief. As a consequence, a vengeful Indian spirit haunts two of these cities to this very day:

1) Winnemucca, where the pale face still waits for his first Black Jack.

2) Pocatello, where the wind blows all the time.

Dr. Purdy probably suspected that nobody lived forever, and Buffalo Horn should have known that the Indians never win. The Nez Perce had just tried it up north where their teepees, made perhaps from second class buffalo hides, collapsed under Gen. Howard's cannon, and Chief

Joseph's hegira through deep snow was further hampered by hungry women and children.

The Bannocks hoped to do better since Buffalo Horn left the missus at home and he had better war paint. The pale face had been around long enough that there were many half-breeds who should be only half-mad, but they too were raging up the Bruneau Valley and heading for the Owyhee mines.

The Bannock War—Idaho's last—was sporadic and pathetic. Whooping braves raided Innskip Station at the Ruby Ranch and worried the folks inside. After the attackers ran out of arrows they burned hay stacks and stole a few horses. (Years later I took my kids there to collect arrowheads, many of which were still buried in the walls of the fortification.) Painted warriors shot up the countryside until they happened to ride by a familiar Jordan Valley ranch. The owner had often hired some of them to break horses, so they dropped in for lunch and a nice chat.

Then the next farmer offered a jug of firewater, and the war was on. Responding to this Indian crisis were the Silver City Volunteers. After his cramped childhood in a church pew, Otis should have known better than to sit in the front row where now he was nominated to lead the SCV who already bristled with fifty caliber Sharps and thirty caliber Springfields.

Twenty-eight Caucasian citizens were joined by Paiute Joe, an Indian who really needed the money after a poker game with a Chinaman the night before. Those with poor eyesight carried shotguns. One sadist packed a knife. Scalps were no longer in vogue, but you never know.

The town doctor was elected as their leader because there is no more formidable foe than a good shot with a death wish.

During the Battle of South Mountain the combatants chased each other over the hills until the Indians ambushed their pursuers in a canyon where the SCV

Unmarked grave. Don't know where. I was lost myself.

encountered bullets instead of arrows; whereupon the volunteers concentrated their fire on the chief. According to Sarah Winnemucca, it was Paiute Joe who killed Buffalo Horn.

This assassination by substitute could ease the Caucasian conscience and really caught on. In July of 1878 a Umatilla traitor brought in a head to claim a reward.

A torso was not worth much unless it was a well-stacked squaw. As if to confirm the importance of doctors in the West, Dr. J. A. Fitzgerald, the army surgeon at Emigrant Springs, verified the head as that of Chief Eagan. The assassin was given to believe that the check was in the mail but something may have been lost in the translation.

It worked again in 1890 at the Standing Rock Agency where Red Tomahawk stood guard over Sitting Bull and shot his famous prisoner in the back of the head. The reward was small because it was such a close shot. Nearby was the chief's circus horse, a gift from Buffalo Bill Cody and trained to perform under the Big Top. During the ensuing melee the horse took his cue and began to perform his tricks. Surrounded by indifferent humans, one loyal animal observed the death of a chief the only way he knew.

Enlisting indigenous warriors began in the French and Indian wars during which Gen. Braddock urged Chief Hendrick and his two hundred Mohawks to attack a much stronger French position. The canny chief responded with an eloquent economy of language which the white man has yet to learn. *If they are to be killed, too many. If they are to fight, too few.* (from "INDIAN WARS" by Robert Utley and Wilcomb Washburn)

Every Mohawk died with his chief but that was way back East and a long time ago.

The volunteers finally holed up at Three Forks where some were wounded and Purdy died. Now Silver City would need a new doctor but even if its citizens found one, would his wife be happy in a small mountain town with no shopping?

The front page of the *Owyhee Avalanche* described the death of Buffalo Horn with those graceless verbs and degrading adjectives which became so fashionable right after Custer's misfortune just two years earlier. Many other Bannocks died but nobody could spell their names.

The *Avalanche* also detailed the final rescue by the cavalry dispatched from Ft. Boise . . . alas, too late, since this was not a John Wayne movie. Here was an opportunity for the editor to vent his vitriol about the territorial governor whom the paper had never endorsed in the first place. There is a portrait of Buffalo Horn at the Idaho

State Historical Library, a handsome countenance much like Anthony Quinn, though perhaps a little too much make-up. It has always been hard to attract doctors to the Owyhees, but it was really tough after the BIG SCARE of '78

It's tougher today since Silver City has a population of ten.

CONSCIENCE: THE MOTHER-IN-LAW
WHOSE VISIT NEVER ENDS
~ H. L. Mencken

Caldwell High School exhorted their Cougars with a stirring fight song for which they claimed originality until a Notre Dame alumnus, who happened to be passing through, insisted that he had heard that tune before.

Boise was even more shameless. They not only plagiarized *The Stars and Stripes Forever* but had never even heard of Sousa. Boiseans also knew nothing about Beethoven, Shakespeare, or Moses. These are provincial folk for whom just living in Boise is quite enough.

Football hopes faded for the mighty Cougars when their finest receiver left to join the Royal Canadian Air Force. Because Goering's Luftwaffe always looked so sharp, Dale's uniform seemed rather drab, but he spent the rest of the war shooting down pilots who were better dressed than he.

Aproned mothers were in a canning frenzy—apricots from Council, cherries from Emmett, and from Sunny Slope, patriotic prunes. But when these zealots shipped asparagus, it was obvious that England was desperate and might lose the war. Fortunately the Basques sent chorizos and the tide of battle changed.

Bundles for Britain jammed the freight depot until they ran out of CARE stencils. Cheerleaders who had just learned how to augment a sweater in the right places renounced pompoms for knitting needles.

Hollywood was cranking out new war movies, but they were slow to reach the hinterland, so Canyon County natives applauded old dog fights between biplanes piloted by actors in leather helmets who had died in their sleep twenty years ago.

"Playing at a theater near you" never meant Idaho, unless Hollywood shipped the can by mistake. Then, one happy day, Errol Flynn finally came to the Roxy Theater, and Caldwell knew they had the right war.

Juvenile students finally got their chance to serve when a group of adults, who should have known better, organized restless seniors into a Citizen's Salvage Corps whose first assignment was to scrounge the hills for usable wood.

To enhance the war spirit, Sam reported for duty wearing medals his uncle had saved after World War One. Unfortunately, these had been bestowed not by Gen. Pershing but Kaiser Wilhelm. This was awkward for Sam, but educational for the rest of us of who had no idea that we had fought Germany long before we were born. During wartime rationing, the government was restricting gas consumption and folks willingly drove on thin tires which, by VE day were quite bald. Citizens accepted this so well that, despite a surplus, sugar was rationed just to make a point. Old planks—if there were enough of them—might defeat the Nazis.

The C.S.C. began with juniper fence posts until an irate rancher explained the difference between salvage and thievery. His persuasive wife carried a 30-30, so they shouldered their crowbars to assault historic Silver City whose aging wood might have won the Crimean War but was certainly too late for this one.

The roofs were most accessible but once these were stripped away the walls could not stand for long. But when haven't vandals posed as patriots? Self-appointed captains—remember, these were full grown men—led adolescent privates in a war effort that excused anything.

Our salvage leader was the high school civics teacher, and students who praised President Roosevelt got the best grades. Since his dad was an ardent New Dealer, Sam's A was assured. By relying on my basic obsequious nature, I was hoping for a B, a dream soon shattered when the civics teacher passed my father's yard which was dominated by a huge poster supporting Alf Landon. Teachers must wield a lot of power, because my family's candidate lost in four successive elections.

Dangerous mine shafts covered old claims where ten thousand souls once labored and one whimsical sign still warned:

DONT FALL DOWN THIS SHAFT
MEN ARE WORKING BELOW

Our next assignment included removal of straining timbers from abandoned mine shafts until one of the smarter kids (not me) wondered if these might be all that kept the tunnel from collapsing. Detecting this uneasiness, the civics teacher promised that they could keep all the gold they found. The captain himself never entered the tunnel . . . something about claustrophobia.

The mine supports grew weaker and Sam suddenly remembered a question he had missed on a history exam concerning collective bargaining. If the mine had been abandoned once, it certainly could be again. Each tossed in a dime for dues and they were instantly unionized.

It would be evening before the truck came to haul the erstwhile miners back to Caldwell, so they puttered around the empty Stoddard mansion wondering why anyone would build a house so big in a town so forlorn. Windows were boarded up with just the lumber we had been hoping to salvage, but better judgment prevailed. Folks this wealthy probably could hire a security guard forever. He could be watching them right now. Sam said he could feel it.

The Stoddards had enjoyed a commanding view of Silver City and since there were still several weathered chairs on the vast verandah, we leaned back and parked our heels on the filigreed railing pretending to be rich mine owners but fooling no one.

Even larger than the mansion was the Masonic Hall above whose door 1862 confirmed the alliance between silver bullion and the Civil War. Just to the north, a white Catholic church had survived a hundred winters and, at least in Silver City, Masons and Catholics were separated by no more than a shallow gully.

Just beyond the rusted tin roof of the Idaho Hotel, a two story plank building had housed the *Owyhee Avalanche* where a Confederate editor exaggerated Indian raids and predicted victory for the South even after Gettysburg. Adjacent to the newspaper was a massive bank. The publisher had intentionally selected this neighbor to impart an undeserved aura of stability to a paper which otherwise had none. Four giant strap hinges secured an iron door to the stone bank walls which separated the *Avalanche* from the ubiquitous Chinese laundry. There had been a few sacs of gold dust under the laundry floor, and stealing this was safer than blowing up a bank. But dynamite works both ways, and burglary took a change for the worse when one crafty Chinaman devised Silver City's first booby trap.

Since zoning was an eastern fad, private homes leaned hard against commercial sites and most were crowded around the town's only fire hydrant.

Names on a dozen homes were too faded to read but it was safe to assume their owners were all dead. Sure enough, they could be reliably identified just across Jordan Creek in a be-weeded cemetery which sadly testified that six children in one family died during a diphtheria epidemic in 1870.

Soon depressed by weathered tombstones, we hiked up War Eagle mountain and sifted an Indian cave for arrowheads. This is dusty work, but considered fun if you're young enough. Then, about two miles down the creek we stumbled across an abandoned frame house which was destined to make us rich for exactly two hours.

Al had found an arrowhead in the cave, and was so imbued with the Indian spirit that he wore a feather and went barefoot until our group crossed the sagging porch which was littered with broken glass. Those pesky shards of lantern chimney can fester subcutaneously for several weeks. We later learned that the smarter Indians wore moccasins. This misadventure became the basis for Al's special report on foot hygiene and the only 'A' he ever got. We crouched through an aperture where leather hinges dangled from a plank in search of a door. Even the cobwebs had cobwebs.

The room was papered with old newsprint which had been makeshift insulation against Idaho wind reputed to be quite crisp at seven thousand feet. The exposed pages were sporadically dated throughout the 1920s when the mines were nearly exhausted; probably the last decade these walls required beautification.

There were many strata and the deeper we peeled the older they got. Most papers were from Pittsburgh, home of Silver City's major investors, and rich ore from The Blue Bucket lode had paid healthy dividends since the 1860s.

Sam remembered that Owyhee gold had helped win the Civil War.

For which side? He wasn't sure.

Ore cart, empty as usual. "Money isn't everything" is a cruel aphorism. It isn't even true.

Midst reading and peeling, they imagined themselves as those archaeologists in pith helmets who excavated eight layers of ruins before discovering the original city of Troy. Very exciting stuff.

Then these latter day Trojans found something even better—a sequestered envelope postmarked 1879 and stuffed with canceled stamps. The ink was too faint to read the address, so the interlopers never knew the name of the long departed-collector. It was uplifting to know that at least one lonely and anonymous miner had found a hobby and from the scattered whiskey bottles, this was not his only one. With such a bonanza every member of the CSC became a potentially wealthy philatelist. Al, who had wanted to be rich ever since he was six, danced on bleeding feet.

With juvenile hilarity, he was dubbed "Cinderella" though glass slippers in that fairy tale had been less traumatic. This cruel sobriquet seemed to cause renewed hemorrhage and the laughs were not worth it. The oath of secrecy was sealed in blood, swabbed from the soles of the reluctant Cinderella. This pact was verified by returning to the Indian cave where a mysterious petroglyph added solemnity to the oath. This was known as THE GREAT OATH OF AL since he alone had bravely faced exsanguination to transform our adventure from ordinary to profound.

As if to prove this story is true, there is a tragic ending.

Our attention span was about average for high school kids who can admire old stamps for just so long. Along with the crowbar each had brought a .22 rifle in case the war in Europe suddenly became global. Only Al and I owned lever action Marlins because Sam was foolishly saving his money for college. His single shot Remington was older than the man who had invented it, and unless the breech was opened carefully the bolt tended to fall to the ground. In case of a rabbit attack, Sam fashioned a bayonet with an ice pick and duct tape.

There were thousands of jackrabbits, the same tularemic-infested rodents so revered in children's books and called bunnies. Every seven years they would explode into a ravenous invasion and strip the country bare. The seven years were just up. The CSC stood unafraid.

History was on our side. Our duty was clear. The hunt was on.

The general theme of the coming adventure was borrowed for a movie about the invasion of Normandy where the rabbits were Nazis and John Wayne played the part of Al. My front pockets were already filled with shells so I jammed the priceless envelope in the rear pocket of my cords. (In those days only real cowboys wore Levis.)

A privy with pride, Silver City. The two story drop takes a while. The thud is conclusive. The relief is worth the wait.

Without taking a vote, I delegated myself as custodian of the stamps. These other kids seemed so unreliable. I came to regret this.

The hunt lasted until dusk and we were late for the truck. It was easy to appease the angry driver who happened to be a philatelist, and openly salivated in anticipation of dickering for rare stamps with dumb kids. Patiently he tolerated a lengthy description of their dramatic discovery in the walls of a Silver City shack. He even made an offer sight unseen, a common tendency among truck drivers.

Alas, it was not to be. My pocket was empty. The stamps were gone. I looked in vain for someone to share the blame, but there were no takers. Sam moaned that this had to be the red man's revenge for desecrating a sacred cave. On that woeful day, I suddenly realized how lonely a ghost town can really be. While the driver honked and fumed, we retraced our steps but cruel caprice intervened with a scattering wind. Darkness did the rest. Even the rabbits had turned in.

Silently, the explorers drove down the mountain, haunted by the vision of some unworthy juniper festooned with a thousand stamps, pretending to be a Christmas tree.

As we huddled in the back of the truck, the only sound was the whistle of wind and the rattle of crowbars.

Nobody talked much.

At least nobody was talking to me.

YOU ARE IN YOUR OWN WAY
PLEASE STAND ASIDE
~ Chinese fortune cookie

It is a state law that every Idahoan must float the Middle Fork of the Salmon River. This was enacted after Carter and Kennedy elevated the Middle Fork to presidential status.

Mountain goats were flattered by the attention as secret service helicopters hovered over Idaho's favorite river. Good fishing was assured as Fish and Game lackeys dashed ahead with a fresh supply of hatchery trout. Since lobster were not indigenous, the White House brought their own which they shared with the easily bribed press corps.

It was not like this for the locals. The prudent Idaho neophyte practiced on more docile water in cautious preparation for the big time rapids of the more violent River of Presidents.

Charlie and I learned river running on the more gentle Owyhee, analogous to learning with training wheels before some older kid pushes your bike over a cliff.

The spires and canyons of the Owyhees were the domain of Doc Jones, a medical patriarch who prowled and prospected this remote and wondrous world. To my children he was the magician who found arrowheads in secret caves and curious artifacts in every creek. Within the Jones domain, chokecherry bloomed on command and sagebrush grew sturdy enough to support a tree house. Indian paintbrush extended to the horizon with a dazzling spectrum from salmon pink to Chinese red. Just as red grew monotonous, balsam and lupine splashed yellows and blues in riotous excess. Ancient junipers guarded the canyon rim and surveyed ravines which shimmered with the variegated greens of scrub mahogany, known locally— and quite accurately—as *Ironwood*. This deceptive shrub thinks it's a tree and can break a professional logger's wrist on the first swing of an ax. Sawing is safer but takes forever.

Charlie and I had taken many hikes in the Sawtooths but this would be our first river adventure, hence an opportunity to apply all those dry land debacles to the water. We reconnoitered the Owyhee in the fall and planned for the spring.

Word spread of the proposed maiden voyage and soon the entire town wanted to join, hoping to conquer the Owyhee, collect arrowheads or worst of all, *write a book.*

But when word leaked that I wanted to be captain, excuses began to pour in. These alibis taxed, and insulted, the imagination. Among the most creative was an epidemic of the Black Plague which was offered on three successive days in black, brown and beige.

Even a plausible excuse can backfire. One of the erstwhile crew feigned gastritis with such conviction that he coaxed it into an ulcer which troubles him to this very day. Serves him right.

This left only the two co-captains who scrounged Army Surplus Stores for a WW-II assault raft but none were to be had. The military had destroyed all remaining U.S. boats after some Californian fell out and sued the government. His vodka was never recovered.

So in the post war market, the only rafts available were flimsy Japanese imitations, barely suitable for children's wading pools. All they had in common with the U.S. variety was air. The really bad ones were water soluble. A duck hunter bought one such raft and we read his obituary a week later.

There were two models based on capacity (laughingly known as two-man or four-man) but their buoyancy was apparently based on a 40 Kg oriental with a small sack of rice. The average Caucasian requires a big boat just to carry his French fries. The adventurers bought what was available, but with a twenty-four hour warranty they had to get to the river fast.

The toy paddles were replaced with ash oars, borrowed from an old row boat but they were too long. Only when afloat was it obvious that they overlapped as did your knuckles.

Because of rain or lack of it, rafting the Owyhee was limited to late May or early June. By mid-June the rocks seem to grow higher and it is not water but lava that can beat your brains out. On June 21st, with two boats that should have been recalled to the orient, we reached the bank at 4:30 a.m. . . . too early in the day and much too late in the year.

A local Basque drove us upriver to put in at the Rome bridge and would later rendezvous seventy miles downstream at Leslie Gulch. We were off to a bad start since A) highway miles are not the same as river miles, B) the driver spoke no English, and C) he had never been to Leslie Gulch. Fortunately we wouldn't know any of this for another week, time enough for a dozen self-created problems to make these pale.

The boats moved well with the current until a breeze swept upstream around four o'clock. This happened every day and the deeper the canyon the stronger the wind.

Head wind is no problem for McKenzie boats, but rubber rafts ride high like a doughnut and, despite steady rowing, they are blown backward where one can enjoy the same scenery two, three, even four times. To avoid this predictable retropulsion we got off the river much earlier than we ever intended, and often settled for whatever campsite the Owyhee offered. The worst was the second night which abandoned us in a deep gorge against a cheerless vertical wall where the sun sank so fast you could almost hear it. We tied to the only shrub available and slept in our rafts.

I craved hot coffee but a nearby petroglyph warned: "Never build a fire in a rubber boat."

By no means rested, we decided to push on until we located a decent campsite, no matter what. This, of course, meant rowing by flashlight.

Fortune smiled with a magnificent sandbar at the mouth of a colorful canyon.

Question: Why all this sand?

Answer: Frequent flash floods. One was due tonight. We had camped on the watershed for three states. Through a long night the endless rush of water flushed down small trees and big rattlesnakes.

Dehydrated food became re-hydrated. Sleeping bags floated away while their occupants clung to American air mattresses which were more buoyant than rubber Yokahama Yachts.

Dawn found us hungry and wet. I wanted my mother.

With one dry match that would still strike, the redoubtable Charlie decided to bake his unforgettable bannock bread, already notorious in Idaho camps and shunned by Indians everywhere. This durable concoction is the ideal survival food. It takes about a week to get it down, a week to digest it and another week to clean up afterward.

I still have an uneaten slice and the rest of the loaf was recently excavated by an archaeologist working on his doctorate at the U of I. Today it resides under a glass dome at the Idaho Historical Museum, inscrutable and inedible.

Despite countless self-inflicted disasters, the days were scenic and memorable. Tall purple spires and orange voodoos were photographed with wet film which imparts an ethereal quality. Later, when we projected them with persuasive dialogue, unsophisticated spectators were led to believe that this foggy effect was intentional.

On June 25th, mid-morning, mid-ship and mid-river the navigator struck a rock and sustained one of those decisive longitudinal lacerations that gave the Titanic an entire paragraph in better history texts. We pushed ashore for repairs and almost ran out of Scotch tape.

For reasons never understood, we decided to float together in my orange boat. We would take turns with the oars and maintain a record in a small waterproof book to keep it fair. The smaller yellow craft was now the designated Supply Boat which we planned to tow. It trailed dutifully but tried to pass the lead raft in fast water in a race that became the source of frivolous wagering. We soon tired of holding the tow rope and—no one knows why— decided to throw it free to find its own route through the rapids to be easily retrieved in still water beyond.

Tossing the tow rope worked just fine. TWICE. Then we looked back in dismay to see a yellow boat completely submerged and firmly wedged between two rocks, each the size of Gibraltar. During a heroic effort to dislodge it, I sustained a spontaneous rupture of my right plantaris tendon. In humans this is a vestigial companion which runs parallel to our gastrocnemeus muscle and attaches at the Achilles tendon. The plantaris is better developed in lower primates who can use an extra calf muscle to swing from the trees. This crude evolutionary reference is unfair because apes are too smart to float down rivers with all their food in another boat. I misinterpreted the tendon snap for the fangs of a rattlesnake and collapsed theatrically. Moaning and groaning echoed up the canyon creating an unmanly scene. I lay down to die until Charlie, always a superior diagnostician, reminded his cowardly companion that a snake would have to penetrate my Levis to get to the calf. The fabric was intact as was the hide beneath.

Bitterly disappointed, I limped back to where we eventually extricated our edible prize only to have the current wrench it away. All the food we owned disappeared in the froth around the next bend. We pushed ahead with more zest than judgment and in our panic ignored a roar with an important message. Suddenly a torrent forced our flagship vertically against a rock where it stuck like a postage stamp. Neck deep in hostile water, Charles struggled to the bank in order to survey the river beyond, while I applied hydrotherapy to an imaginary snake bite:

"What's around the bend?"

"I think I see Omaha."

Whenever we were lost he said clever things like that with the same cheering effect as bannock biscuits for breakfast. With new-found wisdom and pre-existing cowardice, we portaged around bad water but since I still clung to that snake fang theory, Charlie carried the heavy stuff.

Finally we stumbled across our supplies, lodged in a clump of providential willows. Thereafter, we still took a few wrong turns but never lost the entire river.

To ease fatigue there were periodic spectacles. Dominating the west bank was the China Garden, verily a Bryce Canyon without people, with petrified rainbows of purple manganese blended with ferrous crimson and tastefully transected by cuprous greens.

Such colors devoured and deserved two rolls of Kodachrome 25 (f:8 at 1/125 sec.) with a drowned light meter—but Kodak must have screwed up the processing.

Downstream we shared the river with hundreds of Canada geese, preoccupied in disciplining unruly goslings. Fastidious coyotes dined on rodents rather than face the wrath of a gander. An otter tried to chew the raft and got an oar to the head. He skulked away to spread the word that these were river veterans.

The seventy-five mile run climaxed with a wild drop at the Marcum Dam where a roaring cascade ends abruptly in rocks, abandoned concrete, and steel rebars. These have shredded many boats but salvation awaits the inattentive since the Marcum Ranch and its landing strip are in sight. Beyond this, everything was drudgery with a long, hot row across Owyhee Lake to our rendezvous at Leslie Gulch.

The Basque driver looked different and our car had logged 1500 unaccounted miles.

The seat was packed with empty Barcelona wine bottles and on the floor was half a chorizos, though even in their pristine state, most chorizos look partially eaten.

Eaglets, Reynolds Creek. Adult's talons are even larger. Take the photo and get off the cliff.

Through broken English it was learned that next year he wanted more money and a nicer car. Donato adjusted his fifty dollar Stetson and suggested a tip.

When Charles and I began this journey just ten days before, we had said goodbye to a cheerful shepherd in a red beret.

Today his Americanization was almost complete.

Is this not a great country?

THE HIGHER THE DAM
THE BIGGER THE FLOOD
~ Idaho Power

Our first disastrous float down the Owyhee River only proved that doctors are slow learners so we decided to try it again. Since Charlie came from Kansas he liked to suffer and, as an Idahoan, I was naturally gullible. How were we to predict the Big Rain of 1957? This was the government's job.

This torrent finally ruptured the Hardesty Reservoir near Three Forks, and since water moves downhill, the main Owyhee River was soon clogged with juniper fence posts and barbed wire, long considered anathema to inflatable rafts.

This made for a very long day.

Most of the patches were holding when we made camp against a vertical white wall. On the opposite shore, we spied a sheltering overhang under which no rain had fallen. Beneath this was an enormous pile of dry wood about the size of Wyoming.

It made perfect sense for a couple of full-grown men to row over and ignite the stack since no one was using it. With one strike of the match the driftwood virtually exploded. Flames shot beyond heaven, the same heaven we soon implored for deliverance from the intense heat. Planes bound from Portland began circling, believing it to be Boise, only brighter. Flames drove us back across the river where we doused the melting seams.

Of all our lousy campsites this was the worst.

The white cliff became a giant heat reflector from which the only escape would be down river in pitch dark. Bad form. At least if we hunkered by the cliff someone might find two charred bodies and be charitable enough to assume that they were killed by lightning instead of stupidity. We tried to sleep, but the bright flames across the river kept us awake.

Next morning Charlie looked funny with those singed eyebrows, and he spoke through cracked lips: "Whose idea was this?"

After all these years that question remains unanswered.

But the same flood we had cursed became a blessing. The torrent had partially uncovered a long lost artifact and a cast iron leg peeked through the wet sand. Further excavation revealed a miniature Basque stove, perfect in every detail and stamped TOLEDO SPAIN 1886.

It was about 1:10 scale with inlaid tiles of blue and yellow, miraculously unbroken. We speculated on its origin: perhaps a toy for some child, now grown and gone. The original owner probably carried it when he emigrated from the Pyrenees to herd sheep and send money back to his mother. He died forever homesick on the wrong continent wondering why Basque was so easy and English so hard.

From 1839 to 1931 his ancestors suffered relentless Spanish oppression culminating with Primo de Rivera, a ruthless dictator who even proscribed the speaking of Basque. In 1936 a novel technique in death distribution was tested in the Spanish Civil War when the German Condor Legion wiped out Guernica. Since this was the first city ever to be devastated from the air, it was memorialized by Pablo Picasso but from the final painting he must have been in a terrible hurry.

Pablo's buildings are entirely symbolic and even blood—most folks wrongly assume blood to be red—has been splashed on in green. When Charlie finally saw GUERNICA he thought it depicted Marilyn Monroe signing a prenuptial agreement with Joe Di Maggio. Now he knows it is a classic because somebody said so. Charlie always wondered if it was perhaps the green blood that killed those folks.

This wondrous miniature in iron and tile evoked predictable campfire speculation: How did it get here? Who was its owner? We had never seen anything like it before or since and to make room in the boat were willing to jettison food or even each other. We devised a sling to protect the boat floor but the stove weighed about 15 pounds and began to erode the rubber with a small hole that promised to get larger.

Reluctantly we lugged this Iberian trophy away from the river and ceremoniously buried it halfway up the east wall of the canyon. The spot was marked with chunks of lava and streamers of toilet paper (unused). To further identify the location, we climbed to the rim and erected a five foot cairn which could be easily spotted when we returned by jeeping cross country later on. Such a rock pile could be seen for miles over an unending plateau. Hours later we rowed away, determined to return and claim our prize.

We buried that stove in 1957 and haven't found it yet. This is frustrating country with nebulous landmarks and roads alternating between none or too many. Don't look for the horizon. There isn't any. Seductive ruts wander to the canyon rim where the trick is not to fall in. It is obvious that cairns must breed, because where we left only one there were now dozens. Quite honestly, we never expected the toilet paper to last. Western canyons and their myriad clones conspire with cruel indifference to man's disorientation, and last year's landmark makes a liar out of this year's compass. Those Toledo tiles have now entered their second century which is old even for things that don't rust. Charlie never gave up and often flew over the deceptive canyon to photograph the presumed site. Nice pictures but nothing you would hang in your office. He has a treasure map for sale ($4.95 plus postage) but it strangely resembles Venezuela.

If you happen to stumble across this little Basque gem there may be a temptation to claim it. Just remember that two doctors' prints are all over it and can be verified with the F.B.I. Countless visitors arrive to check out western hunting and those who are good shots stay forever. This country also attracts reckless physicians who immediately buy a kayak and take flying lessons.

This is why Idaho will always have a doctor shortage.

DON'T STICK YOUR ELBOW
OUT SO FAR
IT MAY GO HOME
IN ANOTHER CAR
~Burma Shave

Introduction to *Fractures and Joint Injuries*
4th Edition
by Sir Reginald Watson-Jones, FRCS, FRACS, FACS

ORTHOPAEDIC (note that spelling) SURGEON TO
HER MAJESTY THE QUEEN

It may be inferred that, by quoting this jingle, the rigid British occasionally reveal a latent sense of humor, derived largely by watching American billboards. But soon the title page of this two volume surgical classic becomes more pretentious by listing countless other honorary initials after Sir Reginald's name. Additional awards emanated from every university in Europe, including one from the King Oscar of Norway whose regal status can be verified on sardine cans.

Jones is a ubiquitous name, more apt to be remembered if hyphenated and certainly knighthood helps. One of the West's pioneer doctors was a plain old Jones, who never expected to be quoted but is remembered locally for scientific axioms such as: BLEEDING <u>ALWAYS</u> STOPS. Most schools are named after presidents, usually those assassinated or at least having had a close call. A felicitous exception may be found in Arock, a sagebrush suburb of Jordan Valley but worth the trip if the bridge isn't out. This bastion of Basquedom had the good sense to name their school after Walter William Jones. The wrong road takes you past the grave of Jean Baptiste Charbonneau, Sacajewea's son who died at the Ruby Ranch in 1867 and in cold silence waited almost a hundred years for some caring cowboy to mark the site.

So a nostalgic link with Lewis and Clark is not the wrong road after all. Two contiguous and enormous counties, Malheur in Oregon and Owyhee in Idaho, were joined by remoteness and cemented by people as rugged as the terrain, but somehow surveyors divided them at longitude 117 degrees west. Farther north, the Snake River established a more undulating boundary until Hell's Canyon made it decisive.

Renouncing lucrative Eastern enticements, Dr. Jones was drawn to the only life for which he was intended in Malheur's Jordan Valley where, for half a century, he was admired by Basques, Bannocks and buckaroos. Livestock galloped to the gate to greet the man in a checkered suit who made a stable visit before a house call if the horse was sicker. Jordan Valley was no hyperbole. Its meandering streams and knee-high grass created a lush carpet which crept up to the Owyhee Mountains where white subdued the green. For special effects, the biblical Jordan featured a few scraggly camels but this one had fat cattle. Cows have personality. Camels spit on people.

After this build-up, one might think Jordan Valley
was the county seat of Malheur County, but it wasn't.

Walter Jones remembered his first view of the valley:
" Teepees were more numerous than houses . . . and better
built." After Jones treated his first rattlesnake bite he
enunciated safety measures for any five foot reptile with
rattles on one end and fangs on the other:

1) Try to find the snake. Otherwise he might come
back and bite the doctor.

2) No snake in this hemisphere could kill a Basque
but some of us aren't Basques.

3) Whiskey is not therapeutic but some patients will
deplete your supply trying to get well. (One creative alcoholic found that twin stabs with an ice pick can resemble
fang marks, but his duplicity was uncovered when he was
bitten twice in one day.)

4) Patience is paramount: Panic and tachycardia has-
ten the spread of the venom. The victim should lie quietly
under a tree. If there is no tree... *plant one.*

In 1909 the Indians knew a friend when they saw one
and this doctor even spoke their language. SILENCE.
Bannocks and Paiutes had their fill of beads and trinkets,
but this Iowa immigrant won them over with a baseball,
the ineffable symbol of the white man's devotion to violence and preoccupation with rules. The catcher's mitt was
kept in a safety deposit box. This caused no delay on
Sundays because Doc had a key to the bank. In search of
a pitcher, he scouted the territory as far as the Quinn
River Indian Reservation in Nevada.

Smoke signals heralded the doctor's arrival. The tribe
assembled. The chief spoke: " We have just what you need.
A hundred miles is not too far to find a Brave with a rock-
et arm. The missus wants you to stay for dinner. Do you
prefer your venison cooked ? Is there a contract in your
saddle bag ? Don't try to pull a fast one. I have cousin in
Winnemucca who can read English."

Only a few round barns have survived. This is one of the roundest. Harney County.

Doc donned the mitt and handed the horsehide ball to a lad who had never seen one. During an inter-racial game of burn-out he encouraged a six foot Indian with a four foot arm to throw with all his might. Big mistake!

The impact of the first pitch caused the padding to peek through broken stitches. He forced a smile. If Indians saw a white man cry the pitcher's mother might not let him go. On the second throw, the catcher pretended to be distracted and stepped aside—prudence, mind you, not cowardice—as the missile whistled past and singed a swathe of sagebrush that later died. He escaped with his life but when they finally found the ball it was badly scorched. God had blessed Walter with a prodigious pitcher endowed with a Bob Feller arm (Feller was not yet born, but Doc would have said it anyway.) Control of this frightening speed was no problem for the Indian: " Plenty control. I can hit a pale face every time."

So Jones explained the finer points of baseball, that it was bad manners for the pitcher to hit the batter but acceptable for civilized Caucasians to down the clown with beer bottles and collect scalps during the seventh inning.

The Idaho border was barely three miles away, but it was still a long climb toward War Eagle mountain where arch rival Silver City confidently awaited the next game with Jordan Valley. The month before, with more grins than regrets, they had enticed Walter's ace pitcher with firewater and swept the series.

When the Indian finally found the mound he could not climb it. Silver City felt so confident that only the top of the batting order bothered to appear above ground while teammates with carbide lanterns excavated another load of ore—the ultimate Dugout. The hard rock miners enjoyed a unique hometown advantage where no terrain was flat enough for a standard diamond. The two mitts went to the catcher and first baseman so the rest had to improvise. These other positions were designated either downhill (small buckets) or uphill (large buckets). Heavy hits beyond the buckets could even reach the summit where bales of hay stopped the ball so it would not roll beyond the field, or worse, beyond Idaho. A good baseball was hard to come by, and when one tumbled down a mine shaft, it was held hostage while Silver City scored two runs.

Beneath his bare feet, the center fielder could hear the miner's mantra: men without prior piety were praying that Jordan Valley's pitcher would drink again. This cavernous chant was so distracting that they would have complained to the umpire...if they'd had one. But the lad who couldn't find the mound last month, now pitched a shut out. The coach had effectively counseled his red man on the teepee-tequila-tremor-triad and his pitcher was now straight arrow. Caucasian teammates cheered his new-found sobriety and urged his promotion to chief but that, of course, was a tribal decision.

Attendance dropped off when Silver City could no longer rally nine men. The mines petered out and its pop-ulation dwindled to a palsied few. It is rumored that their last winning team is sequestered in a remote Owyhee county cemetery, fenced in by empty ore carts with head-stones that include their batting average. Survivors were sustained by memories of days when miners beat cattle-men on most Sundays, unless coach Jones brought his Quinn River pitcher.

The doctor collected drinking stories which was never hard to do. Once at the height of prohibition his morning was rudely interrupted by a dysarthric stranger who had bribed waiting patients so he could be seen immediately: "Where in this jerk town could a thirsty man find some bootleg booze? I've got plenty of money and you look like you can use some."

He clutched a bundle of bills for their steadying effect. Jones recognized a rare opportunity to enlighten a drunk who (need we say it) drove with California plates. Doc hung his white coat on a silver-plated lineman's spike, pre-sented by Idaho Power in appreciation for servicing bro-ken lines, a useful diversion while his horse rested during long house calls. Walter could still read smoke signals but conceded that the telephone had its place.

"Hop in your car, sir, and follow me."

They drove around Jordan Valley's only block; then west, sort of, and then south, sort of. Finally they detoured, sort of, down the old Antelope Road where the car behind ate dust and could not see that he was actual-ly wandering in a wide circle.

Back in town, both cars parked in front of the Catholic church, barely one hundred yards from the doctor's office. Walter rolled down the window and pointed to the church: "That's the only place you can't buy whiskey." Doc's justice conveyed an unmistakable message that could penetrate even to the most obtuse mind.

Walt set a fracture and sutured several lacerations of a girl who was too humiliated to report the rapist. Confidentiality was respected though the doctor immediately recognized her anonymous assailant as the same bar fly who was not prosecuted last year either. The scum was unconcerned about the law but had not reckoned with JONES JUSTICE. Could Walter make him pay ? He could. Would it be worse than jail ? It would.

That very day, a salacious story spread from Jordan Valley and was re-told by ranchers from Burns to Winnemucca. (And if Jones had his way, Portland and Omaha and Vienna and London. Nothing could bother Paris.)

Revering his oath of silence, but quite by accident, the doctor let slip several small details:

A) A town girl had been violated.

B) Her assailant was some local bum who was still around.

C) He smelled like a goat.

D) He had an extremely short penis

Once seduced by the high desert plateau, the affair lasts forever. Endless sunsets, soaring eagles, and the scent of sagebrush enticed my own progeny who were captured by the vast uncomplicated vistas of the Owyhees from which they never escaped. For a car full of kids, the sixty mile trip to see Dr. Walter Jones was too long without a stop, and their favorite diversion was Jess Strode's spread at the base of Mahogany Mountain where pronghorn grazed with cattle and crimson Indian paintbrush dominated every scene. The creek teemed with voracious trout, but by evening thirsty chukkar owned the banks. Ground squirrels stood at attention near their federally protected burrows. Somnolent marmots guarded preheated rocks.

The children encountered one snake with eight rattles and a badger with none, but young folks just seem to sense that dogs make better pets.

A thousand jackrabbits leaped for joy in celebration of a new population record. At the periphery, cunning coyotes planned their strategy to establish nature's correct ratio of carnivores to rodents. These conniving canines perfected an ingenious relay system where one rested under a juniper while his partner continued the chase. The perspiring rabbit thought all along there was only one pursuer who never got tired.

This works only because all coyotes look alike.

Golden eagles, none bald nor apt to be, wheeled slowly south to survey the food chain in Nevada. The children petted a baby antelope even though that scary white mask more properly belonged on some animal that bites.

The main event of this Owyhee matinee was an acrobatic antelope whose dash began a quarter mile away, letting onlookers believe he was racing to jump the fence. Then, with pronghorn panache, rather than leap over, he slid beneath a menacing low stretch of barbed wire. Careening to a dusty halt, he tipped a hoof to the applause of delighted children. Jess had seen this dozens of times, marveling at an animal who could easily clear eight feet, but would, instead, elect to slide underneath with never a scratch: "It is pure showmanship. They don't take such chances when nobody is looking." Most thinking people would rather crawl in the dirt than risk straddling barbed wire which has a mind of its own.

Mary Strode's mesmerizing Scottish brogue was as thick as her gravy which drowned platters of hot buscuits and almost my entire family. Later we sat on the porch and drank deep from a cold cistern, deeper still from a sunset that went on forever. At least it hasn't ended yet.

Mahogany Mountain signaled that it was not far to Jordan Valley, a dusty town in Southeastern Oregon, hovering on the Idaho border, and supported by one sheriff wearing a scowl and a Wyatt Earp hat. Neither was ever removed.

Since he couldn't write, his wife prepared your ticket the night before in the certain belief that all foreigners will exceed the speed limit before they reach the old Basque Jai Alai court. You can walk faster than the speed limit, so posting it would be superflous. Signs cost money and are embarrassing when so often misspelled.

Anticipationg the sheriff's customary bribe, most of us had a ten dollar bill tucked in the steering wheel, whereas one Boisean paid by offering his wife for the night (though few were worth ten dollars.)

Just beyond the wealthy Wyatt Earp was a Jordan Valley landmark, the mortared rectangle of lava and silver ore built in 1910 by Doctor Jones.

By *him*. Not somebody else.

His office-pharmacy-museum-ice cream parlor included a few cots, since it was sixty miles to a hotel and fifty years to a motel.

When Jones was away tending his flock, we hung around the store while the kids blew their allowance on ice cream cones and colorful geodes.

Doc's office in the rear centered around a roll top desk whose cubbyholes were stuffed with yellowing envelopes from an era when any village of fifty souls had its own postmark. Most of the letters came from Iowa—places like

Red Oak and What Cheer—but most were from Coalfield where he was born in 1876 just four months before Custer's first and last meeting with Crazy Horse at the Little Bighorn.

I would never pry into another man's personal mail so let us share what I read:

"Dear Doc: The missus says you finally decided to cancel our bill which was mostly hers cause pregnancy maked her puny and she is sick all the time. The kids always have a cold. The coats your wife gave them are too thin so it's sort of her fault. The missus is sorry that you had to deliver most of them in the middle of the night but I say you docs get used to no sleep. You let her yell so loud it kept me awake. After you left Iowa we had a lot more kids but she was back on the plow in between. Was going to name a boy after you but forgot your name. How come you wound up in Indian country? Our ball club has been in a slump so the team could use you. I could too since the missus is with child again. Where do kids come from anyway?"

He never returned to Coalfield where payment for service was usually a handshake. And if he coached a losing team, not even that.

In his arcane office teetered a tall medicine cabinet of teakwood and heavy glass. Its owner seemed unconcerned that the jammed doors would never swing again. I never missed a chance to bump into a bare bulb which dangled from a ceiling that was up there somewhere.

Jones rose for all who entered, never excluding children, for he was a gentleman. Even in the dim light, one could identify his constant attire: a suit with a small black and white checkered pattern, a starched shirt, and a black string tie. This characteristic outfit was later imitated by Kentucky Colonels everywhere, but only Jones could really carry it off. Such apparel befit the dignity of his profession but was also adaptable to prospecting or breaking horses. Always commanding yet ever benign, Walter Jones

projected nobility is a suit that could be easily cleaned
with a damp bandanna.

However, his low mumble suggested a detached voice
which caused one to scan the room for a hidden ventrilo-
quist, finding only scores of ore samples. Dominating the
highest shelf were gigantic, sinister apothecary jars.
Below were aligned smaller but equally spectacular recep-
tacles of blue, frost, and amber whose therapeutic contents
were sealed from a prying world with corks, glass stoppers
and beeswax. They were last dusted in 1932 and all were
Smithsonian candidates, including *Larkspur Lotion,
Sassafrass* and *Oil of Tansy.* (Just try to get a refill on
these today.)

The therapeutic array was punctuated with
Asafetida, the stench of which proclaimed that, verily, this
was one powerful medicine. From Spain he imported
Stomalix for the Basques who were suspicious of any New
World nostrum. Walt suspected that the efficacy of
Stomalix was its sixty percent alcohol content. Thirty
proof could cure almost anything if you were careful about
too many refills.

The doctor's gaze hesitated at a small bottle of croton
oil which evoked this useful admonition: "Don't ever con-
fuse castor oil, a standard laxative, with croton oil whose
power defies description. I notice one of your youngsters is
about six, just the right age to remember that castor oil is
taken by the *ounce*, croton oil by the *drop*." These were all
smart kids. They knew what a drop was.

For illustration he recalled the curse of free curbstone
consultations. The families with the most questions never
came to the office where they might have to wait. Their
time was valuable. They should be home procreating.
Anxious patients invariably equated human afflictions
with those seen in livestock and lived in dread of hoof and
mouth disease. After reassurance on this score, the rancher finally focused on grandad whose bowels had not moved

for a month. Granddad was 100, maybe 200. Eliciting a family history in Jordan Valley (or Pittsburgh) is replete with fiction just to keep the story interesting. Had Jones ever seen him? "Hell no. He goes to an herb doctor in Boise." A crowd was gathering and Walt knew there would be no escape until he wrote a prescription for an ounce of castor oil. Or so he thought.

Their paths crossed a few weeks later when the doctor thoughtfully inquired about grandad and wished he hadn't.

"The old bastard (that would be grandad) finally died even after all that CROTON OIL."

The doctor was almost afraid to ask:

"Did his bowels ever move?"

"Damn right. Once before he died and twice afterward."

Every rock, bottle and bone had a story but Doc decided to defer them until the kids weren't around. Finally he paused at a rare treasure, a porcelain amphora with chipped gold lettering: HIRUDA. He considerately interpreted Latin to LEECH.

I pretended to know this. Then the doctor anticipated the next question:

"No. I never used them. Leeches were popular in the Revolutionary War which I missed by just a few months."

I coveted that jar but so did the Smithsonian.

About that checkered suit: he had three just like it.

Surrounded by profligate miners, the Chinese in Silver City huddled in isolated shacks which were no more hospitable than the mines themselves. Here lonely Orientals scrimped, starved and saved to prepare for the promised afterlife, the best life they could ever hope to have. They burned incense and rang tiny bells while praying that they could be buried in their homeland. Since most weighed less than a hundred pounds, perhaps their casket could go to China at a reduced rate. But their frugality would not be rewarded on this continent.

Saving money was a novelty in Owyhee county (one preacher denounced it as un-Christian) and those few who did were targeted for crudely concealed envy, barroom jokes and murder. Protecting his pitiful sack of gold dust (The Chink's Cache) was more hazardous than mine explosions. To steal their sequestered fortune they were seduced to a game called poker but fast shuffling Caucasians learned too late that for five thousand years gambling with a Chinaman was a bad idea unless you too were an Oriental. The queued neophyte held five cards close to his robe, bluffed with a pair of threes and left the game at 2 a.m., driving another man's best wagon. This accomplishment popularized murder which had never been out of vogue. Buried they were, but not in China.

But even this bloody shortcut did not assure success. The same slant-eyed wizard that could fill an inside straight could also hide his gold where you can't find it. Movies provide vicarious adventure and testify to man's innate greed. People with nothing better to do still enjoy re-runs of *King Solomon's Mines* and *The Lost Dutchman,* but Humphrey Bogart personifies the essence of avarice in *The Treasure of Sierra Madre* when he doubles his loot by killing Tim Holt.

Silver City's secret hoards are still somewhere on War Eagle Mountain with legends of lost mines worth millions and Chinese leather pouches worth almost as much. And who would be inclined to suppress these tales of treasure as long as local maps are available for $9.95 plus tax?

With a stethoscope in his pocket and an ore hammer in his hand, Walter Jones pounded inviting rocks until he had pulverized every gully leading to Silver City.

Then he remembered Klondike tales of gold dust filtering through saloon floors but in Silver City somebody else got there first:

"Acting on a hot tip I tore up the floor of a Chinaman's shack and based on what I found began collecting black widow spiders and opium bottles."

Jones was immune to the violence and prejudice which surrounded him:

"Before we got here, great chiefs like Winnemucca and Buffalo Horn had been central to the tribe. We made them a center with no circumference."

Sarah Winnemucca was a very bright girl whose counsel had kept her father's tribe out of the Bannock War. She perceived the Indian's problem of recruitment and replacement. White girls were born with curly hair and every boy came from the womb gripping a rifle. In northern Idaho, Chief Joseph had already discovered that Nez Perce courage was not enough and even the strongest teepee could not withstand a well-aimed cannon. But what Sarah could accept somehow always bothered Walter. Even though he was the product of *Manifest Destiny* he predicted:

"We shall prevail against the Indian but God will give us a headache."

When I first brought my own children to meet Walter—yes, he stood as they entered—they were disappointed to see no scalps hanging on the office wall but kept quiet about it. That was how their father had raised them. Doc appeased them with ice cream cones and a quick peek in an apothecary jar before the leech escaped.

Naturally, most of their questions were about rattlesnake victims:

"I never lost one; had my best results when I was out of town."

They took a shine to him and, renouncing their own father, voted to make Walter their personal doctor, but he graciously demurred since he lived too far away and these kids got sick fast.

My son held out an archaic stethoscope and bared his chest for auscultation. Doc listened with professional deliberation . . . you can't rush these things . . . before he solemnly declared: "Only an Indian's heart could be stronger."

He escorted "Indian Heart" to the swinging door, donated by a bartender who was now a reformed alcoholic, and patted the boy's head:

"Pediatrics is OK unless the stethoscope weighs more than the patient."

His recollections drifted to adventures in dermatology, including that villified cutaneous curse, adolescent acne, commonly attributed to a downright dangerous build up of male hormones. Folklore decreed that unless properly released, the testosterone exploded all over your face in hideous hues of purple and red, usually just before the prom. The source of these unshakable native convictions was the immutable petroglyphs in an Owyhee cave. Medical school was no match for *Learning From Lava*.

To cure the ZIT OF SATAN the swain must lie with a maiden every week, known to Jones as *Catch and Release*. This alleviates pressure in the seminal vesicles and maintains a flawless complexion. For residual blemishes, daily therapy may be necessary because a cowboy's hide cannot be too smooth.

The prudent physician never argues:

"I guess it works. He never had a pimple. She never had a period."

Among his varied encounters was a macho cowboy who slipped out of the saloon just long enough to instigate his wife's annual pregnancy: "He couldn't ride, couldn't rope, couldn't read. He wore a big hat and fought for his manhood until he had more manhood than teeth."

His battered leather bag seemed proud to have accompanied its owner through faithful years of uncomplaining service. Deep cracks testified to a hasty drying over a sagebrush fire after crossing a swollen river on a driftwood raft to reach a sheepherder with spotted fever.

"The patient survived but my horse developed a rash."

No one could guess the bag's original shape and only one man ever knew how to open it.

Out in the wide open spaces many inhabitants saw themselves as *bona fide* characters, but Walter never had to work at it. He somehow found time for anything important and that was everything. After a commencement speech at Arock he would return to patients lined up at the office door. Though it was always unlocked they remained respectfully outside, never quite sure what demons might be inside all those ominous apothecary jars.

He saw a dozen patients that night not counting those treated during graduation ceremonies where one girl had a hysterical fit when she failed to make valedictorian by two votes. Another asked how come she skipped her last menstrual period: "I've always been regular."

Doc wasted no time: "Regular at WHAT?"

The sleuth of Jordan Valley noticed a few worried faces and set out to uncover the real father. Within an hour, three had confessed and two promised to come in the next day.

Don't ever mess with Doc Jones.

Through the years, I would encounter him in the Owyhees—at Three Forks, Silver City or deep in Leslie Gulch—an anachronism in a checkered suit, clutching a gunny sack and swinging a geologist's hammer. The burlap bulged with precious rocks and his pockets suffered the overflow. His jeep was always just over the next hill, a euphemism for five miles.

It too sagged under a load of ore samples gleaned from secret canyons and eventually rolled into the assay office in Vale "before they spoiled."

It wasn't gold. It wasn't silver. It weighed 237 pounds … and cost him a dollar a pound.

One year molybdenum was very big and he even plotted an imaginary road to haul out his fortune: "It has to be molybdenum because you can't get to it." The Vale assayer did eventually report an ore of very high grade but the prospector could not remember where he found it. He did narrow it down to Oregon, Idaho or Nevada.

Eventually his friends grew apprehensive about an old man who prowled deep canyons alone. I came across him once as darkness and rain threatened—rain maybe, darkness for sure—but pressed my concerns too hard and got what I deserved:

"Don't worry, son … I'll look out for you."

He wore out several jeeps climbing impassable roads but never really understood what made them run. He cajoled stubborn engines as if talking to his mare, expecting the wheels to turn with a whinny. His knowledge of human anatomy was somehow never transferred to auto mechanics. The heart resembles a water pump, but not really. He attributed some mysterious personality to anything made of steel. Cars should be corralled and subjugated the same way one breaks a horse. Consistent with his creed, he never changed the oil in any of his jeeps: "After all, nobody changes a patient's blood." Jordan Valley folks cherished any Jones souvenir, but nobody ever bought one of his cars. His proudest achievement was learning how to spell Basque names.

He worried through one particular labor, just knowing that afterward he would have to write *Yturriondobedia* which took more time than the delivery.

"This was a long line on the birth certificate but fortunately I had to spell it only once."

Back in the Pyrenees many Basques had already split these attenuated names but for those still undecided, Jones offered a choice during the first trimester.

Pick Yturri, pick Bedia or pick another doctor.

Dust enveloped Doc Jones and his office-pharmacy-museum when a ranch hand galloped in on a horse that was "rode hard and put away wet."

The breathless messenger brought bad news about his foreman who had tried to outrun a rock slide which killed the horse and broke the rider's leg: at least the bone was sticking out through his levis.

The victim was waiting alone somewhere north of Flint Creek, not much to go on but better than "take the first state on your right."

Doc Jones tossed his grip and a canteen into his buggy with a few hunks of antelope jerky, not ordinary meat but hickory cured from a tender spring fawn which was poached by a grateful father as payment for a midnight tracheostomy during a diphtheria epidemic. As an after-thought, he also threw in his saddle. God took a hand in this but his wife made him do it.

Flint Creek was a rarely traveled route to Silver City but Walter was thoroughly familiar with the area, a myth soon to be dispelled. Out here, there were always more roads than people if one counts the game trails, and one might as well.

It never snowed here in April unless one climbed too high and this was definitely snow. The frigid night found the reluctant mare sharing her blanket with Doc from which he detected considerable resentment.

Next morning the wheels were anchored in deep drifts. His wife was right. He would need that saddle. The antelope jerky was depleted and the mare was in an ugly mood. After sharing her blanket she would now suffer the indignities of a saddle.

Doc began to notice cattle with brands as unfamiliar as the terrain. When a man is completely lost, his horse should offer companionship but this one only aggravated the situation by snickering. They wandered through the blinding storm and crossed Flint Creek twice when once would have been plenty. The Owyhee maps were back in Jordan Valley where they would be safe and real cowboys don't use maps anyway.

Finally, and no thanks to the rider, the mare stumbled across the patient who was nursing the first fire Doc had seen in two days. Its warmth was greeted with a smile and a whinny as Doc's perfidious mare nuzzled up to the keeper of the flame. Walter checked a fractured tibia where it had lacerated the denim. No doctor wants to treat the wrong patient: "Sorry Doc, I already pushed the bone back in."

"Rats, I wanted to do that."

The victim also had rigged a juniper splint: "I wanted to do that too."

Did he intend to charge for mileage? "I guess not since most of it was in the wrong direction."

The doctor was paid in pork and beans so he ate plenty. Without compunction the fickle mare gorged on hay bequeathed by the horse killed under the rock slide. Walter's memory of the Flint Creek disaster was typical Jones:

"I got there late or he wouldn't have made it."

The grateful patient would never tell that the doctor was lost but Walt knew his mare would talk plenty.

Three years later, the unlucky cowboy broke the same old leg but it was not his fault. Any horse that stops that fast could wind up as dead as the last one. This time he did not set it himself because he was not as tough as he used to be.

So Walter got a second chance. He even used plaster.

But you can't please everybody: "The patient liked the leg straight but his horse thought it fit the stirrup better when it was crooked."

After a losing night at the crap tables, the quickest escape from Winnemucca is straight north up highway 95 where soon enough the black ribbon splits McDermitt, already minuscule but now a blur. Once this town fades in the rear view mirror, America's Great Adventure in motoring beckons—unending, unbending, unpatrolled—and now that exhilaration of watching a quivering needle go beyond the numerals of your speedometer.

About one hour later in Jordan Valley, the road makes its first turn after 101 miles. Here you can buy gas if you're lucky, and meet the sheriff if you're not.

Highway 95 was not always that way. Before 1944, the joys of the open road ended a few miles north of Doc Jones' s stone pharmacy.

All of those earlier curves had merely been saved for the next 65 miles where a barely graveled nightmare twisted high above Squaw Creek Canyon and far below were twisted remnants of rusted metal. They looked so different when they came from Detroit.

Drivers hugged the edge, and their prayers that guard rails would keep them from plunging into the void were not always answered. The old Squaw Creek road so thoroughly discouraged passage into Idaho that nothing, land mines maybe, could be more dissuasive.

Trembling Californians photographed a few natives and returned to San Francisco by a longer but safer alternative through Klamath Falls. Early freighters and stagecoaches called anything a road if they made it through more than once; such was the old Idaho-Oregon-Nevada cutoff. When automobiles replaced wagons, new wheels tried to fit in old ruts which only became deeper while the tires grew thinner. In dire emergencies, patients had to hurry down this formidable road where Doc Jones sent them in pairs—one Basque and one interpreter—hoping both did not become victims.

Thus began one man's crusade for a better highway to which he devoted boundless energy and countless hours. Walter Jones became an untiring champion to the glory of asphalt.

At his own expense, he covered the entire state. He exhorted the multitudes. He cajoled civic clubs. He collared legislators. Salem was a four hundred and fifty mile trip, but he made it so many times that every politician knew him on sight. Faint-hearted opponents fled at the sight of a checkered suit, a black string tie and dusty boots. Burdened by pressing affairs of state, entire committees hid behind piles of paper and busied themselves with any legislation *except* Walter's I-O-N highway.

There was no escape from his legendary tenacity. If they closed the office door, Doc would pick the lock. He still maintained a busy practice back home but he always returned. When Walt bought a new set of tires, the desperate governor considered ceding the entire Squaw Creek Canyon to Idaho. This got a big laugh in Boise.

Jones dragged reluctant legislators until they could be identified by shoes that had no heels.

There are so many ways to persuade.

After fifty years of serving a county about the size of Europe, Walter finally locked his office though it took a month to find the key. Since 1906, folks had free access to an open door lest they run out of medicine or some pregnant patient might suddenly crave an ice cream cone at 2 a.m. Also here was one of the few telephones with a nearby Indian basket to leave your dime. Long distance calls were never abused since all their friends lived right here.

At last, the Grim Reaper's scythe had finished its back swing and Walt lived out his final days in Caldwell where my father rendered the care his old friend deserved.

Walt and Will had served a profession they forever respected. Two notably taciturn men found they could reminisce for hours about spectacular Owyhee sunsets, canyons they prospected more for scenery than gold, long hunts on a high desert plateau when the antelope were always just out of range and nobody cared.

Jones used an antique 30-30 with an octagonal barrel which once came close enough to startle a desert big horn. To celebrate the sheep's life, he gave the gun to my father.

On July 17th, 1963, the curtain fell on the stage which had enacted a remarkable western saga where one man played every part and never took a bow.

From Chief Joseph to Sarah Winnemucca, from Irish wranglers to Basque sheep herders, his sustaining spirit was always there. When he died at eighty-seven—much too young—grateful citizens had been traveling his hard-won I-O-N cutoff for twenty years. He had lived just across the border so two states claimed him. Nevada made three.

Ranches covering a million acres were left unattended while leather-faced mourners jammed the Caldwell Methodist Church with a strong scent of sage. Every hand held a Stetson, and all boots were lovingly shined for the first time. Oak pews tried to straighten bowed legs and saddle-callused butts squirmed but gradually accommodated because Doc would expect them to settle down. They frequently checked their hair since most of their life they slept in a hat. Dogs remained outside. Brotherhood prevailed. Sheepmen spoke to cattlemen. Miners stopped criticizing the government. University professors tried to look comfortable in snakeskin boots and legislators pretended they supported The Jones Highway all along. No one cared who they were yesterday because today they were all worth knowing.

Grief takes many forms: the pageantry of a monarch's death, the toys of a lost child, a housewife's flowers that bloom after she's gone, or taps for a battle hero when the sound lingers long after the bugle stops. This day's gathering was all of these but so eloquently understated that every personal memory was intensified.

The ceremonies concluded at Silver City's Masonic Lodge No.13, AF&AM where Walter's spirit joined reminiscing clusters as they re-told favorite tales of sagebrush medicine. Because every rancher wanted to identify with his doctor in the first person, certain familiar anecdotes were allowed modest embellishment as long as the story was recognizable. Pure fabrications were politely corrected since fist fights would show a crass disrespect to the event.

Dr. Walter William Jones left his name on more than an Oregon school house. Small towns can't attract a physician anymore and this man knew he would be Jordan Valley's last. Who else ever willed his patients a highway so they could find a doctor when he was gone?

After he checked the last guard rail for stability, the I-O-N cutoff was dedicated in 1944:

"They even painted a yellow line down the middle. I never expected that."

CHAPTER TWELVE

EVERYTHING FRED DID
I DID BACKWARDS
AND IN HEELS.
~ Ginger Rogers

Eventually, Will had to settle for more sedentary diversions with an occasional movie, but only a fool would pay to sit in the dark and watch two hours of tragedy when he could go to the office and participate in the real thing for nothing. W.C. Fields, Robert Benchley or Fred Astaire offered Will a cinematic escape. The movie must be funny and all actors must be dead.

To avoid that monthly trip to the cinema , he bought a second hand black and white TV and even its eleven inch screen revealed the insidious extent of our Brave New World where logical names were quietly altered to create profitable confusion. Will was surprised to learn that automobiles were now larger on the inside than the outside. Santa Claus was a myth. The tooth fairy, maybe. Health became wellness without the slightest effect on morbidity.

Letterheads from the U.S. WAR DEPARTMENT now read THE DEPT. of DEFENSE, and printed in pink to obfuscate a bellicose image. (In America, a bomb is something that drops from a plane. In Europe, it is something that drops on YOU.) Will had seen this deception coming with Dry Cleaning which, of course, is not DRY but WET. Now all of us are Martinized and don't even know it.

As the years passed — and this could happen to you— nitroglycerin lost its efficacy and my father became a mountaineer emeritus. Will having hiked Idaho from border to border, his advice was sought by neo-adventurers with an aversion to getting lost. At no extra charge, Will also included tips for their camp menu and occasionally referred them to Garber's Shoe Store for a pair of gumsoled Red Wing boots. If their shoe size was not available, these customers were persuaded to forget walking because, just around the corner, Garber also sold cars.

Some consultations were with his own son for whom he patiently sketched the only true route to Enos Lake, step by step, across South Loon Mountain. Even so, my group (I was the leader) failed to find the prize and I complained about the trail.

"Who said there was a trail ?" In my defense, Enos is a rather small lake.Dad's instruction were somewhat nebulous: " Just follow your shadow." If you can't find your shadow, the sun has probably gone down, and you have done something wrong. Try again next year, just as I did.

For the next assault on Enos Lake, another man was elected captain. A unanimous vote, as I recall. Compiling the massive camp menu is a western ritual which emphasizes stuff you would never eat at home. If one packs in ten pounds of bacon and packs out nine—and does this year after year— this should tell the thinking man something about bacon.

After a week in the White Clouds, gastric fantasy becomes colonic reality. Cooking—assuming you have a fire— requires a knife (the macho one in your belt is too big) and a spoon (the bigger, the better.) A trowel is useful to handle ashes and can serve as a spoon. A fork is superfluous. Carry three cheap knives in separate pockets. One to loan. One to use. One to lose.

Neighborhood youngsters could experience camping without leaving town. Behind the doctor's home was every child's time-honored island of adventure . . . a vacant lot. This served as a scientific control study, comparing city parks where games were selected by adults who had forgotten their own childhood. Given the choice between a playground with regulations or a patch of weeds with none, kids knew where to go. My father kept his vacant lot forever because it was never vacant.

The old grammar school class was winnowed and scattered until Will was left with only fragmented memories. Any countenance he might remember would have changed by now, though somehow the face he shaved every morning always seemed about the same. Through the years, he sometimes thought he glimpsed the old thirty-four star flag and during town parades, this doctor not only saluted but counted the stars just to make sure. The stripes were no problem. Clocks also evoked memories, especially the big one in the Caldwell train depot which suddenly became that relentless Regulator clock which once had held every Falls City pupil hostage as it ticked the terms of confinement. While waiting for the train, it was as if he still had unfinished home work, seriously overdue after fifty years. Clocks may mesmerize but bells can wake you up. Every bell was a school bell. Will could even taste the past when any hint of iron reminded him of the battered school yard pump, commanding him to keep both lips inside the cup. Most likely, the rest of Will's class still heard clocks and bells but there was one olfactory jolt: For his generation, the smell of chalk dust would endure forever.

The Falls City he left was a dozen small houses hidden by a mountain of sawdust. Entire families—school drop-outs for several generations—were still married to the mill with its promise of perpetual security. Their progeny, with high hopes and low credit, still waited for the blades to spin again. But whatever makes small towns tends to keep them that way. Restless kids were anxious to see the rest of the West, huge chunks of which were states waiting to be admitted. The world of 1895 had shrunk to the size of that blackened globe which dangled from the schoolhouse ceiling, and once they wiped off the soot it was a world worth seeing.

Their hegira was hastened by a couple of wars which killed some and dislocated the rest. Old Latin scrolls describe how Caesar's legions willingly fought the Gauls but always bitched about the food. The true spirit of Rome lives today, when latter-day draftees brag about those homemade biscuits like mother used to make. The mother of record was always a gray-haired angel in a flour-covered apron, dispensing selfless love from a wood stove. Actually some angels never opened the oven door except to look over her shoulder and pull out a sequestered pint of gin. After enough wartime hyperbole, the soldier hesitated to go back to that sagging house on Main Street which was not a mansion after all.

Will could not escape the ancestral magnet that pulled him for the last time back to Falls City. He wanted his son to see it. We retraced the ancient path from where his house had been, beyond where the mill had been, to where the school had been. It took ten minutes so it wasn't ten miles after all. Even the few remaining buildings had shrunk, probably from that perpetual rain which on this nostalgic day seemed to make Will's eyes a little moist.

Unchanged were the waters of the Salmon, where John Flynn's red-crowned image resurfaced to play new roles in old stories. I thought he had been fictionalized just for bedtime stories when it was not Mother Goose but John Flynn and a night light that made it safe to go to sleep.

I knew everything about my father's childhood friend except what became of him. Then one day, many long years out of grammar school, an imposing figure knocked on Will's door and was quickly admitted because he avoided society's sickest game of "Guess who I am." Only thus did he escape a response used once by Mark Twain: "You tell me who you are, and I'll tell you if you're right." Elegantly framed by the door was Captain John Flynn. His luxury liner was the flagship of the Pacific Grace Line. I thought he had just cruised up the Boise River, though when my father and I were duck hunting, we had seen nothing this big. Braid raced across the bill of his white hat, over his shoulder, down the sleeve and probably covered his underwear.

It was obvious that the captain had a good job with better charts than Columbus, less scurvy than Magellan, and a richer clientele. Whenever folks were ready to travel, John would gladly take them on his big boat. He cruised the sparkling islands of the South Pacific where grass-skirted maidens beckoned behind every palm and beachcombers sold driftwood and collectibles from Woolworth's. John had grown up surrounded by Idaho timber, but now he floated through an exotic world where the trees were smaller and the girls more expensive. In 1778, Capt. Cook tried to pass the word on the wonder of it all but, except for a penal colony in Australia, nobody came. The captain was here to invite Will to be his guest for a month. He could be polite. He could be persuasive. He could be insistent. But real captains never beg. Will would be pampered in the finest cabin on the top deck. He would dine at the captain's table and every detail would be arranged including travel from Idaho to the Port of Los

Angeles. The doctor already knew that would be in California. He ate their oranges.

"Will, you never took a day off in your life. Don't mistake gratitude for charity. Most people have a provincial view of sailors, but I don't even have a mistress in Tahiti. My wife would kill me." The uneasy doctor tried to buy some time: "Why don't you come back in a darker uniform so I can get used to it?" John never traveled without a sea chest full of clothes: "Maybe just the trousers. In full regalia I am too elegant, especially this far inland." For years, Will had been long troubled about an unresolved childhood disaster and here stood the only man who had the answer: "Whatever happened to your brother, Mr. Judo?" The answer was unexpected:

"Pat's a wealthy inventor, moved to California, and invented parking. He is so rich that he should get a divorce."

Will was still stalling: "To be honest, I am not the cruise type and would be uncomfortable even with you there." Any good captain knows how to change his tack: "I did not knock on your door without some preliminary research. I have learned that you love golf. NOW HEAR THIS—You can hit practice balls from the stern." Will winced: "Good grief, do you actually have something that extravagant?"

"Not yet Will, but the Lure Line does, so I've been thinking about it. I could even send a diver down to retrieve them just to assuage your parsimony. We'll be in this together. Sin is more bearable when it's shared. (The captain was part preacher.) You can keep all balls that don't splash, those that stay with the ship, so to speak, unless that's too nautical for you." Golfers by nature are a suspicious breed. Did John somehow know about an embarrassing duck hook that had recently plagued his drives? Had someone in his foursome squealed or was this just a lucky guess? Maybe sea captains are naturally clairvoyant. That would certainly be handy around icebergs: "John, I do appreciate your magnanimous invitation but doesn't dining at the captain's table mean eating grapefruit with one hand?"

"I could teach you. Most amateurs practice secretly in their stateroom. With a ship full of strangers you can even hide under a blanket if that makes you more comfortable. The steward does what I tell him. It's my ship and my blanket. If the cabin boy talks, he'll be thrown overboard. You can even bring the grapefruit home. I understand folks in Idaho often smuggle the rind into their garbage just to give it class."

It was uncanny how right this man could be. John even threatened to circulate a rumor that this doctor had once tried to separate Siamese Twins and wound up with three kids. But Will didn't think he would.

One enticed while the other demurred and soon they leaned back in overstuffed chairs to thoroughly enjoy the stalemate. The captain was curious about the doctor's early days in Caldwell to which Will remembered one itinerant salesman with a foot fetish who called himself a doctor and always included Caldwell on his vigorous western campaign against corns and bunions. His arrival was always heralded by a three line ad in the *News Tribune* which denounced orthodox medicine and ended with the slogan: *Limp in and Leap out*. From a rented corner in the Botkin-Harmon Drug store, he sold foot plasters for a dime and peddled what was left from the curb at Main and Kimball.

In those days, medical advertising was considered unethical and Will compared him to a pitch man in a carnival. "Will, if I didn't know better, I'd say you were describing Dr. Scholl." "That's the guy. Whatever became of him?"

In the 1930s there was big money in feet. Progressive shoe stores featured the new fangled fluoroscope to assure perfect fit for children's shoes. Curious kids stood in line to giggle at their metatarsals, but thirty years later this same radiation was correlated with an epidemic of papillary carcinoma of the thyroid.

Drug detail men made their pitch for Dicumarol, a potent anticoagulant which required careful monitoring. Will logically suspected that this name would be confused with Demerol, a time-honored pain medication, administered every four hours. Sure enough, it was not long before some poor soul developed massive bleeding from an overdose of Dicumarol. "He was not my patient."

He had another close call when a wealthy chiropractor was murdered near Succor Creek Canyon, but it was also opening day of pheasant season and Will was miles away in another county. Succor Creek was OK for chukkar and sage grouse but lousy for pheasants. To clinch his alibi, Will was hunting with the sheriff who found birds so plentiful that it was the next day before he could investigate the murder. John Flynn suppressed a yawn. After a life at sea, he preferred tales about sex, not murder, but Will's salacious stories were classified so he switched to the alimentary tract.

Sinner and priest shared one last confession: "I have been forever wary of delicate medical terms and, try as I might, I could never be sure when *irregularity* became honest-to-God constipation." The captain was happy to resolve the confusion: "Irregular refers to verbs and people who worry about this suffer constipation." Flynn was decorating his ship's salon and sought expert advise from Will who served on the Art Committee for the Carnegie Public Library: "Don't ever buy the Mona Lisa. They are asking too much for a picture so small. Mona doesn't even have any eyebrows. She was a contrivance of crass French publicity when the Lourve pretended she was stolen and later returned. Only then was her smile truly inscrutable, a term usually reserved for an Oriental . . . which she isn't."

Will predicted that da Vinci's scam would be perpetuated with an air-conditioned Mona smiling from behind bullet-proof glass. No flash allowed. John extended his hand: "That was a close call, Will. You saved me a bundle."

The South Pacific of John Flynn differed significantly from that of James Michener. Did John ever run out of gas? Did he force diners to walk the plank for using the wrong fork? Does caviar make good bait? Should it be eaten with ketchup? The answers were instructive: "I have one officer whose only job is to watch the needle on the gas tank. Nobody walks the plank anymore though sometimes the hoist motor gets stuck and slows debarking. I merely phone the shore to keep the shops open. Every passenger expects two hundred pounds of Polynesian art. A good captain can mollify any irate shopper at dinner with a corsage, usually orchids since they are dirt cheap over there. Then I personally cut her grapefruit. And, in view of your profound lack of sophistication, caviar is eaten with mayonnaise or taco sauce." The captain grew contemplative.

"Once I forgot my compass and tried to guess direction from the stars but, Will, there are SO MANY. Occasionally, a pearl diver got caught in the propeller but my biggest scare came while shaving. As the years passed, I kept the skin increasingly tight to iron out the wrinkles and guide the blade. Then, one day, I must have pulled too hard. Suddenly my entire face disappeared. It had slipped to the back of my head."

Will had the solution: "Forget the wrinkles. Grow a beard. Then you could play a captain in the movies."

Both were kids again back in a one-room schoolhouse, drinking from the same cup and saluting the flag which during two wars had draped the coffins of several classmates: "Did you eventually realize that Miss Lane was a real doll?" "What do you mean, eventually?" What a relief! Will had not passed through puberty alone. In that reminiscent glow each took turns piecing together a long-scattered puzzle. Occasionally, some irregular fragment of hazy truth had to be trimmed and honed until it fit just right. Will remembered an evening in the kitchen, one of the few times Grandad let him sit down, when they had answered a barely audible knock to admit John's barely audible sister. All the Flynns sported red hair and she was all Flynn but because her brothers were so effusive, Sally compensated with an economy of words. Strangers thought her mute. After an awkward pause, Grandad wondered if perhaps she had knocked on the wrong door but in her own good time she spoke:

"Your barn's on fire. I just had to tell somebody." They dashed out where neighbors with their own buckets had already doused the flames. Sensing disaster, they had chased after Sally or maybe just followed her alarming hair. It certainly wasn't anything she said.

Since yearbooks were unknown, nobody had ever been voted most likely to succeed. None ever made Who's Who but John nominated the school yard bully for What's What: "He could have been on the cover of TIME as Primate of the Year." John recounted Will's notorious Judo Toss when Billy the Beast learned manners on a pile of conspiring rocks. There was not much to remember because he didn't bleed long. "But you threw that jerk all wrong. My brother was almost ashamed of your sloppy technique." The doctor insisted he knew a fracture when he saw one but John persisted: "That arm didn't break. It just bent funny. Was it the guilt of hurting some defenseless dolt that drove you into medicine?"

"Not really. I had bad sinuses." The captain paused to wonder if the Mayo brothers began with such pathetic motivation. After five minutes in a losing argument, it was Will's policy to change the subject. The five minutes were just up: "What attracted you to a life at sea?" Only a lousy captain could not answer this.

"After north Idaho rain, I wondered if any place was wetter. Now I know." That same weather drove Will to the Boise Valley and he was just now getting dry: "It's a long way from here to the sea and an Idaho boy commanding a big ocean liner seems incongruous." John reacted with typical honesty which was the curse of the Flynns.

"I wouldn't even know what incongruous means if I hadn't left home." Will decided a minor insult might minimize the glare of the captain's braid.

"You probably learned lots of big words dining with passengers in tuxedos, all eating grapefruit with one hand." "Doctor, I hate to brag but, at last count, I knew thirty-seven big words. But I never use feckless. It's much too dangerous. I'll admit I have to look up a word now and then, whereas Yale types, like Wm. F. Buckley, open a dictionary just to add one." Will considered tossing out a few medical terms but what's the use? John took pity and returned to his ship.

"I knew you would decline even before I left the home port, and please don't fret about your empty stateroom. General Eisenhower is on the waiting list and he—Mamie actually—has been pestering me for the first vacancy. Ike will be overjoyed. He may send you a medal so watch your mail."

"Captain, you have real style. Can the ship sail without me?"

"Frankly, she can even sail without me. I am only there to take the blame if she sinks." John now confessed that his cruise offer was partial payment for a secret debt he owed Will since childhood: "We drew straws to fight Billy but I palmed mine so you were falsely elected. During a family huddle we decided that you would be killed but saw no reason to mention it. Pat thought it might shake your confidence. After you flipped Billy his head hit the rocks but you closed your eyes and missed the finale. It only fractured his skull so he was barely stunned.

The monster started to get up so Pat stood on his throat. This probably fractured his larynx but he never talked much anyway. That final touch was rather crude and Pat knew how sensitive you were. It was for merely surviving that you were elected an honorary Flynn."

Will should have suspected this because the only other time he ever saw the monster he noticed a peculiar heel mark on his Adam's Apple (Pomun adami indentus). Strangely enough, Billy didn't seem to say much about it.

The captain had a fancy Swiss chronometer and a wrist strong enough to hold it. The gold dial included barometric pressure, moon phases, tide schedules and the interest on his mortgage As a curious bonus, it even gave the time which was now late:

"Will, we have been reminiscing for most of the day. I believe we must have covered everything."

"Yes, Captain, I believe we have." Unlike most reunions, they didn't even pretend they would ever see each other again, so it was important to get everything right. The pride of the Grace Line, glimmering in white, stood at the threshold.

"John, your epaulets are too wide for the door." So he saluted and eased through sideways. All things considered, no man could be more fondly remembered . . . or made a better exit.

OBJECTS IN THE MIRROR
ARE CLOSER THAN THEY APPEAR

I have never aspired to design a golf course but Will and his cronies built two and had the calluses to prove it. But a doctor, a merchant, a barber, and a car dealer could not do it alone. With an artful blend of flattery and coersion, they mobilized what was laughingly called a community effort. Those were the days of house calls but laggards soon came to realize that the doctor might forget their address until the next fairway was levelled and seeded. By then, you could really be sick. (Critics claim doctors want to play God but, in all honesty, who better?)

Generosity was rewarded and the farmer who loaned his tractor could expect an extension of his bank loan.

Caldwell's Carnegie Library had nothing on golf and very little on grubbing sagebrush and blasting lava. Will's was a low budget construction with dynamite left over from abandoned Silver City mines. The nearby Boise River provided sand which was mixed with crank case oil to create a smooth putting surface.

During today's Masters Tournament at Augusta, sports narrators (usually with British accents) modulate to *sotto voce* when describing slick greens. Will's were slicker.

My father's links had no score cards but, since golf is a game of honor, each player entered his score before the game began. This primitive layout was so unorthodox that even the fairways were out of bounds. Animals outnumbered people. Players learned to distinguish between a coyote chasing a rabbit and a wolf dragging a child. Rescue parties finally rebelled after saving so many lost golfers and the Curtis Park links was finally abandoned . . . too big to put in a museum, too small to create a new state.

The second course had real grass which eager citizens manicured as part of their green fees. Today's golfer insists on a matched set of irons. Back then, a matched set meant a hoe and shovel.

February golf should be tempered with palm trees but most golfers (and the best ones) live up north where orange, not white, was the color of winter and any time a spray-painted ball could peek through the snow was a day for old veterans to play. A curling rink would have made more sense. Yet there they were: Will's thickly clad foursome gripping clubs through two pair of gloves. The ritual included scrounging for wood along the ditch (out of bounds left) after which they huddled over a fire in the middle of the sixth fairway.

Such behavior would never be tolerated at the Arizona Biltmore . . . nor would it be necessary. After the spring thaw, they replanted the circle of blackened grass. There were a few complaints but these were referred to the city council where Will was perpetual chairman of the golf committee. Patiently, he explained the mystique of this legendary game. When reason failed to silence critics, he threatened to kidnap their children.

After three heart attacks, a light stroke and a touch of leukemia, Will played his last round in 1974. He carried dimes won yesterday in one pocket and nitroglycerin in the other. Dim eyes obscured the ball but his partner's cataract surgery had been more successful.

Most of the group were just deaf enough that garbled insults were mistakenly interpreted as compliments.

Will outlived several foursomes, none of whom ever failed to pay on a bet with a single exception: one player, with an otherwise exemplary reputation, had doubled up on the last hole, sliced out of bounds, collapsed before reaching the green, and left the skin game intestate. When octogenarians play, there are no carry-overs.

When my father died that June, he already had a celestial tee time. Luke and Ray were waiting on the putting green, where Ray's stroke was occasionally interrupted to scratch residual welts, cutaneous reminders of his incarceration long ago in a mosquito-infested tent at Ship Island Lake. Even God is hesitant to forgive a game hog.

Both men had been plotting a strategy, certain to lead to victory over their old golf nemesis. When putting for a birdie back on earth, Will usually whispered: "I have never seen the righteous forsaken, nor his seed begging bread." The scripture source was always different but Luke and Ray were so intimidated that they often conceded the putt. Misquoting the bible up here was serious business and two TV evangelists had been severely reprimanded and another de-winged. Will was met in the clubhouse by an angel who spoke with a Scotch brogue and promised they would never play behind a slow group . . . most of whom aren't admitted to heaven anyway. Not every life on earth had been blessed with golf and those non-players were introduced to the game by shagging balls while a few satisfied their work ethic by re-shafting golf tees. Something for everybody.

God Himself decreed that all anecdotes be limited to golf. This was not the actual voice of God, but dubbed in by Richard Burton whose elocution was more commanding:

A) Steel spikes are prohibited because they puncture the clouds.

B) Any club thrown in anger will boomerang with an accuracy never seen on earth.

C) "Improving your lie with a surreptitious nudge of the ball is prohibited," announced Burton with a voice that reverberated across eighteen fairways. Because second offenders could expect a bolt of lightning, precise golf etiquette soon prevailed.

The golf angel (he played to a seven handicap) also operated the clubhouse, made great hamburgers (nothing for vegetarians) and greeted all newcomers: "Your grandfather has been here for some time. When he isn't grubbing stumps, he reads Plato in the original Greek and his omniscience is second only to You Know Who. He certainly looks like George Bernard Shaw, our only socialist except for three popes. He wins religious debates with Brigham Young but has yet to convince his harem.

"During his life in Falls City, Hugh never understood women and heaven can't change everything. As an implacable champion for hopeless causes, your grandfather is a natural for golf. Why don't you talk to him? Up here we supply everything: custom made clubs and balls by the gross. Titleists, of course. But please, no wagering."

And Will hurried to tee off before the angel said something about Methodists.

If Hugh was aware of Will's fishing, the old man never said a word, though silence would be flimsy evidence from a grandfather who spoke about twice a year. Nobody would suspect such a furtive diversion from a fine Christian lad who spent Sunday in church (God's work), unloaded wagons (hard work), bucked bales (man's work), and always made dinner on time (no big deal). It is no surprise that any sport based on deception has long endured. Qualities usually considered odious are not only laudable but carefully cultivated. After the trickery of catching a trout the fisherman then unabashedly exaggerates its size to whoever will listen. Finding a listener is a separate specialty and keeping him is another.

A Methodist conscience gnawed at Will without actually drawing blood, and the guilt of fooling a nice old man was never quite enough to make him turn in his pole. On the other hand, family meals in Hugh's kitchen were so meager that his grandson's riparian devotion put more food on the table than any crop on the Falls City farm.

Since the pole was kept hidden Will could always say he found the fish along the bank. Indeed, were it not for its secretive nature, fishing definitely built character. Then one day by a deep pool on the Salmon it happened. A blurred figure barely stirred on the far bank and the boy's eyes soon focused on a bearded form: Rigid. Stern. Forbidding.

It *looked* like Granddad.

Silence enveloped the scene. Not a word was spoken. It *sounded* like Granddad.

Uneasily, he searched the face. There was no smile. It *was* Granddad. Something strange had materialized where nothing had been, yet this was so like him. Hugh's long beard projected an apparitional quality which was handy when he intended to impart heavenly significance to his earthly pronouncements. An eerie nimbus outlined his back-lit beard though the sun was not shining. Did this form rise from the mist or descend from the clouds? Might this be some angel (all fishermen believe in these) here to bless the pool? If so, was the benediction for the water's inhabitants or the hopeful intruder on the shore? That was in 1896, and Will never dared to ask that formidable guardian if he had been down on the river that day, but this was not his last unexplained appearance. The old man pulled this ghost trick for the rest of his grandson's life. Invisible arms pulled him away from falling snags in logging camps. Hugh lightened the heavy grief when Will was somehow spared while tuberculosis stole his sisters one by one. With logs and baling wire, Will built a raft to explore the Salmon River and, as the craft disintegrated on the first rapid, he heard a distant voice reminding him how to swim. The voice was distorted by the water's roar but the erstwhile sailor thought he also heard something about *saving the wire* if he had time. Hugh patched up a malnourished boy after school yard fights and watched him grow until a Finnish sawyer could look after him. Will heard Shakespeare in English, Goethe in German and Ecclesiates in Greek but it was Hugh's homey aphorisms that fit more occasions and drew the most admiration, words King Solomon meant to say but forgot.

Will quoted his grandfather for the rest of his life. Anybody (well, almost anybody) could recite an appropriate passage from the Bible but only Will could quote his personal oracle with a three-word punch line which instantly overcame every disaster from the death of a president to a missed putt. Hugh buoyed sagging spirits in medical school and quoted scriptures during embryology, though he could never quite reconcile Creationism with Darwinism. Grandad was there to turn the pages of Gray's Anatomy when the nights were long and the book was heavy. The student listened attentively to whispered words that only he could hear because this teacher would say it only once.

The solicitous mentor made sure his grandson survived sleep deprivation and guided the pen during every exam, except psychiatry, where there was really nothing to know. When they graduated together this stern overseer discarded his white garb . . . or maybe sent it to the cleaners . . . and attended the ceremony in a dark suit. Nobody noticed his halo.

When times were good, Will never saw him, but during trouble Hugh stood in reassuring silence, looking exactly like George Bernard Shaw. Of course it wasn't, because Shaw always had a lot to say. During my father's final days, I heard for the last time those haunting stories about an omniscient ancestor who was never heard but often quoted. Apparently, Hugh did speak now and then, because the day my father died I overheard their last conversation.

George Willis Montgomery, M.D. 1889-1974